Praise for
All Who Go Do Not Return

"Harrowingly recounted. . . . Deen's wishes are fairly modest—all he wants, he writes, is 'a world in which I was not lying or hiding'—but what it takes to achieve them illustrates just how much power religion can wield."

—*The Boston Globe*

"[A] page-turner of a book. . . . Moving and vivid throughout."

—*Haaretz*

"To the end, Deen searches for a new kind of faith to guide him into the future and also to help him make sense of his past choices. But a resounding lesson of his book is that once doubt creeps into your life, certainty never returns."

—*Maclean's* (Canada)

"Deen is an achingly expressive writer and an honest and caring man. He has written a wonderful first book that really explores what it feels like to lose God and then your family, and then for a brief time, feel like you are losing your mind."

—*The Jerusalem Post*

"A clash of cultures made fascinating and personal."

—*Booklist*

"A heartbreaking read as Deen fights to reconcile his identity and love for his family with his loss of faith in God. But it is also one of great courage and hope as Deen aspires to live openly and without fear for the first time."

—*Publishers Weekly*

"In this moving book, Deen lays bare his difficult, muddled wrestling with his faith, the challenges it posed to everything he thought he knew about himself, and the hard-won redemption he eventually found."

—*Kirkus Reviews*

"[Deen] delves into the challenges of his past with such careful honesty. . . . A solid memoir that will be of interest to fans of that genre, as well as to readers curious about Judaism and Jewish life."

—*Library Journal*

"A fascinating, disturbing memoir of loss. . . . An unforgettable story of the power of belief—both the beliefs that bound Deen to his community, and the questioning and unbelief that broke those bonds. Heartbreaking, it is absolutely spellbinding."   —*The American Jewish World*

"Deen's is an unflinchingly honest book—a work of remarkable intro-spection, punctuated with a healthy dose of Jewish self-deprecation. . . . Riveting."   —*The Jewish Daily Forward*

"Gripping. . . . A fascinating glimpse into a largely unknown world."
                    —*The Rumpus*

"I understand that even if I did visit New Square I would have no greater access to Hasidic life than my occasional walk through Williamsburg, where I can see but can't penetrate its appeal, or its secrets. Deen's mem-oir, however, does grant me that access. It is the book's ticket to mass appeal as well as the seat of his disquiet in his writing. Though he writes because he has a story to tell, Deen's work . . . is clearly crafted to benefit others dealing with a wavering faith."   —*Tablet*

"[Deen's] narrative flows beautifully. . . . His memoir keeps the reader glued to the page from beginning to end. . . . Those who long to be accepted, who have felt lost, should pick up this book. This is a book for the nomad, the explorer, the insatiable."   —*Jewish Book Council*

"Mr. Deen is a heretic now, he says, but he still is a Jew. He is a gifted writer too, so his memoir—unlike so many others from people who are off the derech, who have left the straight, clearly marked path that was laid out for them—is not filled with cartoon villains and gaudily signposted emotional reactions. It is, instead, the rueful, painful, deeply reflective story of a man whose heart and brain, working together, left him no op-tion but to quit the only life he'd known."
                    —*The Jewish Standard* (New Jersey)

"*All Who Go Do Not Return* is an extraordinary memoir. The writing is beautiful. The journey it chronicles is poignant, relatable—and also un-like anything most readers will ever have experienced."   —*ZEEK*

"Shulem Deen's new memoir, *All Who Go Do Not Return*, surprises. Instead of condemning his former life as a Skver Hasid from his current, secular views, Deen inhabits equally the multiple selves that appear in the memoir: credulous child, mystified teenager, and fatefully curious adult.... [A] measured and sensitive account."   —*Jewniverse*

"What makes this book an unflinching example of the 'off the derech (path)' genre is its rare glimpse into life in New Square.... It is a society which can be warm and enveloping or vile and repressive. Written in an admirable unobtrusive style, *All Who Go Do Not Return* achieves emotional truth and plot-driven suspense."   —*Killing the Buddha*

"Heartbreakingly honest and unaffected."
          —*Kveller*, "Top 15 Summer Reads for 2015"

"This is an atypical memoir, not a crude or feckless narrative of religion lost and meaning found . . . but something far more heartfelt, genuine and—here's the word—believable.... Though Deen and I have very different perspectives on religion, there is something deeper here, a need and hunger for authenticity, for rigor, for freedom, that I could relate to."
          —*The Muslim Observer*

"Deen is the poet laureate of ex-chasidim. His sentences flow with originality as he unveils his story with passion and sensitivity."
          —*The New York Jewish Week*

"The richly depicted Chasidic world of Shulem Deen's new *All Who Go Do Not Return* . . . feels as transporting as any travelogue.... As a reader, one feels privileged to be along for the heartbreakingly beautiful ride."
          —*Arizona Jewish Post*

"This well-written book takes the reader through little-known aspects of a Hassidic community, both its strengths and vulnerabilities. At once a wealth of psychological, sociological, and just plain interesting episodes as Deen grows and matures, *All Who Go Do Not Return* rewards the reader with distinctive insights into the ultra-religious world of the Hassidim."
          —*New Books Network*

"Deen's narrative is steady and dedicated, his keen eye for detail and the drama of his life never bogging the book down in mawkishness or anger. The narrative is brimming with Deen's strong, even destructive, emotions and impulses, but he does not succumb to angry polemic. Even when depicting unsavory people he makes a good faith effort to portray them as rounded characters. He is also uniquely gifted at interlacing narrative past and present to provide a complete portrait of his complicated, messy life. He does this capably, without getting lost in asides or tangents, and the story always maintains a sense of urgency. . . . *All Who Go Do Not Return* stands as a testimony of how to live with our ultimate, lasting decisions no matter what the cost." —*Colorado Review*

"Outstanding. . . . A story of great courage in the face of unrelenting pressure to conform." —*The Atheist Rabbi*

"Shulem Deen has a fascinating story to tell, and he tells it with exquisite sensitivity. *All Who Go Do Not Return* gives us not only an insider's glimpse into a shrouded world few outsiders get to see, but also a movingly told narrative of one man's struggle toward intellectual integrity. The setting may be the world of Hasidic Judaism, but the drama and the insights are universal." —Rebecca Newberger Goldstein, author of *36 Arguments for the Existence of God: A Work of Fiction*

"*All Who Go Do Not Return* is a deeply honest and moving story about a man's decision to do something both so simple and so radical—to live in accordance with his own beliefs. Shulem Deen has written an enormously powerful and important memoir about faith, doubt and freedom." —Tova Mirvis

"On the eve of his marriage, at eighteen, Shulem Deen knew how to slaughter an ox in Jerusalem's ancient temple, but he knew less than most seven-year-olds do about sex and movies and technology and literature— about the world that lay only miles away from him. Among the Skver Hasids, all who go do not return, but in writing this memoir, Deen has returned, and brought us, his lucky readers, with him. This is a heartbreaking book, and an important one, about the consequences of being true to yourself, and about a world and a community few of us know." —Joshua Henkin

All Who Go Do Not Return

All Who Go
Do Not Return

••

A Memoir

SHULEM DEEN

Graywolf Press

Copyright © 2015 by Shulem Deen

This publication is made possible, in part, by the voters of Minnesota through a Minnesota State Arts Board Operating Support grant, thanks to a legislative appropriation from the arts and cultural heritage fund, and through a grant from the Wells Fargo Foundation Minnesota. Significant support has also been provided by the Jerome Foundation, Target, the McKnight Foundation, Amazon.com, and other generous contributions from foundations, corporations, and individuals. To these organizations and individuals we offer our heartfelt thanks.

Disclaimer: This is a work of creative nonfiction. Many of the names, and some minor identifying details, have been changed to protect the privacy of individuals. All the people in the book are real and the events described actually took place. The events were written mostly from memory, and, when available, from the author's personal journals. Scenes and dialogue were rendered as closely as possible to how the author remembers them. In a very small number of instances, the order of events given is not the exact order in which they occurred; this was done chiefly to maintain thematic cohesion between chapters, and only in such cases where, by the author's judgment, the substance of the story was not affected.

Published by Graywolf Press
250 Third Avenue North, Suite 600
Minneapolis, Minnesota 55401

All rights reserved.

www.graywolfpress.org

Published in the United States of America

ISBN 978-1-55597-705-4

6 8 10 12 11 9 7 5

Library of Congress Control Number: 2014950983

Cover design: Kimberly Glyder Design

Rabbi Yochanan said: Once a man has lived
most of his life without sin, he is unlikely to sin ever.

—TALMUD, YUMA 38B

Do not trust in yourself until the day you die,
for Yochanan was the High Priest for eighty years,
before he rejected the teachings of the sages.

—TALMUD, BRACHOT 29A

♦♦

On a ship's deck, in the middle of the sea,
Stands a teary-eyed Jew from the Holy Land.
From Jerusalem, his home, his life,
that sacred land he has been forced to leave,
and his brothers, his children, his dearest kin.
He travels now to America. Oh, how bitter it is.

—FROM "WILLIAMSBURG," BY YOM TOV EHRLICH

Note on the Uses of Yiddish and Hebrew

Yiddish words are rendered phonetically as they are commonly spoken among contemporary American Hasidim. This is generally known as the Southern (or "Polish") dialect of Eastern Yiddish, although there are occasional exceptions.

Hebrew words are rendered using popular conventions for Hebrew-English transliterations, which often differ markedly from typical Hasidic pronunciations; for example, *Torah* rather than *Toyreh*; *Rosh Hashanah* rather than *Rosh Hashuneh*.

The word *rebbe* might cause some readers some confusion, as the term can mean either a dynastic leader of a Hasidic sect or a male teacher of elementary school boys. Generally, however, the term can be properly understood from its context.

All Who Go Do Not Return

PART I

Chapter One

I wasn't the first to be expelled from our village, though I'd never known any of the others. I'd only heard talk of them, hushed reminiscences of ancient episodes in the history of our half-century-old village, tales of various subversives who sought to destroy our fragile unity. The group of Belzers who tried to form their own prayer group, the young man rumored to have studied the books of the Breslovers, even the rebbe's own brother-in-law, accused of fomenting sedition against the rebbe.

But I was the first to be expelled for heresy.

The call came on a Sunday evening, while Gitty and I were having dinner with our children.

"Shulem, this is Yechiel Spitzer," a deep male voice said, and then paused. "Can you be at the *dayan's* office for a meeting at ten?"

Yechiel was a member of both the Education Committee and the Modesty Committee, which were, together, tasked with looking after the behavior of individuals in our village, ensuring that they wore the right clothes and attended the right synagogues and thought the right thoughts.

"What kind of meeting?" I asked.

"The *bezdin* would like to speak with you," Yechiel said.

The bezdin was our village's rabbinical court, a three-member body that issued regular edicts on urgent religious matters—banning Internet use, or condemning unauthorized prayer groups, or regulating proper head-coverings for women—at the head of which sat the dayan, our village's chief rabbinical judge.

Yechiel waited for my response, and when I said nothing, he said, "You might want to bring someone along. You may not want to be alone."

His tone was oddly flat, which sounded like a deliberate affect, as if to underscore the gravity of his call. I didn't know Yechiel well, but we were friendly enough when we passed on the street, or if we happened to be sitting next to each other at a shiva or a bar mitzvah. Clearly, though, this was not a friendly call.

When I returned to our dinner table, Gitty raised an eyebrow, and I shook my head. *Nothing important.* She pursed her lips and held my gaze for a moment, and I turned back to my plate of leftover chulent from yesterday's Sabbath lunch. The children seemed happily oblivious. Tziri, our eldest, had her eyes in a book. Hershy and Freidy were giggling into each other's ears. Chaya Suri and Akiva were squabbling because Chaya Suri had looked at Akiva's dinner plate and Akiva said he couldn't eat food that Chaya Suri had looked at.

Gitty continued giving me silent glances, until I looked up at her and sighed. "I'll tell you later."

She rolled her eyes, and then stood up to clear the plates off the table.

I looked at my watch. It was just after six.

I wasn't entirely surprised by the call. I had heard from friends that word was getting around the village: *Shulem Deen has become a heretic.*

If heresy was a sin in our all-Hasidic village in Rockland County, New York, it was not an ordinary one. Unlike the yeshiva student who ordered a taxicab each night to get away for an hour of karate lessons, or the girl spotted wearing a skirt that didn't fully cover her knees, or the schoolteacher who complained of the rebbe's lengthy Sabbath noon prayers, heresy was a sin our people were unaccustomed to. Heresy was a sin that baffled them. In fact, real heresy, the people in our village believed, did not happen in our time, and certainly not in our village, and so when they heard there was a heretic in their midst, they were not sure what to make of it.

"Doesn't he know that the Rambam already answered all questions?" the rebbe had asked.

The Rambam, also known as Moses Maimonides, was a twelfth-century Jewish scholar and philosopher, perhaps the greatest of all time. His gravestone in the city of Tiberias, Israel, declares: "From Moses to Moses, there has risen no one like Moses." In our study halls, we pored over his legal codes and his famous Commentary on the

Mishna. We told tales of his righteousness and his scholarship. We named our children after him.

But we did not study his philosophy.

It was said that the Rambam's most notable philosophical work, the *Guide for the Perplexed*, was so great and so brilliant that it was meant only for the most learned. For everyone else, to study it was unnecessary. The important thing was to know that it contained all the answers, and so all further questions were pointless.

"Doesn't he know that the Rambam already answered all questions?"

I don't know if the rebbe in fact said that. I had heard it from friends, who heard it from other friends, and rumors in our village weren't always reliable. What I did know was that the rebbe was the village's supreme leader, and nothing of consequence happened without his direct involvement. And so when I was told to appear before the bezdin, I knew that the order had come all the way from the rebbe.

At exactly 10:00 PM, I walked up the dirt path to the side entrance of the dayan's home. The dayan's authority came from his extensive knowledge of Torah, but his office was an extension of the rebbe's. If the rebbe was our chief executive, the dayan and his bezdin were our judiciary and law enforcement.

The gravity of his office notwithstanding, the dayan was a kind and gentle scholar. Back when I was a yeshiva student, more than a decade earlier, I had spent hours with him in talmudic discussion. During the years following, I had walked this very path hundreds of times for various personal and familial matters, bringing palm fronds to be inspected before the Sukkos holiday, undergarments to be inspected for menstrual blood, chickens with discolored flesh to be inspected for signs of injury.

Now, once again I walked up the familiar flight of stairs onto the weather-beaten wooden porch and knocked on the door. Through a window I could see the light on, and from inside came voices, vehement ones, argumentative, disturbed. I waited a few moments and knocked again, and the door was opened by Yechiel Spitzer, who gestured to a small room off to the side.

"Wait there," he said curtly, and disappeared into the dayan's office across the hall. I sat in an old chair near a small table and listened to the hum of voices coming from the next room. After a few minutes, Berish Greenblatt joined me. Berish and I had been close for years, ever since he had been my teacher at a Brooklyn school when I was a teenager and he'd invited me to his home for the Sabbath when my father was ill and in the hospital. Now, years later, we had grown apart—he, still the pious scholarly type and I the rumored heretic. Still, his presence was comforting, even though neither of us knew what to expect.

Soon we were summoned into the dayan's office. The dayan sat at the center of a small table strewn with religious texts, surrounded by two other rabbis of the bezdin and four other men, leading members of the community.

The dayan smiled warmly, almost beatifically, his face framed in his sprawling gray beard.

"Sit, sit," he said, and pointed to an empty chair facing him across the table.

I sat and looked around, while Berish took a seat behind me. The men facing me were pressed tightly together, nervously fingering the books on the table, stroking their beards and tugging at their mustaches. A few exchanged whispered remarks, and soon one of the men began to speak. His name was Mendel Breuer, a man known for both shrewdness and piety. It was said that he was as comfortable negotiating a voting bloc for an elected official as he was delivering a Talmud lecture to a group of businessmen each morning.

"We have heard rumors," Mendel began. "We have heard rumors and we don't know if they're true, but you understand, rumors alone are bad."

He paused and looked at me, as if expecting me to show agreement of some sort.

"People say you're an *apikorus*. People say you don't believe in God." He raised his shoulders to his ears, spread his palms, and opened his eyes wide. "How does one not believe in God? I don't know." He said this as if he were genuinely curious. Mendel was an intelligent man, and here was a question that, given the time and inclination, one might seek to discuss. But now was not the time, and so he went on to tell me more about what people were saying.

I was speaking ill of the rebbe.

I was no longer praying.

I disparaged the Torah and the teachings of our sages.

I was corrupting other people. Young people. Innocent people.

In fact, people were saying that I had corrupted a yeshiva boy just last week. Corrupted him so badly that the boy left his parents' home, and—Mendel didn't know if this was true, but so people were saying—went to live with goyim in Brooklyn. It was rumored that the boy planned to attend college.

People were saying, Mendel further informed me, that something must be done. People were very concerned, and people were saying that the bezdin must act.

"If people are saying that the bezdin must act, you understand, we can't very well do nothing."

Yechiel Spitzer, sitting at the very end of the table, twirled a few hairs beneath his lower lip and absentmindedly placed one hair between his front teeth. The three rabbis sat with their eyes downcast.

"You understand," Mendel went on, "that this is not about causing pain to you or your family."

Here he paused and looked at the dayan, before putting his palms flat on the table and looking at me directly.

"We have come to the conclusion that you must leave the village."

I was being expelled, though in those moments, I wasn't sure how to feel about it. My initial thought was to defend myself, to declare it all lies, hateful gossipmongering. But the truth was, I no longer belonged here. This was a community of the faithful, and I was no longer one of them.

And yet, to be expelled was different from leaving voluntarily. To be expelled is to be rejected, and to be rejected is to be disgraced. There were also Gitty and the children to think about. This village was the place Gitty and I had called home for the twelve years of our marriage. It was where our five children were born and where they had dozens of cousins, aunts, uncles, grandparents, all within a ten-minute walk from any point in the village. This was our hometown. Only two years earlier, we'd purchased a four-bedroom semi-attached townhouse, imagining we'd be living there for a good portion of the rest of our lives. It was not a luxurious home, but it was spacious and sunny and fresh—we bought it new, the smell of paint and polyurethane still in the air the day we moved in—and we had grown fond of it. We'd planted a tree in the front yard. We'd gotten a good price on the house and an excellent rate on the mortgage.

And so I told the rabbis that it wasn't at all a straightforward matter.

"I am happy to go home and discuss it with my wife. And then, if we agree to leave, I would have to find a buyer for my home."

I knew the rabbis wouldn't be pleased with my response, but unlike those who had been expelled in the past, I was bolder. I was more informed. This was America in the twenty-first century. You couldn't force people from their homes unless you were the government, and the bezdin wasn't the government.

The men looked at one another gravely. Even the dayan—who had been nodding along throughout Mendel's little speech, occasionally glancing my way with a faint smile, his expression empathic, as if to say, *I'm sorry, my friend, sorry it has come to this*—now looked perturbed.

Mendel looked at one of the other rabbis, who seemed to think for a moment and then said, "*Nu.*" Mendel withdrew a folded white sheet of paper from the breast pocket of his coat. "This," Mendel said, pushing the document across the table, "is what we will have to publicize if you don't comply. You may read it."

The document took the form of an open letter, the kind that could be published in newspapers, hung on synagogue doorways, and stuck to the walls above synagogue sinks. It was written in florid rabbinical Hebrew, heavy with biblical and talmudic wordplay.

> To our brethren, the children of Israel, in all their places of residence:
>
> This is to inform you that the man Shulem Aryeh Deen has been found to hold heretical views. He has engaged in the manner of Jeroboam the son of Nebat, sinning and causing others to sin, an inciter and an agitator, who has openly and flagrantly violated the laws of God and His Torah, has denied the tenets of our sacred

religion, has mocked our faith in God and in the law of Moses,
and continues to encourage others to follow in his wicked path.

The document went on to call on all God-fearing Jews to dissociate from me in all matters. I was not to be hired as an employee or allowed residence in their homes. I was to be excluded from their prayer quorums and denied entry to their synagogues. My children were to be denied admission to their schools.

My hands trembled as I finished reading the document and laid it back on the table.

"We're not sending this out *yet,*" Mendel said, as he placed the document back in his coat pocket. "Comply with our orders, and we'll keep this to ourselves. Otherwise, you understand, we'll have no choice."

I looked around at the rabbis. The dayan looked at me with sad eyes, while the other rabbis looked away.

"That is all," Mendel said.

I waited for the rabbis to rise. But they just sat there, and so I sat there, too, vaguely stunned.

One of the rabbis looked up at me. "I hope you'll come back to visit," he said.

The dayan nodded along: "Yes, yes, come back to visit."

"You can stay at my place, your whole family," the other rabbi said, and for a moment I thought, how kind of him, this rabbi who hadn't said a word through the whole meeting and with whom I'd never spoken before. But I didn't yet know how to feel about this, and I didn't yet know how to feel about this rabbi or the bezdin. But mostly, I was thinking about how I would tell Gitty and the children. There would be tears. There would be cries of shame. There would be pleas to ask the bezdin to reconsider.

But it was just as well. I no longer belonged here, in this village, in this community, among these people. It would not be easy, but this was bound to happen. It was time to go.

Chapter Two

I have an image in my mind of the moment I realized that I was a nonbeliever. I don't remember the day, or the month, or even the exact year, but only where I was and what I was doing. It was morning. I had woken late and was rushing through my morning routine. I was no longer praying at the shul, but I still prayed, alone at home, choosing only the important passages—the first and last sections of the Verses of Song, the Shema, the Shmoneh Esreh—and skipping the rest. I no longer found prayer meaningful but still kept up the routine, partly out of habit but also out of fear of displeasing Gitty. If she knew that I no longer prayed, there was no telling how she would react.

I remember that I was in the dining room, and through the thin walls I could hear Gitty busy in the kitchen: "Akiva, finish your toast," "Freidy, stop bothering the baby and get dressed," "Tziri, brush your hair and get your backpack." The sounds all blended together. One by one, each of the children recited the morning blessings, groaned about unfinished homework assignments, lost shoes, misplaced hair accessories. I swung my prayer shawl over my shoulders, whipped up my sleeve, and wrapped the leather straps of my tefillin around my arm. And as I stood there, the black leather cube on my left arm bulging against the sleeve of my starched white shirt, my body enveloped in the large, white, black-striped shawl, the thought came to me:

I no longer believe in any of this.

I am a heretic. An *apikorus*.

For a long time, I had tried to deny it. A mere sinner has hope: *An Israelite, although he has sinned, is still an Israelite*, the Talmud says. But a heretic is lost forever. *All who go do not return.* The Torah scroll he writes is to be burned. He is no longer counted in a prayer quorum, his food is not considered kosher, his lost objects are not returned to him, he is unfit to testify in court. An outcast, he wanders alone forever, belonging neither to his own people nor to any other.

It was at that moment, sometime between fastening the knot of my tefillin against my occipital bone and racing through whatever chapters of prayer I still chose to recite, that I realized that my heresy was simply a fact about myself, no different from my brown eyes or my pale skin.

But being a heretic was not a simple matter. Gitty and I, along with our five children, were living in New Square, a village thirty miles north of New York City inhabited entirely by Hasidic Jews of one particular sect: the Skverers. The village had been established in the 1950s by the grand rebbe of Skver, Reb Yankev Yosef Twersky, a scion of the Chernobyl and Skver Hasidic dynasties. Stepping off the boat in New York Harbor in 1948, the rebbe, who had been raised in the town of Skvyra, Ukraine, took in the city's aura of decadence and said to his followers, "If I had the courage, I would get right back on that boat and return to Europe." Instead, he set out to build his own village, an American shtetl. He was told that it was impossible, that America was not a place for shtetls, and that his plan would surely fail. It almost did.

For decades, his followers would tell of endless obstacles in building the village: hostile neighbors, an uncooperative town board, building materials stolen by the very truck drivers who delivered them, endless problems with sewage systems and badly paved roads. But the rebbe persisted. According to legend, a county clerk, listening to a group of bearded Jews declare that they wanted their new town called "New Skvyra," wrote "New Square" instead, and this Anglicized form of the name was now official.

But if the name sounded American, the village itself was anything but. Some people would later say to me: "Of course you became a heretic. You lived in a place so sheltered, among such fanatics." It was often Hasidim who said this: Satmars and Belzers and Lubavitchers, no strangers to fanaticism. New Square was a place that even extremists thought too extreme, where even fanatics shook their heads in dismay. *This*, they seemed to say, is taking it too far. *This* is just crazy.

At first, I questioned only the authority of the rebbe, the wisdom of the Hasidic masters, and the particulars of our ultraconservative and insular lifestyle. Soon, however, I was treading on more fraught territory: I wondered whether the Talmud truly contained the word of God, and then I wondered about the Torah itself. Was any of it true? And God Himself, where was He and who was to know what He wanted or whether He existed at all?

In the beginning, all I had were questions. But even asking questions was forbidden.

"Isn't Judaism all about asking questions?" people would later ask. "Isn't the Talmud filled with questions?"

The Judaism that is familiar to most liberal Jews is not the Judaism of the Hasidim, nor is it the Judaism of the Baal Shem Tov, or Rashi, or Rabbi Akiva. The Judaism of our ancient texts allows for questions, true, but they must be of a certain kind and they must be asked just so. *He who inquires about these four things*, says the Talmud, *it is better if he were never born: What is above, what is below, what is the past, what is the future.* If one is plagued by questions for which there are no answers, it is not the fault of our faith but the fault of the questioner, who has surely not prayed enough, studied enough, cleansed his heart and mind enough so that the wisdom of the Torah might penetrate his soul and make all questions fall away.

"What made you change?" people would ask in later years, and the question would frustrate me because the things that made me change were so many and varied that they felt simply as life feels: not a single moment of transformation but a process, a journey of inquiry and discovery, of beliefs and challenges to those beliefs, of uncomfortable questions and attempts to do away with them, by brute force if necessary, only to find that that was not possible, that the search was too urgent and necessary and giving up was not an option. Yet I found no neat answers but only muddled and contradictory ones, until hope gave way to disillusion, which would in turn give way to hope once again, but dimmer and weaker each time, until I would swing back to confusion and disillusion in an endlessly maddening cycle.

I remember one of the first times I had questions that I could not ask. They were not questions of faith but of more mundane matters—about the girl proposed to me in marriage. What I wanted to ask was chiefly this: Is she pretty? Is she smart? Is she personable? And if she isn't those things, can I say no?

The questions I would eventually ask—Does God exist? Does our faith really contain the universe's essential truths? Is *my* faith truer than someone else's?—would, on the surface, seem of greater consequence. But at the age of eighteen, I had no big questions, only relatively small ones. And those small questions seemed so trivial that I was embarrassed to voice them. *Charm is deceptive and beauty is vain; a woman who fears God, it is she who is praised.* I was told that the girl was very much a God-fearing one. Did I really need to know more?

◆◆

I was in the middle of doing laundry when I was told of the girl I was to marry. I was a student at the Great Yeshiva of New Square, when the washing machine in the dormitory had stopped working and students scattered to the homes of friends and relatives to do their laundry. I dragged my laundry bag to the home of the Greenblatts, family friends who lived at the edge of the village. My father had died several years earlier, and my mother was still trying to rebuild her life after my father's death. So the Greenblatts were standing in as family, providing meals, laundry services, and the kind of meddling ordinarily reserved for family members.

It was close to midnight, and Berish and the children had long gone to bed. The only sounds were of Chana Miri finishing chores in the kitchen, cabinets gently opening and closing, the careful clinking of dishes being placed in the sink, running water. Soon these sounds died down, and I heard the soft tap-tap-tap of Chana Miri's slippers as she came toward the laundry room, near the stairway to the bedrooms upstairs. I imagined she was heading to bed. I would let myself out, as I often did.

Chana Miri appeared in the doorway to the laundry room, and I raised my head in her direction without meeting her gaze. She wasn't family, and to look at her directly was forbidden. From the edges of my peripheral vision, I could see the cloudy image of a diminutive female form, a kerchiefed head, a shapeless floral-print housedress.

"Did Berish tell you about the *shidduch?*" she asked.

I shook my head, my eye fixed on the motion of the iron. Chana Miri fell silent.

"Well," she said finally. "Berish can give you more details tomorrow, but I might as well tell you now." She paused, and then said haltingly, "I know . . . this might not sound like a great proposal. But . . . give it some thought."

I nodded as I moved the iron across the white polyester fabric, watching the soft creases disappear under the gentle hiss of steam. I was hoping to appear nonchalant, although I felt my heartbeat quicken with a tick of excitement.

"Chaim Goldstein's daughter," Chana Miri said finally.

I must have looked crestfallen because Chana Miri's next words were, "I know what you're thinking. But it's not as bad as you think."

I didn't know the girl, but I knew her male family members. Chaim Goldstein was a portly man who prayed exuberantly and unself-consciously in the back row of the shul. During Friday night services, I would see him making his way through the synagogue aisles, silver snuff box in hand, while the cantor's twirling voice filled the high-ceilinged sanctuary. Shuffling from table to table, he would offer worshipers a pinch of his peppermint-scented snuff, while behind him trailed three of his young sons, with unkempt sidelocks, mud-crusted shoes, snotty noses. He was not the kind of man I imagined as my father-in-law, and I turned away now, not wanting Chana Miri to see my disappointment.

I thought also of Nuchem Goldstein, Chaim Goldstein's son. I remembered a day when, my study partner absent, I had asked Nuchem to be my partner for one study session. This was during my first year at the yeshiva, and I'd thought it kindly to reach out to the boy who sat day after day without a study partner, idling over his Talmud, drumming his fingers on the table for hours, never once letting his gaze fall to the open volume before him.

Nuchem seemed to have little aptitude for Talmud study. In fact, I had never before encountered a partner like him. "Why did the sages ask all these questions if they already knew the answers?" he asked, as if the entire form were unfamiliar, as if he hadn't been studying Talmud since the age of six.

"It's a process," I said, scarcely believing I was having this conversation.

"Why does the process matter?" he asked, scowling and indignant, as if personally affronted by the sages' lack of consideration, putting him through the grind and toil of rediscovering conclusions that surely ought to have been known by now. "Why don't we just study the conclusions?" It was a startling question, and I felt bad for this boy, who was clearly not enjoying his time at the yeshiva. But what I felt mostly was contempt; he was asking that which we knew must not be asked. Was he so dense as not to know that?

"I know what you're thinking," Chana Miri said again now. "You know her father, you know her brothers. But I was told she is different." She stood in the doorway, and the silence hung heavy between us.

"What's her name?" I asked finally.

"Gitty," she said, all too eager. "Gitty Goldstein."

Gitty. From the Yiddish, *git*, good. It had a pleasant ring, suggesting femininity, innocence, devotion.

Still, all I could think of was her family—Chaim's simpleminded mannerisms, the dim look on Nuchem's face, the little boys following their father at the shul, shy and timid, as if aware, even at that young age, that some people were more worthy than others and that they, by virtue of some arbitrary social code, had been placed among a lower class.

"I need time to think about it," I told Berish the next day. I said the same to my mother after Berish asked her to speak to me. Only Chana Miri seemed to understand. But still, she thought I shouldn't dismiss it.

"She's different from her brothers," Chana Miri said. "I hear she's very normal." I couldn't help thinking: *Normal?* Is that her best quality?

Several months earlier, my classmates and I were taken by surprise when the first of our friends got engaged.

"*Hust gehert?*" The news went from table to table and bookstand to bookstand, sweeping through the vast study hall within minutes. "Have you heard? Ari Goldhirsch is engaged!" The studious looked up from the tiny letters in the margins of their Talmuds, and the idlers halted their conversations. We were stunned, hardly expecting one this soon. Most of us were only seventeen, some even younger.

"*Bei vemen?*" was the question on everyone's lips.

Bei vemen. Not *with whom* but *in whose home?*—into which family, and within which extended clan of aunts, uncles, cousins, grandparents.

"Mordche Shloime Klieger."

The name of the bride didn't matter, only the name of her father. It wasn't just a girl that a boy married but an extended set of family relations, with all its respectability, if one was lucky—or its grim ordinariness, if one wasn't.

It was April 1992, and I'd been hoping that the engagements wouldn't start until the following year. It was said that the rebbe didn't approve of these early engagements but that families sometimes rushed them when the match was too good to let pass. Sometimes, if the boy or the girl was not yet eighteen, the engagement was kept secret; but soon enough, word would get out. The first engagement brought with it the pressure to be among the first. Early engagement was a sign of desirability; extended bachelorhood, a mark of shame.

With Ari's engagement, the race was on, and other classmates soon followed. Moishe Yossel Unger and Burich Silber were engaged within a week of each other to two sisters, granddaughters of the rebbe's personal secretary. Of course, none of us knew what the girls were like, but the girls themselves were hardly the point.

Aron Duvid Spira was soon engaged to the daughter of Avigdor Blum, the wealthiest man in the village. Zevi Lowenthal followed soon after, to the daughter of a prominent scholar. My afternoon study partner, Chaim Lazer, was engaged to the daughter of his uncle Naftuli. As one friend after another was paired off, I, too, waited for the matchmaker's call. I congratulated each of my friends at their weddings, accepted in return their gracious smiles—*mertzeshem bei dir,* your own engagement soon, if God wills it—yet my heart ached, anticipation seasoning into dread. On Friday nights, as I prepared to lift the glass of sweet wine to recite the kiddush, I prayed that soon I might be doing so with a wife at my side, rather than alongside hundreds of other hungry yeshiva students. *King of kings, command Your ministering angels to commend me with mercy.* Let it be soon. Let it be with a good girl from a respectable family.

At the *tischen,* the rebbe's public Sabbath meals, we stood on six rows of tall bleachers to the rebbe's right. Each year, the yeshiva students shifted one set of bleachers nearer to the rebbe himself, until the yeshiva seniors, the eighteen- and nineteen-year-olds who would be married that year, stood nearest. All eyes were trained on the latest group of eligible students, appraising each one, wondering which daughter of which community member he might be paired with.

"What is wrong with Chaim Goldstein's daughter?" Berish asked a few days later.

I said only that I needed more time to think, unable to formulate the torrent of thoughts into words.

"She has everything a wife should have," Berish persisted. "What's to think about?"

I didn't know what there was to think about. If at first, I was not drawn to this match because I was not drawn to this girl's father or brothers, I soon found myself wondering about the girl herself. But the questions I had in my mind could not be asked aloud. I wondered: Was she pretty? Was she intelligent? Was she thoughtful and charming with a pleasant smile and an endearing laugh? Or did she have none of those qualities, and maybe even decidedly unpleasant ones? I wondered if I might ask for a photo of the girl, but since none was offered, I thought it improper. I imagined that Berish and the matchmaker and the girl's family would wonder: What kind of boy is this, who needs a photo of a girl before deciding to marry her?

"I hear she is very sweet," my mother said, after making her own inquiries. "The fourth child of twelve, takes very good care of her younger siblings. That says a lot. She'd make a good wife and mother."

"She's very social, too," my mother added brightly. "Attends weddings and other family celebrations very eagerly. Joins in the dancing. Has friends. She's very well spoken of."

When none of these bits of information had the desired effect, Berish suggested the obvious solution. "Why not ask the rebbe?"

Of course. The rebbe. The rebbe would have the answer.

Late one night, several days before Chanukah, Berish and I went to seek an audience with the rebbe. The *gabbai,* Reb Shia, the rebbe's elderly secretary, sat in his office adjoining the rebbe's chamber, while several dozen Hasidim waited in the large, brightly lit waiting room, pacing nervously, reciting Psalms, or brooding in silence. Reb Shia wrote my *kvittel*, a request note scribbled onto a small white square of paper, and ignored Berish's query of how long the wait might be. Hour after hour passed as, one after the other, the men were summoned for their turn with the rebbe, soon emerging with smiles for the surly door attendant, slipping ten- or twenty-dollar bills into his palm, now pleased, with hearts and minds unburdened.

Finally, Berish and I were ushered in. I'd only been to see the rebbe for hurried blessings and rushed handshakes, never for advice on a personal matter. Now, for the first time, I was to make a decision based on the rebbe's guidance. It was a comforting thought. This was the special privilege of the Hasid, having access to the divine inspiration channeled through the tzaddik, the perfectly righteous individual.

The rebbe sat at the head of a long table on an elaborately gilded chair upholstered in rich blue fabric. I could see him observing the door, fingering a gold pocket watch. His forehead was misty with sweat, his stout frame and graying beard appearing so close, so lifelike—unlike in shul, where he seemed only a blurry impression beheld from afar. Strewn across the table were piles of request notes from earlier visitors, mixed with the traditional money gifts—twenty-, fifty-, and hundred-dollar bills.

"*Nu, gei shoin!*" the attendant shoved my arm when I hesitated at the door. "Go already." There was no time to be awed; others were waiting. Berish stood off to the side as I handed the rebbe the *kvittel* and watched as he read it: *Shulem Aryeh the son of Bracha. For blessings and redemptions.*

Berish stepped closer and told the rebbe why I had come: a girl was proposed, and I was here to seek the rebbe's advice. The rebbe looked at me for a moment, and then, with a flash of recognition, grew animated.

"Ah, yes, yes, yes. Of course!" He'd been consulted about it by the other side, he said. "A good match, a wonderful match. Yes, yes. Wonderful, isn't it?" The rebbe smiled, his eyes twinkling, crinkling along the edges.

"He isn't sure," Berish said softly. "He has some doubts, some questions about it."

The rebbe regarded me from above his gold-rimmed eyeglasses and raised his bushy eyebrows with a look of surprise. "Questions?" he asked. "What kinds of questions?"

What *were* my questions? Here I stood in front of the *righteous foundation of the world*, who was asking me to tell him why I might not desire a match that he had already declared "wonderful." I looked from the rebbe's inquiring eyes to the heavy brocade tablecloth to the piles of *kvitlech*, but the words did not come. It was then that I realized, I didn't have questions, not really.

I just didn't want this match.

I knew in my heart that it was not the right one, that the things that were *not* said about Gitty Goldstein were as significant as those that were, and that I was unlikely to hear anything that would change that. Perhaps I had been hoping that the rebbe would tell me something new and delightful about this match, but what I really wanted was permission to refuse it. I wanted the rebbe to say that if I did not want it, it was OK, that something better would come along and that saying no was not shameful, or cruel, even as I knew that Gitty Goldstein was at that moment anxiously awaiting word from the matchmaker. I wanted the rebbe to tell me that I did not need a reason to say no but a reason to say yes. But the rebbe had already declared the match *wonderful*; one did not tell the rebbe what one wanted to hear. One listened, and accepted.

The rebbe waited with raised eyebrows, then looked back at the *kvittel* in his hand, then back to me. Finally, he spoke: "Chaim Goldstein is a very fine man with a very fine family." And, the rebbe added, he had heard very good things about the *keren*. "The *keren* is a good *keren*," the rebbe said.

Keren is the principal sum in a financial investment, and it took me a moment to grasp what he meant. But of course, the rebbe would not say "girl," a word so blatantly feminine that to speak it was improper. Instead, the girl was the *keren*, the principal. This investment, the rebbe was saying, was a good investment.

"It's a good *thing*, this *keren*," the rebbe said again, and waved his hand with a sweeping, exuberant motion. "A good *keren*. A fine *keren*. Eh. Nothing to worry about."

He reached for my hand with his fingertips. "May the one above bestow you with good graces. May the match be concluded favorably."

Several days later, I sat in the backseat of a car, on the way to the home in which my bride and I were to meet. It was early December, the third night of Chanukah, and a snowstorm had come early that year. Snowdrifts were piled along the side of the road, and I watched as children sledded down a driveway on Lincoln Avenue.

"Nervous?" Berish asked from the front passenger seat.

I shrugged, avoiding his gaze. I was not nervous, not in the way that he meant it. I had been told they wanted me. I was not concerned about being rejected.

The car pulled over to the curb. The front door of the house was slightly ajar, and through a thin curtain I saw people milling about inside. My mother, in the foyer when I entered, looked at me with what looked like forced cheer.

"She's a lovely girl," she said, smiling.

There was a hint of sadness in her voice, as if she sensed the heaviness I felt, but she, too, knew that refusing the match was no longer an option. The rebbe had given his blessing. There was nothing left to say.

Chaim Goldstein appeared from one of the back rooms. He smiled and shook my hand, and then he and Berish led me into the dining room, with my mother following behind.

The girl, my future bride, stood at the far side of the table, next to her mother. Her hair was short and curly, dirty blond. Her clothes were simple, a long pleated skirt, a V-neck button-down sweater over a white blouse and ruffled collar. She looked away as I entered, and only after a moment did she let her eye wander toward me, offering a stiff smile, then looking away quickly.

Our elders left the room, and Gitty and I sat down on opposite sides of the table. For the past five years, all conversation with girls had been forbidden, and it felt odd being in a room alone with a girl, vaguely inappropriate. I had been told that it was my role to initiate conversation, but the strangeness of the circumstances left me bewildered. For a full minute, I could not think of a single thing to say.

"Smile from ear to ear," a friend had said to me earlier that evening. I had confided that I was having my *beshow* that night, and I needed some tips. "Smile from ear to ear. The whole time. You must show her you're happy to be there."

"The *whole* time?"

"From ear to ear, the whole time." He was certain of it.

I wasn't sure what to make of his advice. Smiling from ear to ear would require an unnatural stiffening of the facial muscles, which would be impossible to maintain for the full fifteen minutes of our meeting. Also, it would make me appear insincere. Yet it was all the advice my friend had to offer. He'd used it himself, he said, and he could vouch for its success. When I asked for topics of conversation, he said, "Talk about anything." But what does one talk about to a girl who has never studied Talmud, never attended a rebbe's tisch—whose life, in fact, seemed so far removed from mine that we could not possibly have anything in common? My friend didn't know, he wasn't sure, he no longer remembered, really, his own meeting was so many months ago. Anyway, he said, in his case, the girl did most of the talking.

Gitty, however, was not doing much talking at all. Fumbling for conversation topics, I finally asked about matters I already knew: whether she was still in school, how many siblings she had, whether she wanted to remain living in the village after our wedding. No, she shook her head, she'd already graduated some months earlier. Eleven siblings, she mouthed in a barely audible whisper. Yes, she nodded, she wanted to remain living here. I offered a few remarks about myself. I said that I hoped to continue my studies after we married, at least for a couple of years. She nodded in response. It was a given. Two years of study was mandatory for all married men in the village.

She kept her eyes downcast at the table in front of her. When she glanced at me at one point, I quickly flashed the ear-to-ear smile my friend had advised, and she returned it stiffly. I thought she might offer a few questions or remarks of her own, but she seemed to have none. Soon I ran out of questions, and we sat in silence until Chaim Goldstein entered the room.

"Are you done?" he asked.

It wasn't a question. Clearly, we were done. I had imagined a fifteen-minute meeting, but this couldn't have been more than seven minutes. I was relieved it was over.

We rode to the rebbe's home, a short distance away, Gitty and I in separate cars. A few close friends and relatives milled about and greeted me cheerfully. They had been notified already, and they seemed happy for me. The rebbe's attendant smiled, too, his usual gruff manner set aside for this joyous occasion, a new engagement.

The men entered first and the women followed, while the rebbe smiled and waved his hand in a gesture of joy. The men gathered around the table, clearing a space so that the rebbe had a view of the bride, who stood among the women against the far wall.

The attendant closed the door.

"Mazel tov, mazel tov!" the rebbe said. "May it be a steadfast union. May you merit lasting seed to bring forth upstanding and blessed generations."

The engagement was final, the rebbe's blessing like a judge's gavel.

The attendant placed a small tray of chocolate pound cake in front of the rebbe, and the men lined up to receive their portions from the rebbe's hand while the women watched from the edge of the room. The men sipped from small cups of wine and lined up for blessings of *l'chaim*, "to life." As the person of honor, I was first, and the rebbe held my fingertips for a long moment, mumbling a blessing, the same one he had mumbled to thousands of grooms before me. It felt cold and impersonal, the rebbe's eyes shifty and restless as they searched for and then lingered on my bride, as if to include her from afar. I told myself that this was what I truly wanted. The rebbe had approved of the match. I told myself that I was pleased with it, that I *must* be pleased, because clearly the rebbe was pleased. I told myself what we, the rebbe's followers, always told one another: The rebbe cares about us more than we do ourselves. Our joyous occasions bring him more joy; our sad occasions, more sorrow. I believed this, had repeated it to myself countless times, and had *made* myself believe this. I knew it must be so.

Chapter Three

The first time I saw the rebbe, I knew little about him. I was thirteen years old, a student at the Skverer yeshiva in Williamsburg, Brooklyn, when I was told: "The rebbe is coming." I responded with a shrug, and watched, amused, as a frenzy of anticipation took hold among students and staff. Broken table legs in the study hall were frantically repaired. Floors were cleaned and waxed. Guatemalan day laborers worked overtime to replace the wainscot paneling in the hallways and repaint the lecture rooms. We were instructed to scrub our dorm rooms clean. Even the bathroom stalls were cleared of graffiti: *Reb Moshe Lazer is a chazzer. Touching your bris is worse than smoking.*

I had enrolled at the yeshiva not as a follower of the rebbe, like most students, but because the Skverers didn't ask too many questions, and I needed a yeshiva in which few questions were asked. While most of my elementary school friends had sought Talmud academies with reputations for producing impressive young scholars, my own goals were less lofty. I had heard of the entrance exams at the more prestigious institutions, hour-long oral exams covering many pages of Talmud along with their major commentaries, and the tales inspired dread in me. The summer after my bar mitzvah, after my friend Chaim Elya told me that the Skverers were in need of students for their modest-size Williamsburg yeshiva and that they weren't very selective and administered no entrance exam, I told my parents that I wanted to study with the Skverers. My father looked doubtful, curious about my uncharacteristic initiative; but ultimately, he was pleased. "They're *ehrlich* people, the Skverers," he said. *Ehrlich.* Pious. Good Jews.

But the Skverers and their ways were strange to me. I had spent my childhood mostly among the Satmars. The Satmars, too, had a rebbe, but I'd seen and heard little of him. My Satmar schoolteachers rarely spoke of him. My father embraced the teachings of the previous Satmar rebbe, the firebrand Reb Yoel, who died in 1979, but never visited his successor.

"Ah! The rebbes of old!" my teachers would exclaim, and from them I learned that modern-day rebbes were only quaint relics of a once-glorious era. There was a time back in the old country, in the towns and villages that speckled Russia's Pale of Settlement and the mountains of Carpathia, when a rebbe could make an anti-Semitic landowner perish in a freak accident, make a childless couple bear children well into old age, gaze into the eyes of his followers and see every one of their deeds, good or bad, past and future. But times had changed, it was understood.

There were rumored exceptions. Reb Yankele from Antwerp, people said, performed miracles so great and so frequent, they were near daily occurrences. There was talk of the Tosher, near Montreal, who was good for marriage blessings—it was his specialty, they said. But these rebbes and their Hasidim were not in Brooklyn, and so they didn't seem quite real to me.

Now, observing the Skverers as they prepared for the rebbe's visit, it was clear that they thought their present-day rebbe to be of equal stature to the great rebbes of old, and all I could do was scoff inwardly.

"Did you see your name on the lottery list?" Chaim Elya asked one day. Anticipation was mounting as the rebbe's visit drew near.

"What lottery list?"

"The lottery for the rebbe's visit," he said. "The lottery for who gets to do what. You won Psalms."

As I was to learn, a lottery had been held in which all students were entered for the privilege of serving one of the rebbe's needs: opening the doors to the rebbe's shiny black Cadillac on his arrival, holding his sterling-silver pitcher and washbasin, pulling out his chair when he stood or sat. It seemed as if the rebbe did not move an inch or raise a finger without a predetermined set of assisting maneuvers. I won the privilege of handing the rebbe my book of Psalms, from which he would recite five chapters at the end of morning prayers.

At first, I was indifferent. Sure, I thought, the rebbe could use my Psalms if he wanted to, although it was just the same to me if he didn't.

"Can I see your Psalms?" a classmate asked the next day.

Several students gathered around as I withdrew the modest faux leather-bound volume—a bar mitzvah gift from a family friend—from my navy-blue velvet tefillin pouch. My friends leaned in to examine it, but with one quick glance at its puny ordinariness, they shook their heads. It was not the right kind, they said.

"What's the right kind?"

"The rebbe uses only a *Shloh* prayer book."

The *Shloh* prayer book was a special prayer book for the mystics and the ultra-pious, filled with kabbalistic commentary in the margins. Because the rebbe used one, most self-respecting Skverer Hasidim used one, too. I, of course, did not.

One of my classmates pulled me aside. "I'd be happy to exchange privileges."

"What'd you get?"

He bit his lip. "Holding the towel after tefillin—but the rebbe can't use your Psalms anyway."

Chaim Elya, my source for all things Skver, explained it to me: "When you hold the towel," he said, "the rebbe wipes his hands, and that's it. The towel is still the rebbe's. But with Psalms, it's your Psalms. You make a note inside that the rebbe used it. You get to keep it for life."

Other students, too, offered to exchange privileges, always making sure to emphasize that the rebbe couldn't use my Psalms anyway, and so I'd best take what they offered or I would end up with nothing.

Suddenly, my indifference was gone. I had won the privilege fairly. I approached the dean, Reb Chezkel, to ask if my Psalms was good enough for the rebbe, and he waved his hand to dismiss the critics. "Your Psalms is fine. The rebbe won't care."

Still, some of the students would not let the matter rest. "You're not even a Skverer Hasid," one argued, "What does it matter to you?"

One student offered me ten dollars in exchange for the privilege, and for a moment I wondered whether I might capitalize on the affair, sell it to the highest bidder. I thought of the chocolate Danishes at the corner grocery store, the shelves of Yiddish books at the Judaica shop on Bedford Avenue, the hot dogs turning in the window of Landau's delicatessen on Lee Avenue. But selling the Psalms privilege would be unseemly, an insult to the rebbe. Besides, now it all seemed like a pretty big deal. I was keeping my privilege.

I stood with the rest of the student body, lined up in the study hall waiting for the rebbe to appear. The door opened slowly from the outside.

"Shh, shh," the crowd hushed.

An elderly man with a salt-and-pepper beard and bulbous nose, looking both morose and self-important, appeared, and it took me a moment to realize that he was not the rebbe but his attendant. He began brushing away imaginary specks of dirt on the floor with the tip of his shoe and shoving aside students whose elbows stuck too far into the cleared path. Several paces behind him came a stout man with a reddish beard gone slightly gray, his brow wrinkled, his wide-brimmed hat pulled low over his forehead, his eyebrows narrowed into an insistent scowl. This, evidently, was the great man himself: His Honorable Holiness, Our Master, Our Teacher, Our Rabbi, the Righteous Foundation of the World, the Rebbe of Skvyra, May He Live Many Good and Long Days.

He did not look like a rebbe. He did not look regal, he did not look scholarly, he did not look *rebbish*. His beard was not white, and not nearly long enough—fist-length, at most. He did not sport long flowing white sidelocks but small reddish ones, and he kept them tied in a small knot in front of his ears. I had always thought rebbes were supposed to have a languid air, eyes downward or lightly closed or rolled upward, otherworldly. But this rebbe's eyes looked shrewd and present. When he walked, his head pointed forward, but his dark eyes, under thick, slanted eyebrows, shifted with alertness. He said not a word and made no unexpected gestures, and yet, his presence in the room was thick; I felt it in the utter silence, in the unblinking, staring eyes and the bated breath of all around me. The rebbe approached the special lectern prepared for him, then whipped his densely woven prayer shawl out of its cowhide pouch and flung it in one sweeping motion over his head and torso, sending a gentle breeze over our sweaty foreheads.

Prayer began moments later. We stood in a tight semicircle around the rebbe, whose face was obscured, only the bulk of his large, swaying body visible from behind. A handful of burly students were stationed in the front row, creating a force field of empty space around the rebbe while behind them the rest us elbowed for a better spot.

He who makes peace among the heavens, may He make peace among us. The prayer leader called out the last verses of kaddish, and I readied myself with my little Psalms.

With the last chorus of "Amen," I pushed my way through the tight semicircle and approached the rebbe. My hands trembled as I laid the book on the lectern and watched as the rebbe's thick hands reached for it. From behind the folds of his tallis, his eyes met mine for a quick second, piercing me with their silent scrutiny. I took several steps backward and watched as he glanced at the volume, flipped the front cover, and read my gold-embossed name. For a moment I held my breath, waiting for the rebbe to turn and say that it was not the right kind. Instead, he glanced once again in my direction, and I saw a hint of a smile, as if an acknowledgment of my boldness in offering a volume so ordinary. I felt a flutter of victory.

It was all over very quickly. After prayers, the rebbe was led around the premises by Reb Chezkel as the student body surged several paces behind. As soon as the rebbe's car left, taking off with its strobe lights flashing and siren shrieking to announce the rebbe's departure to the Hasidim of Williamsburg, we took to analyzing each moment of the visit. Every step, every glance, every twitch of the rebbe's eyebrow, had been carefully observed and scrutinized, and for the rest of the week, it was all the students talked about.

Inside the front cover of the little volume, following the guidance of my friend Chaim Elya, I wrote: *In this Book of Psalms, the Rebbe of Skvyra, may he live many long years, recited chapters 91 to 95 on Thursday, the 27th day of Cheshvan, 5748.*

It wasn't until my first visit to the village of New Square that I came to understand what really set the Skverers apart. The death anniversary of the rebbe's grandfather, Reb Duvidel of Skvyra, was approaching, and the yeshiva organized an official trip to the sect's headquarters. The rebbe would be leading a memorial tisch, a traditional communal meal.

I wasn't eager to attend. Rebbes were still not on my mind much. In Borough Park, where I lived, there was no shortage of those who laid claim to the title. They all seemed indistinctive and uninspiring, caricatures of pietistic pretense, each with his gauzy white beard, glazed eyes under thick eyeglasses, blue or white floral caftans: the Munkatcher, the Bobover, the Stoliner, the Skulener, the Rachmastrivker; Hungarian and Polish, Romanian and Galician, even the occasional Lithuanian. On the rare occasion that I would attend one of their tischen, I would listen as they spoke, mumbling in odd singsong voices, always variations on the same themes, about Torah study and prayer and the Sabbath kugel and good Jews and bad non-Jews. There were songs, on occasion, as often as not uninspiring, tepid melodies sung halfheartedly and off-key by sparse crowds. Usually, I would attend only with friends, if it was a special occasion and there was the promise of entertainment—a Purim play in Munkatch, the menorah lighting in Rachmastrivka, dancing till dawn at Bobov on the seventh night of Passover, which was pleasant enough for about five minutes but surely not for five hours. For the most part, little of it held my interest; I was far more concerned that my black caftan would become creased, that my polished black shoes would be scuffed, and that my Sabbath beaver hat would get knocked into a bowl of chicken soup.

Reb Chezkel, however, made it clear that attending the tisch in New Square was mandatory.

The shtetl was only an hour from Brooklyn, but as our yellow school bus made its way through the strange village, I found myself intrigued. Young boys wore black suspenders over dull-colored shirts and black pants, their unkempt sidelocks down to their chests—unlike us Brooklyn boys who snipped our sidelocks at chin-length and kept them perfectly curled. Their hats appeared rain-speckled, and every man and boy appeared to be wearing "Medicaid glasses," cat-eye frames of thick black or brown plastic. Their *gartels*, thin black prayer sashes, were wound tightly around their waists over ill-fitting gabardines; their shoes looked worn-out, scuffed at the toes and encrusted with mud. Even the women had a more pious appearance, kerchiefs bound over their wigs more tightly than in Brooklyn, their expressions more se-vere. There was something slightly repellent about these people and, at the same time, strangely enchanting. I half expected to see a yard full of squawking chickens and a milk cow at pasture.

The bus stopped in front of a large, plain-looking rectangular struc-ture in the center of the village, its only adornment a narrow roofed porch and two concrete square columns at its entrance. This was the village's main synagogue. Inside the sanctuary, an enormous table was set up, made up of dozens of smaller tables, each covered with what was once a white tablecloth but was now grease-stained and yellowed. Seated on benches with tall backrests along both sides of the table were elderly men, and behind them, leaning on the backrests, were more men, middle-aged, some with small children in their arms or standing beside them. Behind them were rows of bleachers, five stories each, about fifteen feet tall. On the bleachers, young men and teenage boys stood pressed against one another, and more were climbing to take their places among them, all of them looking toward the head of the table, where the rebbe was soon to appear.

I felt a tap on my shoulder. A thin, tall man stood behind me and extended his hand.

"*Shulem aleichem*," he said. "Welcome."

I looked to see if I knew him, but he took off without another word. Soon another man approached to shake my hand, and then another. Some smiled but most didn't, as if these welcoming gestures were a solemn duty. Some asked for my name and where I was from, but most moved on quickly. The handshakes were as varied as those who offered them: limp, firm, pumping—even a two-handed one from a middle-aged gentleman who smiled broadly as if we were old friends, but he offered no words at all.

Suddenly, there was frantic hushing, and I watched as men and boys of all ages made a final dash for their places. I tried to get a peek between the many hats and heads and shoulders but couldn't see much past the jostling men in front of me. The rebbe, I presumed, had just entered from a room at the front.

Another tap on my shoulder. Chaim Lazer, one of my classmates, stood behind me.

"Come up onto the *parentches*," he said, and pointed to the bleachers, rows and rows of boys our own age.

"It looks full," I said.

"They'll make room for you. In Skver, there's always room for another."

I followed Chaim as he climbed to the top row of the last set of bleachers. Already cramped, the boys squeezed together to make room for us and reached across to shake our hands. There was a faint musk in the air, from the compressed bodies and layers of clothes; on occasion, my nostrils were hit with a strong whiff of it.

The hall fell silent. All focus was on the rebbe, who now sat on a tall gilded chair at the head of the table, its seat and back of rich red leather, a gold crown in wood relief rising from the chair behind the rebbe's head. I watched as he raised a large loaf of challah, the size of a small child, and cut a slice for himself. He ripped a small piece and chewed slowly, his head swaying from side to side, as if in prayer. Meanwhile, the attendant took the rest and cut it into smaller pieces. The challah chunks, soon shredded into hundreds of pieces, were passed from hand to hand all the way across the shul. Some received only crumbs, and those crumbs were split into even smaller crumbs. These were the traditional sacred morsels, *sherayim*, leftovers of the tzaddik's food, each morsel bringing untold blessings: it healed the sick, brought good fortune, and instilled in one the fear of God.

More food was placed in front of the rebbe, all of it in enormous silver dishes: a whole cooked salmon, chicken noodle soup in a covered silver tureen, a large platter piled high with dozens of chicken legs, and another with brightly glazed carrots. From each dish, the rebbe ate only a few morsels, swaying from side to side as he chewed, after which the attendant passed around the leftovers, which were then passed, hand to hand, through the rest of the crowd.

An elderly man began to sing a familiar song, a coarse and boisterous melody, its simple notes taught in every Hasidic kindergarten: *Grant us the good inclination, to serve You with truth, with awe and with love.* The rebbe rested his forehead on his right hand, covering half his face. His cheeks were flaming red over his reddish-gray beard as his body swayed softly to the rhythm.

The crowd joined in, and slowly their voices grew louder, more robust, the song filling the sanctuary. Moments later, the rebbe removed his hand from his forehead and began to pound his fist on the table. The crowd responded, stomping their feet in time to the rebbe's pounding. Even the brass chandeliers vibrated to the beat of the song. The simple passage was repeated over and over, until the crowd was like a single massive organism screaming its desperate plea: *Grant us, grant us, the good inclination! Grant us, grant us, the good inclination!*

During a pause in the singing, men removed kerchiefs from their pockets and wiped the sweat from their brows. Above us, latticework panels covered the balcony areas, the women's section, and here and there a slender finger gripped a wooden strip from behind the partition. Through the slats, I could make out the vague outline of faces, the few women who cared to attend, to observe this otherwise male-only event.

Another dish was placed in front of the rebbe, and then quickly removed for disbursement. The crowd grew tense with anticipation, soft murmurs followed by expectant silence. The rebbe gestured to one of the elderly men at the table. The man began to sing a slow tune set to words I remembered from the penitence prayers of the High Holy Days, a prayer not to God but to his ministering angels:

> *Remind Him, make it heard before Him,*
> *the Torah study and good deeds*
> *of those who rest beneath the earth.*

The crowd took up the tune, again starting out weakly, their voices growing stronger with each stanza. The song came to an end, and the crowd took it up again from the beginning. Some of the men appeared to be weeping. The boys around me swayed vigorously with their eyes closed. Even the children stood remarkably solemn, all eyes on the rebbe:

> *Let Him remember their love, and keep alive their seed,*
> *so that the remnant of Jacob will not be lost.*
> *For the sheep of a faithful shepherd has been put to humiliation,*
> *Israel, one nation, to scorn and mockery.*

The last part was directed to God Himself, as if our restraint had dissolved, the passion of our cry warranting the bypass of heavenly bureaucracy:

> *Answer us speedily, God of our salvation,*
> *Redeem us from all harsh decrees.*
> *Save, with Your bountiful mercy,*
> *Your righteous anointed one and Your nation.*

There were more songs, slow tunes and lively ones, some set to words and others only a steady stream of *ya di da di dai.* I found myself swept up in the energy, joining hands with the boys beside me, lifting my feet with them and stomping on the floorboards, sharing in their exuberance, smelling the sweat of their bodies and tasting the *sherayim* of their rebbe's food.

For the first time, I understood the tisch, not as something a teacher or parent declared important but as something experiential and inexpressible. It was some combination of the people, the food, the bodies pressed tightly together swaying in unison, the Hasidim's warm smiles that inexplicably captivated me. For the very first time, it occurred to me that being a Hasid allowed for more than the daily grind of studying Talmud and adhering to the minutiae of our religious laws.

Here was the ecstasy and the joy. Here was all that I had been told that we Hasidim once had and lost. "The teachings of the Baal Shem Tov have been forgotten," the old rebbe of Satmar had famously said, but here among the Skverers, they appeared not to be forgotten at all.

It was soon after that evening that, if anyone asked, I would say, "I am a Skverer."

Other Hasidim, those I had grown up among in Brooklyn, were different. They cared a great deal about their crystal chandeliers and Persian rugs, their summer bungalows in the Catskill Mountains and the prestige of their children's marital arrangements. On Sabbath afternoons, the men paraded through Borough Park in their finest clothes, the tassels of their silk, handwoven gartels flapping at their sides, their gleaming fur *shtreimels* tall on their heads, with the outer edges shooting up in circles of tiny spires. But they did not cry as they stomped their feet: "Grant us! Grant us! The good inclination!" as

the Skverers did. Hasidim in Borough Park remodeled their kitch-
ens frequently and got the best deals on late-model cars, but never
had I seen them squeeze together to allow another Hasid to experience the song and dance of a rebbe's tisch. "Animals!" my friend Shloime
Samet's father screamed when he discovered a light scratch along the
side of his brand-new tawny Oldsmobile, and I stood stunned that a
scratch on a car could enrage a man so. "Don't ruin my furniture," my
friend Nuchem Zinger's father growled as I brushed lightly against
the mahogany china cabinet in their dining room. In Borough Park,
I had been told tales of men who embraced asceticism and poverty
and want, who did not go to bed until they had given their last coin to
the poor, and yet we lived as if those tales had taught us nothing. But
the Skverers were different; they appeared to live exactly like the pious
and modest folk of the old European shtetl, and now I longed to be one
of them.

Several months later, my parents sent me for a year of study at a yeshiva
in Montreal. The dean was a Satmar Hasid, as were most of the students, but there were also Belzers and Vizhnitzers, and Bobovers, and
even one Lubavitcher. I, along with only two others, was a Skverer. A
year later, at fourteen, I would return to study with the Skverers, first
in Williamsburg, and later, at sixteen, in the Great Yeshiva in New
Square. But it was during that year in Montreal, among Hasidim of so
many different sects, that my new identity took firm hold.

On the Sabbath, at the third meal, as evening blended into night,
we would gather around the tables in the dining room over pickled herring and cooked chickpeas, and I would think of New Square, where
the same meal was held in the rebbe's great synagogue, the lights ex-
tinguished, as if it were a Ukrainian town a century earlier, when the
candles of the previous evening were burned out and new ones could
not be lit until nightfall.

"*The sons of the inner chamber, who yearn to gaze at the countenance
of Ze'er Anpin,*" the boys in my Montreal yeshiva would sing, while I
would not sing with them but only chant mournfully, as I had among
the Skverers in their shtetl, where hundreds of men and boys would
stand pressed together, the blackness of our coats and hats blending

with the blackness of the dark hall, creating an eerie otherworldliness, at once melancholic and strangely joyful. *"Rejoice! There is goodwill in this hour, no anger or fury,"* the rebbe would cry, his sobs reverberating through the pitch-black chamber. A chill would go up my spine until I felt the hair along my temples go straight. *"Come near to me, behold my strength, for there are no harsh judgments."*

"Hey, Skverer, where are your boots?" one of my Satmar classmates would taunt me. Skverer men, once married, wore tall peasant boots on the Sabbath instead of the knickers and white stockings of other Hasidim. But I felt not taunted but proud. I would wear those boots, too, when the time came, when I found a girl from a Skverer family to marry, and raise our children as Skverers.

Chapter Four

A dozen of us attended each of Avremel Shayevitz's sessions of "groom instruction." Beneath the harsh white light of two long, naked fluorescent bulbs, we sat around a brown Formica table in Avremel's dining room. Through the closed door to the kitchen came the sounds of children playing, crying, laughing, bursts of raised voices followed by a woman's scolding: "Shh, Tatti is studying with the *bucherim*."

"*Respect her more than your own self!*" Avremel would cry during those sessions, quoting the Talmud, his jerky arms and fists slicing and pounding the air. "But how do we *understand* this passage? What does it *mean* to respect a woman?" Avremel would twist a hair from his scraggly black beard around his finger, pull it out, and drop it absentmindedly on the table between us. "What it *really* means, esteemed young men, is that we must be vigilant! Respect what *she*, a *woman*, can do to a man if he does not remain careful." He would wag an index finger over his head, "Let down your guard, and she will lead you into *sheol tachtis*—the abyss of sinful temptation!"

There were other "groom instructors," too.

There was Reb Noach, with his mangy blond beard and his springy step and ever-present smirk, who would teach me about the female body and the many laws related to its function. There was Reb Shraga Feivish, who would, on the afternoon of the wedding, teach me the mechanics of how to perform "the mitzvah." There was Reb Srulik, with whom I would consult after the wedding on various questions—embarrassing ones, mostly, about body fluids, and shades of red and brown and ocher, anything that might interrupt our "family cleanliness."

But before, after, and in between all the others, there was Avremel, the facilitator and clarifier of all that information, casting it in its appropriate light, ensuring that it was properly understood and acted upon.

Avremel's mentorship had begun nearly three years earlier, in our first year at the Great Yeshiva, not to prepare us for marriage but as a general counselor. He was a thin man, with hollow cheeks and dark eyes that opened wide to reveal the whites and narrowed to slits so intense that they were frightening. Avremel was one of a cadre of men chosen by the rebbe to serve as special mentors. In later years, I would see Avremel as a caricature of religious fanaticism, a Savonarola of the Hasidic world; but at the time, I idolized him. His speeches were masterful: he was able, in a single breath, to weave talmudic passages about hell and the afterlife into a scathing comedic rant against one sort of wickedness or another, scorning the sheer idiocy of those who could not resist temptations of the flesh, who veered from "holiness and purity."

Once a month, for the New Moon feast, scores of young men would squeeze into Avremel's small dining room and sit around his table or on the battered divan by the wall or cross-legged on the floor. We would dip chunks of challah into bowls of *yishke*—a concoction of overripe tomatoes, diced onions, and bits of schmaltz herring, drenched in vegetable oil—and wash it down with flat seltzer while Avremel spoke of the evils of gluttony and earthly temptations, sinful thoughts in our sleep, insufficient devotion in prayer or to the rebbe. We would enter through a rear door, to avoid glimpses of Avremel's wife or his young daughters, but we'd hear their disembodied voices from other parts of the small apartment. Occasionally, one of Avremel's young sons would join us, and even the youngest knew to close the door behind him quickly. It was the perfect Hasidic home, and Avremel, clearly, was a paragon of Hasidic manhood.

The groom instruction sessions were different: intimate and secretive. Only the soon-to-be-married were invited, and we were instructed to speak with no one about them. These were sensitive matters, and we would slip away from the study hall in the evening, aware of the furtive glances in our direction.

The first session took place two months before my wedding, which was to be held in early June. When the session was over, I waited until the others left, and then asked Avremel if I might speak with him. We sat on opposite sides of the table, and I remember struggling for words. What came out was a croak, a lame attempt at verbalizing my tempestuous swings from anger to melancholy to resignation during the last four months. "I am not happy."

Avremel's eyes went wide in response, fiery, almost scolding. "Why?" he asked.

Again, as in the rebbe's chamber, there was a question and I had to come up with an answer. I thought that with Avremel it would be easier, but now I realized that here, too, I couldn't speak my thoughts. They felt inappropriate, almost sinful. I was thinking the wrong thoughts, feeling the wrong things.

"I don't know why," I said. And then I felt an explosion of despair, my face suddenly awash with tears. I did not want to marry this girl. The day, the hour, the moment was approaching, and I could not stop it. I wished I could escape, take off to some unknown place, where I could start a new life and be spared the shame of what I really wanted, but where would I go? Overwhelmed, I buried my face in my arm, unable to contain my sobs.

When I raised my head again, Avremel was staring at me, his eyebrows narrowed, his brow creased, as if he now realized that, yes, we had a problem. But he needed more information, he said. "Perhaps you can think on it some more."

"I don't know," I remember muttering. "Maybe—I just don't think she and I have anything in common."

Avremel nodded slowly, then looked at the table for a long time. Finally, he said, "You were hoping for a friend." He stroked his beard, beads of spit trapped in the edges of his unkempt mustache.

I shrugged with a half nod. Perhaps that was it.

"A wife isn't a friend." Avremel shook his head emphatically. "*Eizer kenegdo,*" he said, quoting Genesis. "A wife is to be a helpmate. Your friends will still be your fellow students."

Avremel looked at me while I stared at the faux wood-grain patterns in the Formica tabletop and I thought about his words. After several minutes of silence, he began to speak again, more assuredly this time. I had misunderstood the whole marriage thing, he said. A wife is not a friend. A wife is not something to think about excessively. To take a wife is a biblical commandment, and so we do God's will by taking one. A wife is there to assist with one's service to God, nothing more.

In later years, I would have words for that which I could not articulate to the rebbe or to Avremel, words from beyond our cloistered world of tischen and Talmud study and groom instruction: Attraction. Chemistry. Compatibility. I would later learn other words—passion, romance, arousal, desire—that I wanted as well, but to want those was an unquestionable sin; those feelings and thoughts and behaviors that passed between sexes outside of our world were anathema to us and our sacred ways.

I remember when I first became aware of a world filled with forbidden passions. I was nearing fourteen, during my year of study in Montreal, and I had a curious thought.

"Have you noticed," I said one day to my friend Avrum Yida, a Satmar boy from Williamsburg, "that here in Montreal, wherever you turn, there is a man and woman walking together?"

Avrum Yida didn't understand what I meant, and I tried to point out what was to me unmistakably apparent. In our world, fathers walked with sons and mothers with daughters, but here, everywhere, were men and women in pairs—strolling down leafy Avenue Saint Viateur, past the many shuttered Roman Catholic churches; sitting on the benches in Outremont Park, resting hands, heads, legs in each other's laps; eyeing the jewelry store displays in the small row of shops along Avenue Bernard, eyes glittering toward each other through the fog of their breath in the frigid January air.

It must be a French thing, I remember thinking. I had learned that Quebecois were French, and the French, I had heard once, were the most decadent of all people. Paris was the source of all *shmutz*, our teachers had told us. It was the place from which immodest women's fashions were conceived and sent to the rest of the world, to tempt men to sin. This uncouth display of intersex courtship must have something to do with that.

Avrum Yida, when he finally understood my observation, dismissed it. "It's just how goyim are," he said. "You can see it in Manhattan, too." Avrum Yida thought himself wise and worldly, and I was inclined to take his word for it. Not a French thing but a goyish thing.

French or goyish, however, it was sinful to gaze at. Yet I could not look away. From the second-floor window of our yeshiva, I would watch as they passed, hand in hand or with their arms on each other's backs, heads leaning on shoulders, pecking at each other's lips and nuzzling noses. My jaw would go slack as I observed them, until I would catch myself and turn to check that no one was watching me.

Shield your eyes, our teachers would warn us. *Your eyes are the doorways to evil thoughts.* From the day of my bar mitzvah, matters of *holiness and purity* became the obsessive concern of my mentors. If at twelve, I might have played a game of cat's cradle with my sister's friend Rachy from down the block, by fourteen, such interaction was strictly forbidden. If at thirteen, I could still spar with Bruchy Feldman over a book, by fifteen, I would avert my eyes entirely when a girl or woman entered a room or passed me on the street.

Guard your covenant, my teacher warned during my private bar mitzvah lessons. I was not sure what he meant until he looked at me sternly, and warned me that if I touched my covenant and it became long and hard, it could lead to the greatest of all sins: *the well-known sin.* And I couldn't help wonder: If it was so well known, why did I not know it? Did it have another name, maybe? Was I allowed to ask?

"From tomorrow onward," my father said on the evening of my bar mitzvah, "you must immerse in the mikveh each morning before prayers." He made vague allusions to impurities occurring during the night, which the purifying waters of the ritual bath were to cleanse.

"You went to *Eichler's?*" my sister, Chani, two years older than I, asked in horror when I returned home one day with an Eichler's shopping bag. Eichler's was a Judaica bookstore on Thirteenth Avenue, Borough Park's main shopping thoroughfare. "You shouldn't be anywhere *near* Thirteenth Avenue!" Thirteenth Avenue was filled with housewives and schoolgirls. Even my sister knew that was too much temptation for a thirteen-year-old boy to handle.

Eleven-year-old Bruchy Feldman, the sister of my friends Nusy and Eli, knew it, too, and attempted to give me a lesson about it when she caught me reading a book I had quietly taken from her room. It was during one of my return visits from Montreal, while visiting the Feldmans next door, when I wandered into Bruchy's bedroom to browse the collection of books she had—mostly Holocaust memoirs, tales of ancient sages, and novels about Orthodox Jewish schoolgirls. On the floor near her bed, as if discarded, was a tattered, dog-eared volume, on its cover a drawing of a boy holding a pair of binoculars. Before I knew it, I was slouched on the hallway floor outside Bruchy's room, riveted.

"You shouldn't read that," Bruchy said, appearing suddenly at the top of the stairs and smiling coyly as she approached. "It's not for boys."

I grunted in response, then inched away as she reached to take the book from me. I was thirteen, a yeshiva boy and budding Talmud scholar. I didn't take orders from eleven-year-old girls.

Bruchy left but returned several minutes later.

"You shouldn't read that," she said again, her tone now reproachful, certain of her righteousness. "It's not for boys!" she cried as she lunged for the book, her straight, unstyled, dirty-blond hair flapping across her face.

But the book *was* for boys. It was not one of *our* books but a secular book, with the stamp of the local public library on the edges of the page. The book told the story of a boy who would gaze through binoculars to the house across the street, in which there lived a girl his age who kept her window shades open. The boy would watch her undress, then think about what he saw, and later he would find that in his pants he felt an odd feeling, a tightening bulge that he was certain everyone noticed and that he tried to cover up by wearing a raincoat at all times. He also experienced what one of his teachers called "nocturnal emissions," which described exactly that terribly embarrassing thing that I had begun to experience over the past few months.

If I was surprised that this book was to be found in the Feldmans' home, I didn't give it much thought, although I was dimly aware that Bruchy had probably sneaked it into her home without her parents' knowledge. Her father was a rabbi and scholar who spent his days absorbed in his studies and paid little attention to his children's reading habits. Mrs. Feldman, a book lover herself, must have been lax about supervising her daughter's reading.

But Bruchy knew, as anyone with any sense did, that this was certainly not a book for boys. Boys were to keep their minds pure and spend their days with Torah study. Girls were not required to study Torah. *He who teaches his daughter Torah,* the sages said, *teaches her foolishness.* Girls, we were told, didn't have the urges and temptations that boys did. Girls were allowed to gaze at boys, but boys were not allowed to gaze back. Some said that women possessed loftier souls than men and therefore didn't need to study Torah, weren't obligated with as many commandments, were allowed to study English literature and history and even a little art and science, too, because their souls were so lofty that those subjects couldn't hurt them, or not nearly as much as they could boys. I knew this, and Bruchy knew this, and so we both knew that it was her duty to keep me from reading a book that she, too, should not have been reading but was far more sinful when read by a boy.

It would be several decades before I learned that the book was *Then Again, Maybe I Won't,* which, along with other books by the same author, Judy Blume, was seen as transgressive even by non-Hasidic standards and was banned from schools and libraries across the country. At that time, however, I knew only that the book addressed so many mysteries of my private world that I could not contain my desperate desire to keep reading it. Except, Bruchy would not allow it. Over the next few days, whenever I returned to the Feldmans' home, I would plead with Bruchy for another glance at it, only just to hold it in my hand, and each time I would face again her righteous hissing: "It's not for boys!"

A week later, I was back on the bus to Montreal, squeezed into a window seat beside a heavyset rabbi who spent most of the eight-hour trip offering me chulent-making tips—he claimed to be a world-class expert—while all I could think of was the boy with the binoculars. I wondered whether he ever got to speak to the girl across the street, or whether he learned anything more about the mysteries of his body. As the rabbi went on about choosing the best kinds of beans and how to cut the potatoes just right, I wondered why some books would be *not for boys,* what made boys and girls different, and why I was beginning to feel a strange stirring whenever this rabbi's daughter, a pale, thin girl with a long dark braid sitting across the aisle, glanced my way.

"Perverted thoughts only enter a mind devoid of wisdom," my teachers would remind me, and so, throughout my yeshiva years, I would try to fill my mind only with Torah study. And yet, those other thoughts still came, often when most unexpected.

If the woman plants the seed first, the child is male, I read in the Talmud, and I wondered about the ways in which such a seed might be planted.

In the Bible, I read the tales of ancient people and their many acts of "lying with"—Pharaoh and Abraham's wife Sarah; Reuben and his father's concubine Bilhah; Judah and his daughter-in-law Tamar—and I tried hard not to let my thoughts wander to what such "lying with" might entail.

Then there was that mysterious term: *tashmish hamitah.* It appeared on occasion during my studies but was never explained. Teachers mumbled it without elaborating. I knew the literal meaning: "service of the bed." I knew some things about it: It was forbidden on Yom Kippur. It was the thing—referred to by the Bible as "playing"—that Isaac did with his wife, Rebecca, while the Philistine king Avimelech watched through the window. It caused ritual impurity, requiring immersion in water before being allowed into the temple in Jerusalem or partaking of the sacred meat of ritual sacrifice. But I did not know what it was.

When I was twelve, several months before my bar mitzvah, I turned to my father one day as he headed to his study with a glass of tea in hand. The question popped out of my mouth, as if on its own: "Tatti, what does *tashmish hamitah* mean?"

My father stopped, startled. Standing tall and thin in his faded black *chalatel,* the light gabardine he wore around the house, his *gartel* wound snugly around his waist, he looked at me as if trying to read some secret intent behind my question. Then he asked me to follow him into his study, where he sat down in his chair and asked me to close the door.

Tashmish hamitah, my father said, refers to something very private between a husband and wife. "It involves touching in a way that expresses feelings," he said.

He looked at me thoughtfully to see if I understood, and I nodded, feeling for a moment as if I had actually learned something. I had never seen Hasidic husbands and wives touch, and so what I now heard was so new and startling that I did not think to ask anything more about it.

"You'll understand more when you get older," my father added, and it was only after I left his study that I wondered what such touching might look like. My father said it expressed feeling, and so I wondered: Did they hold hands? Caress each other's cheeks? And why was a bed needed?

Several weeks later, our rebbe, Reb Meshulam, gave his afternoon Bible lesson.

"*And you shall enter the ark, you and your sons, and your wife and your son's wives*," he read from the Bible text. It was the tale of Noah and the flood, and few students seemed to be paying attention. We'd studied this portion each year, for nearly a decade, and the story never changed. Noah built his ark. God sent the flood. Everyone perished, except those in the ark. We'd heard it all before.

"Let us study the Rashi," Reb Meshulam said, and pointed his finger to the lower half of the page.

Rashi was a medieval French rabbi who wrote the most essential commentaries on both the Bible and Talmud. But we'd already studied this portion of Rashi, too, many times.

From across the room, Shloimy Rubin doodled in the margins of his Bible reader. Eli Green rested his chin lazily on his forearm. Next to me, one boy yawned followed by another. It was late on a Sunday afternoon, and class would end in an hour.

Reb Meshulam read from Rashi's commentary: "*The men and women entered the ark separately. And so we know that* tashmish hamitah *was forbidden in the ark.*"

Suddenly, my mind was alert. There was that term again. *Tashmish hamitah*. Service of the bed. This was a passage of Rashi I hadn't noticed before—as if it had been newly placed inside our texts. So startled was

I by its newness, that I blurted a question aloud: "*Tashmish hamitah* was forbidden in the ark? Why?"

Reb Meshulam fell silent. Shloimy Rubin stopped doodling in the margins of his Bible, and Eli Green raised his head from resting on his forearm.

Reb Meshulam looked away. "The world was in sorrow," he said after a long pause. "It would have been inappropriate."

Reb Meshulam continued his lesson. Shloimy returned to his doodling. Eli rested his chin back on his arm.

"You know what *tashmish hamitah* means?" Shloimy and Eli came running after me, when school was over. I was heading down Forty-Third Street, past a schoolyard in which a group of non-Hasidic kids were playing softball.

"We heard you ask your question," Eli said, catching his breath. "We figured you must know."

"I do know," I said.

They waited for me to elaborate.

"I can't really say. It's not proper to talk about it."

"We think we know," Shloimy said, looking at me intently. "Eli saw a picture in a magazine."

Eli nodded along.

"Tell me what you know," I said, "and I'll tell you if it's correct."

Shloimy looked at Eli, who smiled sheepishly. Then, as Eli could not bring himself to mouth the words, Shloimy offered it instead, speaking the words almost in a whisper: "The man puts his front into the woman's behind."

It was now five years later, with my wedding nearing, and Shloimy's words niggled in my mind. Could that have been what my father meant? It was hard to believe, and yet, what if Shloimy was right? Anxious to have it either confirmed or denied, I proceeded to the next level of groom instruction, a series of lessons with Reb Noach.

At Reb Noach's dining-room table, sitting on a sweaty, plastic-upholstered chair for two hours each afternoon, I listened to instruction on a whole new set of laws: *To a woman impure from menstruation, thou shalt not approach*, Reb Noach read from the Hebrew Bible in front of us. *A man who lies with a menstruating woman, both will be cut off from their people.*

A woman emits a bloody discharge each month, Reb Noach explained; during that period, it is forbidden to approach her. It is forbidden to share utensils, to pass her any object directly, to touch her or even her garments, to gaze at her body parts that are generally concealed—upper arms, thighs, shoulders, even her hair. It is forbidden to sit on her bed, to pour her a glass of wine, or to exchange words of affection. Detailed records must be kept to allow us to be vigilant during days that her period was likely to arrive.

It was all just another elaborate set of laws, not unlike the requirement to fast on Yom Kippur, cut a newborn male infant's genitals, or tie your left shoe before your right. Many volumes had been written on the subject. And still, the great mystery of the *touching* was not revealed.

My wedding day arrived a month before my nineteenth birthday. At three o'clock in the afternoon, I was to meet with the last of all groom instructors, Reb Shraga Feivish.

I awoke early that morning to recite the entire Book of Psalms. I would be fasting; the wedding day was a personal Yom Kippur for the bride and groom, a sacred day of atonement and repentance. After morning prayers, I had a brief audience with the rebbe, who sat wrapped in his prayer shawl as he read my *kvittel,* and then extended his hand. "May your celebration arrive at a good and auspicious hour," he said, as he held my hand with the tips of his fingers.

Reb Shraga Feivish, an emaciated-looking rabbi with a beard down to his navel, led me into his study. Religious texts were strewn about on every available surface. He opened a large volume on the table and read aloud: *One who marries a virgin takes possession of her, and separates from her immediately.*

Reb Shraga Feivish went on to teach me about all the laws that come after "taking possession," and as the minutes passed, I felt a rising panic. Had he flown right past the obvious? Had I missed a crucial lecture with no one realizing it? I needed the basics, not the laws on what came afterward. I wanted details of the act itself, but Reb Shraga

Feivish seemed too absorbed in his stream of instruction, and I was too anxious and too stunned to interrupt him.

After about twenty minutes, Reb Shraga Feivish closed his book. "When you get home after the wedding, begin preparing right away."

"*Tonight?*" I gasped in alarm.

"Yes. The mitzvah must be performed before daybreak. It'll probably be very late when you get home, so don't waste any time."

I hadn't been expecting this immediacy. I had thought that whatever it was, I would have time to process it all. Reb Shraga Feivish, however, only continued with his instructions. The mitzvah, he said, must be performed twice a week, on Tuesday and Friday nights, after midnight, in total darkness.

"Have you been to your apartment?" he asked. "Does the bedroom have a heavy window shade?"

I had been to the apartment but hadn't thought to check the window shade.

"Well," Reb Shraga Feivish said thoughtfully, "don't worry about it now. If necessary, you can put a quilt over it."

Then, at last, he described the mechanics of the sexual act. He used a series of hand gestures, and finally I understood, more or less. Shloimy and Eli had been wrong, I was relieved to learn.

Reb Shraga Feivish wasn't finished, though.

"Before the act itself," Reb Shraga Feivish said, "lie beside her and chat for a few minutes."

"Chat about what?" I asked.

"It is recommended that one tell tales of the righteous. Only a few minutes are necessary. Until she gets comfortable."

"What kinds of tales?" I asked.

"Doesn't matter. Any tale about a righteous man. About his fear of God, or his love of his fellow Jews. The usual tales." He paused to make sure I understood. "Then you get on top, and tell her you love her."

"How?" I asked simply, and the question felt stupid on my lips.

Reb Shraga Feivish paused, as if startled by so direct a question. "Just say, 'I love you.'"

The notion of loving my wife had never occurred to me. Marriage was a duty, no more. To pretend otherwise seemed ridiculous.

"It is the law," he said with a shrug. "The law says you must tell her you love her."

There was no arguing with the law.

"You must kiss her twice," he continued. "Once before the act and once during."

The "mitzvah," Reb Shraga Feivish explained, must not be done when in a state of anger. It must not be done during daytime hours. It must not be done when drunk, or after eating, or before using the bathroom. It must not be done if she is brazen ("she must not ask for it explicitly; she may only hint at her desire indirectly"). It must not be done in the presence of sacred books, or in the presence of a child. Most important of all, the mitzvah must be done the way it was done by the great sage Rabbi Eliezer: *with awe and with fear, as if forced by a demon.*

By the end of the lesson, I had more questions than answers, but there was no more time. It was four o'clock. The wedding was to begin at six. Reb Shraga Feivish gave me a reassuring look and a warm smile, and then led me to the door and shook my hand. "Mazel tov," he said. "If there are any problems, call me."

Later that evening, I sat at a narrow table covered with a white plastic tablecloth, my shtreimel perched heavily on my head, etching a deep red ring into my forehead, my tall black boots stiff and painful. The betrothal agreement was read, a glass plate was broken to the joyous cries of "mazel tov." The white shroud, in remembrance of death and the day of judgment, was pulled over my head, and soon I was led out to the street, accompanied by my friends' singing:

> Once again will be heard in the cities of Judah and the streets of
> Jerusalem,
> Cries of joy and cries of gladness, cries of bridegrooms and cries
> of brides.

We moved to the women's section of the wedding hall, for the *badeken,* the ceremonial covering of the bride's face. I was led there as if in a daze by Gitty's father and Berish Greenblatt, who stood in for my father, who was no longer alive. I walked tall but kept my eyes dutifully averted from the sea of females that parted in front of me. Gitty sat on her bridal throne as I approached, and our eyes met for a brief moment. During the six months of our engagement, we had neither met nor spoken even once, and we were still strangers in every way. Her eyes shifted downward quickly. A white veil was placed in my hands, and I laid it across her forehead, allowing it to fall over her face. My mother stood to Gitty's left, her eyes glistening. My sister, Chani, at my mother's side with her two young daughters, looked at me and smiled. Gitty's mother, standing just to the right, stared at me, expressionless.

The chuppah, a canopy of deep-blue velvet with gold fringes, was raised outside the shul, where a crowd of men had already gathered. "Right foot forward," my father-in-law said as I stepped under the canopy beneath the clear June sky.

I would later remember the ceremony only vaguely, with the dayan officiating and the rebbe swaying silently nearby, and from my eyes an ocean of tears flowed as Gitty circled me seven times. I remember being surprised when, weak from the day's fast and emotionally spent, I stepped on the glass cup and it did not break. The second time, I raised my foot and brought the heel of my boot crashing onto the glass as if in anger. "Mazel tov, mazel tov," the crowd cried, and burst into song.

Gitty and I were driven the short distance back to the wedding hall, together in the backseat, riding in silence. After a brief period in a small room at the wedding hall, where we broke our fast and exchanged pleasantries, we parted again, I to the men's section on the first floor, and Gitty to the women's on the third.

The rest of the wedding passed in a blur, a constant throb of music and throngs of men dancing ecstatically. Around midnight, the crowds thinned as we prepared for the *mitzvah tantz*, the ritual dance. Gitty came down to the men's section, and then held the end of a prayer sash as the male guests, holding the other end, shuffled before her, fulfilling the words of the sages: *He who gladdens a bridegroom and bride, it is as if he rebuilt the ruins of Jerusalem.*

The very last dance was for the bride and groom alone. Among other sects, the sash was laid aside and the groom took his bride's hands as they danced together, for the first and only time in their lives. But in Skver, there were no allowances for such improprieties, and so

I took the end of the sash and performed the ritual dance while Gitty, swaying as if in prayer, held the other end.

At three in the morning, we arrived home to our new apartment. The gifts were hauled in, our parents said their good-byes, and Gitty and I sat down at our new dining-room table, completely alone together for the very first time. We regarded the mountain of wrapped packages piled up around us and counted the checks we had received. We spoke hesitantly, cordially, asking each other how it went—"Did you dance?" "Did you eat?"—and hoping to postpone the awkwardness of what was to come next.

We didn't have much time, though. It was early June, and dawn would break soon. From my prayer-shawl pouch, I retrieved a small booklet given to me by Reb Noach, a summary of instructions and prayers for the evening.

> *Lord, grant me pure and sacred seed, blessed and good. Purify my body and sanctify my soul. May I gather strength to fulfill Your sacred will.*

There was also an incantation advised by the kabbalists, not in sacred Hebrew but in Aramaic, a warning to Lilith, the deviant first wife of Adam. Refusing to submit to her husband, the kabbalists wrote, Lilith was banished from Adam's side. Ever since, she lies in wait for men who spill their seed, which she gathers up, greedily, hungrily, impregnating herself and giving birth to demons.

> *In the name of the Lord:*
> *Do not enter and do not appear. Return, return, the sea beckons.*
> *I am clasped to a sacred allotment, I am cloaked in sovereign holiness.*

It was a matter of duty, the last ritual of a long day. A quilt hung over the window to ensure total darkness. We fumbled our way into bed, moving about each other shyly as we adjusted to this unfamiliar intimacy.

"Call me if there's any problem," Reb Shraga Feivish had said, and as we lay in bed some time later, we found that not all had been made clear. We needed more guidance. We looked over at the clock—4:30, the green numbers read—and I hesitated but made the call anyway. Reb Shraga Feivish picked up on the first ring, as if he'd been waiting, then listened carefully to my questions, about anatomy and friction and physiological responses of various kinds. He suggested we keep doing what we were doing, that it wasn't so difficult and we should, given enough time, figure it out.

It took several tries, that night and a couple of nights after, with several more consultations with Reb Shraga Feivish. The act was laborious and clumsy and entirely devoid of the erotic. But there were moments of tenderness—fleeting, but present—of shared frustration and deep sighs and suppressed giggles, even bursts of laughter. In hindsight, it was a bit like assembling a piece of furniture. You turn repeatedly to the instruction manual, to verify the shapes of parts and how they fit together, and it all seems kind of baffling, the screws and the holes appear to be sized differently from the diagram, and you're not sure which goes into where, and as you place your index finger on your chin and contemplate it further, your partner reaches out and gives something a tug and a twist and you think, "No, that can't be right," and then, "Oh, look, it snapped into place." And you look at her with a self-satisfied grin, as if you actually knew what you were doing.

Chapter Five

"GENTLEMEN! THERE IS A FIRE BURNING!"

The whites of Avremel's eyes were blood-red, his eyeballs protruding, his bony hands tightened into fists as he raised them beside his head.

"The flames are rising from within these very walls! This sacred edifice, built by that sacred smoldering ember saved from the inferno of the Holocaust, our saintly old rebbe, is now crumbling from within! And our present rebbe carries the weight of preserving it. . . ." His voice cracked and we, too, held back the sting in our eyes, our hearts melting for the rebbe's weary shoulders.

It was shortly before dawn on a Sunday morning. Fifteen of us sat around two old tables in a dank room in the yeshiva basement. We were the elite, handpicked by Avremel to be part of a special group. Once a week, we would gather here to read from one of our mystical texts and Avremel would provide elucidation and commentary sprinkled with condemnation of all things impure. The timing was deliberate, to weed out those who preferred warm bedsheets to the fiery words of the Hasidic masters. All of us were married—a condition for inclusion. Marriage allowed that extra measure of *holiness and purity*, the pent-up virgin energy released, the lustfulness of adolescence appeased.

Avremel was known for dramatic pronouncements, but now he seemed gripped with genuine panic. It was the dead of winter, and our sidelocks, which had frozen into solid strands during the sixty seconds it took to walk from the mikveh to the yeshiva building, were dripping onto our books and into our laps, as we sat there stunned.

Avremel continued, his face flushed crimson, blue veins on his neck straining through his skin. "It has come to my attention that within these very rooms are students engaging in abominable behavior! And they are sweeping others with them to the depths of *sheol!*"

He told of students watching television on small, compact devices, sometimes within our very study halls; students listening to secular music, or sneaking out of the village to watch movies in darkened theaters; students taking taxicabs to sinful places where no decent human being should ever be found. It was up to us to stop it. To take up the spear of Phineas, and smite the evil within those who blasphemed within these sacred walls.

We headed to our morning prayers, each of us stirred with the call to action. The sun was now up, and the sanctuary filled with students donning prayer shawls and tefillin. It was the Tenth of Teves, a fast day, which included a special reading of the Torah.

> *And Moses beseeched God, his Lord, saying:*
> *Why, my Lord, must You be angry with Your people? They are*
>   *a stiff-necked nation.*
> *And God said, I have forgiven them.*

But only God could forgive. Man must act against those who anger God. Watching television and reading magazines and listening to secular music angered God; so when we finished our prayers, we huddled in a corner of the prayer hall for hushed consultations. We conveyed the urgency of our task to those who hadn't been at the meeting, and the outrage grew.

A half hour later, in one of the large lecture rooms off the building's main corridor, two dozen of us sat around a list of names we had drawn up, names of those we suspected of sin—peers, classmates, friends with whom we'd shared countless hours of study. There was little time for establishing facts. Vague suspicions and Avremel's talk were all we had and all we needed.

Nuta Margulis was the first to be summoned.

"Please sit," someone said when he entered. Nuta looked confused, but complied. It was a pitiful sight, Nuta alone on one of the long cast-iron benches, his palms resting on his knees, the rest of us standing against the walls, an impromptu tribunal.

Somebody spoke. We, as a group, would not tolerate the kind of activity we'd heard about. Any one of our friends caught with a forbidden device, a radio or a portable television, or a secular magazine or forbidden musical cassettes, would be wrapped in a prayer shawl and beaten. Association with certain undesirable persons, known transgressors, would also be forbidden. This time, it was only a warning. The next time, we wouldn't be so tolerant.

Nuta tried to protest: "I didn't—I have never—I don't—" We silenced him quickly. His words did not matter.

Other friends were summoned, each told to sit and given the same speech. For each student summoned, before he entered, there was a call around the room—"Who's speaking this time?"—and someone would volunteer. The things said were the same. The reactions, too, were similar, always the same look of horror as each of those summoned sat wondering what could have turned longtime friends into inquisitors. Only Yossi Rosen declared that he would not be cowed.

"*Mi somchu le'ish?*" Yossi shot back at us, citing the verse in Exodus. "Who appointed you as master?"

Menashe Steiner, who was doing the talking, held up his hand and said: "That's what the cursed Dathan said. And what happened to *him?*" Swallowed into the pit, of course, along with all the other Israelite rebels in the desert, and the thought hung heavy in the air as Yossi was shown out of the room.

A half dozen of our friends had been summoned and released, but we weren't pacified. Unsatisfied with the relative moderation of warnings, we wanted more.

Mendy Klein had not appeared when summoned, so a handful of students were dispatched to find him. They checked the synagogue, the study hall, the lecture rooms, and the basement dining room, but Mendy was nowhere to be found. His dorm room was reported locked, the persistent knocking on the door unanswered. The thought of Mendy's locked door ignited our imaginations. A locked door meant something hidden, something forbidden.

"Let's get in there," someone said.

We looked at one another in silence. "We can't go into the dorms," someone said finally.

All of us in our righteous clique were married, and yeshiva policy—as ordered by the rebbe himself—forbade married students to enter the dormitory area. The reasons were never made clear, but like the rule that two students alone were never to lock the door, this hinted at fears of sexual transgression.

The sense of urgency was now heightened. An opportunity for acting on our zeal was slipping away on a technicality. As we stood outside the study hall, Reb Yankel Gelbman, a rabbi at the yeshiva and one of the village's foremost scholars, came up the stairs carrying a stack of texts. One of us left the huddle and approached the rabbi to ask the question.

Reb Yankel furrowed his brow, and looked around at our group. *"And thou shalt be rid of the evil within your midst,"* he said finally, quoting the Bible. "An unequivocal biblical command!"

A ransacked room is an ugly thing, but for us it was a thing of beauty. The door smashed in, blankets and linen ripped off the mattresses, dressers overturned, its contents on the floor in disarray, the mob of dozens searching, picking through items, certain that somewhere in that room lay the evidence of transgression and abomination, proof that our zeal had not been in vain, our impassioned assumption of a sacred guardianship justified.

A locked cabinet was discovered, a hammer procured, and the lock smashed. We didn't know what we were looking for but were sure that the evidence existed somewhere. A cheer went up when someone found a pile of unmarked audiocassettes. A cassette player was found and one of the cassettes inserted. Hebrew music by a male singer came out of the tinny speakers, and someone hit the Stop button in disgust. The singer sounded secular, Israeli, though we weren't sure; even so, it was not a sin worthy of our zeal. If the singer was female, that would've been something else, but it wasn't, and the cassette was ejected with disappointment. A second unmarked cassette was inserted but was only a scratchy recording of one of Avremel's old talks.

Someone discovered a pile of photographs, and leafing through it found a photo of Mendy and several other students wearing T-shirts and baseball caps. It was quickly taken as evidence of something illicit. Why else would they discard their long black coats and wide-brimmed black hats for the vulgar sartorial habits of common Americans? Later we learned that Mendy and the others had been on an outing to cut phragmite weeds from the New Jersey Meadowlands to cover the sukkah booths for the Sukkos holiday, and had simply donned clothing more suitable to the task.

We found little else. Soon we heard the sound of an emergency siren. Someone came running from the outside: "Mendy called the police!" The room had all but cleared out in seconds, and my friend Mayer Goldhirsch and I were the last ones in the room. Mayer was still looking through the scattered mess on the floor and I grabbed his arm. "Mayer, let's go!" But he wouldn't leave. I let go of his arm to leave on my own, and he looked up and grabbed me. "Shulem, we *have* to find something. I *know* we'll find something."

"Find *what*, Mayer? We don't even know what we're looking for!"

Reluctantly, he stood up, looked around, and followed me out of the room. The wailing siren had stopped, and we heard hasty footsteps coming up the stairs.

"Quick, the other side!" Mayer cried, and we ran across the corridor to the other stairway. As we pushed open the door, we looked back to see Mendy angrily leading two police officers to his room. Mayer and I bounded down the stairway and ran, panting, back to the yeshiva building.

‥

It hadn't always been clear that this was to be my path. My father was a pious Hasid but of a gentler, more tolerant sort. He was not a Skverer but a mix of Satmar anti-Zionism, Breslov mysticism, and his own brand of humanism. He was a scholar and teacher, and spent much of his time reaching out to secular Jews to teach them about Orthodox Jewish observance.

And yet, there was much about him that was unorthodox.

One Saturday night, when I was around eleven, my father allowed me to accompany him to a lecture he gave at a Jewish Community Center somewhere on Long Island. My father and I entered a room filled with people who did not look particularly religious, men in bare heads and women in short skirts, knees and elbows showing. It was shocking to me to see that the sexes were mixed. I looked at my father to see whether he, too, was disturbed, but I could tell nothing from his expression. He pointed me to a seat off to the side as he took his place at the podium. The sight of my father, a tall Hasidic man in a fur shtreimel, a caftan down to his calves, and white stockings, brought silence to the room.

"*Gut voch*," my father began. Some in the crowd nodded and smiled. "Before I begin," he continued, "I would like to ask that men move to one side of the room and women to the other." I watched the changing expressions in the crowd—astonishment, indignation, bemusement. People looked at one another for hints on how to proceed. My father was not finished. "I would like to say," he added, "that I understand and respect the desire to avoid such separation. But I do not agree with it." He repeated his statement a couple more times for emphasis: "I respect it, but I do not agree with it."

I watched as the audience rose slowly, shuffled around, and took new seats, men on one side of the room and women on the other. I remember that my father thanked them for it and then made a remark that drew laughs, and whatever tension may have lingered appeared to dissipate. After that, he gave his talk, of which I understood little but from the attentive expressions of the audience, and the eager and lengthy question-and-answer session that followed, I knew that his talk was received with satisfaction. A woman later approached me in the corridor, her face glowing, her palm against her chest, her torso bent from the waist as she leaned—almost bowed—to my own eleven-year-old height, and said, "Your father is an amazing man!" I knew then that he had touched his audience in a deep way.

I respect it, but I do not agree with it. Those words would embody what I saw as my father's ability to stand by his principles while acknowledging that others lived by different ones, their convictions as strong as his own. Those words provided a counterbalance to the more prevalent view expressed by my teachers and others, of utter contempt for everything but our own worldview. And so I couldn't help but wonder: Who was right, my father or my teachers? Were we allowed to respect others, or were we obligated to vilify all who believed differently?

My father seemed to embrace the former, and my teachers the latter. Which, then, was I to accept?

It wasn't only other Jews my father had unorthodox views about, but also people of other faiths.

"Judaism accepts," my father said to me once during a walk to shul on the Sabbath, "that non-Jews have their own faiths. That other religions, too, for their own adherents, can provide a path to God."

I told my father what my rebbe had told me: *The kindness of the nations is for sin.* A goy, even when he does a good deed, its purpose is for evil.

My father shook his head. "That is not correct," he said. Later, at home, he took me into his study and opened a book on his desk. "Read this passage," he said, and I read aloud the row of tiny letters at the tip of his pointed finger: *So said the Prophet Elijah: I testify before heaven and earth, each Israelite or Gentile, man or woman, slave or maidservant, each according to his deed, so rests upon him the holy spirit.*

My father sat down in his chair and drew me close with his arm around my back and his hand on my arm. "I know this isn't what you always hear, but you must still always remember it."

"But don't all goyim hate us?" I asked.

My father thought for a moment, and then said: "There are some who do. And throughout history, there were many. But no, not all."

Yet why did my father choose to raise me among people whose views he disagreed with? I did not know the answer to this question, nor did I know how to ask it, but I knew that I could not accept my father's view. He was only one against the many who preached differently.

It is a well-known dictum that Esau hates Jacob, the sage Rabbi Shimon Bar Yochai said. As my rebbes explained, it was a law of nature: The non-Jew will always despise the Jew. History proved that principle correct, my rebbes would remind us. The Spanish Jews in the fifteenth century and the German Jews in the twentieth bore witness to the same thing: a Jew might think himself assimilated, but the goy will always—secretly, if he must, and openly, if he dare—despise him.

The non-Jews in our neighborhood, the *Talyayners* and *Portrikaners*, seemed to reinforce that view. They lived not among us but along the edges of our neighborhoods, and when my friends and I would pass them on the street, they would jeer. "Jews!" one of the Puerto Rican boys would always shout, laughing. If I was walking alone, one of them would approach and flick my yarmulke off my head, his buddies cheering. I'd be sitting on the stoop in front of our home, eating a Popsicle or reading a book, and if one of them passed, I'd cast him a nervous glance.

"Ya motha!" the boy would shout at me.

"Why do the goyim say that?" I asked my mother once. "*Ya motha.* What *about* my mother?"

"It's a goyish thing," she said, her eyes on the pot she was stirring on the kitchen stove. "Just ignore them."

Passing the Catholic church on Sixteenth Avenue, my friends and I would cross to the other side of the street, spit in the direction of the church, and recite three times: "*Thou shalt utterly detest it, and thou shalt utterly abhor it, for it is a cursed thing.*"

Thou shalt not walk in the ways of other nations, we read in the Bible. This, our rebbes explained, meant that we should not play baseball, wear Western-style clothes, or sport popular hairstyles.

On occasion, our non-Jewish neighbors surprised me. At age eleven, two friends and I, overcome with curiosity, asked an Italian boy near our school to tell us "the meaning of F."

"The meaning of F?" the boy asked.

"Yes," we said. "You know. The F-word. What does it mean?"

"Oh," the boy said, a grin spreading across his face. "You don't know?"

We didn't. The boy maintained his grin but wouldn't tell us. He said that it was a dirty word. And we couldn't help but wonder: Why would that bother him? Didn't all goyim use such words freely, issuing profanities as casually as they walked their dogs or fiddled with the undersides of their cars?

"Is the rabbi home? Can he spare something for the baby?"

The woman would stand by the door, and one of us children would run to our father's study and say, "The lady from the corner is here." We knew her only as that, because she seemed at all times to be sitting on the corner stoop, in front of a decrepit, graffiti-covered apartment building beneath the elevated subway line, chain-smoking and drinking something out of a paper bag. She would often come with her teenage daughter, bringing with her the stench of something we could not identify. Sometimes they would be carrying an infant, although I never knew if the baby belonged to the mother or the daughter.

My father would rummage through his pockets and withdraw a crumpled bill, and then walk to the door and hand it to her. He would ask how she was doing, and she would moan about her miseries and my father would wish her the best and say that he hoped she felt better.

"Dovid!" my mother would cry. "Why?"

My father would say only, "She says she needs food. It isn't for me to question her." And my brother Avrumi would say, "But she's a goy." And my father would simply say, "So she is."

My father's generosity frustrated my mother, but I thought of him as a tzaddik, his manner reminiscent of the saintly men one heard about in legends. When he prayed, my father would stand for hours on end, often with his eyes half-closed, only the whites visible, as if in a deep meditative trance. I had seen him pray in that same way as far back as I could remember, and still it was mystifying to watch him. For most of my childhood, I had assumed that when he prayed, he, or some essential part of him, went elsewhere, traveling through some exalted and spiritual realm. I have a vivid image of myself at age four, standing next to him in the empty synagogue after prayers, looking up to him and pleading with him to recognize a truth that appeared to have failed him: "Tatti!" I would cry. "All the people have gone home!"

I remember wondering why his erect but still body made no effort to respond as I pulled on the tassels of his gartel, attempting to awaken him from whatever unconscious state he was in.

Over time, I came to realize that our family was different. While my brothers and I spoke to one another in Yiddish, picked up at the schools we attended as far back as our memories reached, our parents spoke to us mostly in English. They showed odd interest in matters no one we knew cared for, their values acquired elsewhere. Unlike my friends, whose homes were elegantly furnished, crystal chandeliers gleaming above their dining-room tables, Persian rugs in their living rooms, late-model cars in their driveways, our family lived modestly. As I grew older, I became aware that my clothes were often a size too small, that our dining-room chairs were mismatched and rickety. I felt embarrassed to have friends over, worried they might notice that we lacked the piece of furniture that existed in every Hasidic home: a china closet, which was a glass-enclosed polished-wood breakfront that typically held a family's collection of silver—menorahs, *ethrog* cases, cylindrical megilla containers, kiddush goblets. We had little silver, no china or heirlooms or other precious objects, and so we had no need for a china closet.

Once a week, my parents would take the subway to a place they called "the Village," where my mother claimed that no Jews lived. They went there to buy organic fruits and vegetables, which were unavailable in Borough Park. I remember frustrating visits to our local supermarket, where I would gaze at blood-red tomatoes and football-shaped green grapes, and my mother would wave her hand dismissively: "If you only knew the chemicals they put in those things." As if *those things* were clever plastic imitations. Sugared cereals and candy bars and sweet soda drinks never entered our home. My mother's notion of American food manufacturers was of fat, cigar-chomping men who put toxic ingredients into their food products to make children want more, more, more, and rot their teeth and poison their bodies while the fat evil men laughed and laughed and raked in the profits. Her attitude was unusual in Borough Park, where middle-class comforts and consumerist attitudes were as entrenched as any other place in America.

It wouldn't be until late adolescence that I would understand what set our family apart. My parents had spent their youths not in the ultra-religious world of the Hasidim but in secular environments, where they were raised not with fur hats and flowing caftans and floral kerchiefs but with movies and boyfriends and secular educations. They spoke little about their pasts, preferring to shelter us from the knowledge that they had not always been Hasidic, to keep us from knowing that my mother, as a teenager in Queens, was a Beatles fan, and that my father, raised in Baltimore, had spent his twenties in San Francisco participating in civil rights protests and getting high on psychedelics. Both of my parents had spent several years as hippies, and their choices—my

mother in her late teens and my father in his twenties—to join the
Hasidic community came with high-minded idealism. They retained
their disdain for societal conventions.

"Is it true your father is a *baal teshuvah*?" my friend Yochanan Fried
whispered to me in the school bathroom when I was ten. We were
standing at the urinals when he said it, and I looked at him in horror
over the partition. *Baal teshuvahs*, or "returnees," were those raised as
secular Jews who later joined the Orthodox. They were given lip service
for their courage, but it was no secret that *baal teshuvahs* were odd for
giving up the temptations of their former lives and joining a world of
endless rules and restriction. They must suffer a psychological ailment
of some sort, it was assumed. Or they were those who couldn't make it
among the goyim and came to try their luck among the Hasidim.

I denied it to Yochanan Fried. I had not learned the truth yet. I
knew that my parents were different, and my father's behavior was unorthodox in a world in which piety and righteousness were to be lived
within the parameters of convention. I thought only that he was a man
who lived in a world unto himself, extending himself for a few hours
a week to interact with the world—to attend shul, to teach his classes,
and grant audiences for those who sought his counsel—but soon with-
drawing back into his little study with his many shelves of sacred texts
and his hours of prayer.

I would realize later that my parents had joined the Hasidic world
with knowledge of only its pious exterior. They found its teachings
profound. So much love. So much joy. Such inner peace. In their
idealism, they overlooked its harsher realities. They hadn't grown
up in this world, hadn't seen the gruff attitudes with which children
were raised, hadn't been subject to schoolteachers who routinely beat
students for not knowing the meaning of an Aramaic word in their
Talmuds, or for removing their fingers from the tiny text of the Rashi
script in the margins.

"Ich bin a chusid fun aybershten," my father said one day, when I asked
what sect he belonged to. "I am a Hasid of God."

The boys in my class at the Krasna cheder in Borough Park were
from families that belonged to small Hasidic communities—Kasho,

Sighet, Tzelem—groups that had no bona fide rebbes of their own but were, by their shared Hungarian and Romanian origin, loosely affiliated with Satmar. And so, at the age of ten or eleven, I wondered: What were *we*? Being a Hasid of God was all right between my father and God, but it wouldn't do if the question of our *belonging* was raised by a friend, a teacher, or an acquaintance.

"Where does your father belong?" Reb Shimon Mauskopf asked one day during lunchtime, as he poured warm cocoa into a row of plastic cups on his desk.

I made a snap decision. "My father is a Breslover," I said.

My father studied the teachings of both Breslov and Satmar, and those, I thought, were the plausible options.

In truth, though, I wasn't happy with my father being a Breslover, even if, as the case was, he was not one. Breslovers were the eccentrics of the Hasidic world. *The dead Hasidim*, some called them. They'd never chosen a rebbe after their first, Reb Nachman, died in the early nineteenth century. They were the misfits within our world and were known for attracting the misfits from without: former hippies, druggies, ex-convicts, and other social outcasts, all of them drawn to the intensity of the Breslover message, the psychological insight of its long-dead leader and his whimsical tales of beggars and forest dwellers and its New Agey embrace of meditative practices.

It would've been better to be Satmar. The Satmars were arrogant and superior and bombastic and proud and entirely scornful of all but their own. They were disdainful of other sects, even friendly ones, and fiercely hostile toward those who opposed them. They were the winners, and it was good to be a winner. Better to be a bully than to be bullied.

But I couldn't plausibly say that my father was Satmar. Unlike the Breslovers, the Satmars had a rebbe who was very much alive, Reb Moshe, the late Reb Yoel's nephew and successor. To declare oneself Satmar would require a nod to Reb Moshe's leadership. Unlike my friends' fathers and grandfathers, who took occasional pilgrimages to the Satmar rebbe's shul on Rodney Street in Williamsburg, my father never visited him. It would be too contrived to declare him Satmar. It was more plausible to turn my father into a Breslover, even if at the same time, I would resent it.

I knew little about the Skverers back then. The Krasna school I attended was around the corner from the Skverer school, our backyards back to back, with occasional exchanges of water balloons hurled over the barbed-wire fence between us. "Skverer *chenyokes*," we shouted. "Krasna bums," they shouted back. And then our bells would ring and recess would be over, and we'd all go back to the same volumes of Talmud, the same rods and switches and rubber-wire casings in the hands of our rebbes.

Word on the street was that Skverers burned Breslov books in annual conflagrations along with the pre-Passover burning of the *chometz*. It was said that Skverers refused even to utter the word "Breslov," hissing instead the phrase *yene chevre*, "that notorious group." No one really knew the reason for the centuries-old hostilities but only that they had been passed down from generation to generation and were now a matter of tradition.

It was this animosity that would cause me some consternation later, when I thought I might attend the Skverer yeshiva. Given that my father had Breslov sympathies, he might not approve. But my father, calling the Skverers "*ehrlich*," had no objections.

The Skverers, I would learn, were *ehrlich* but also idiosyncratic, with a kind of provincial piety that was uncommon among American Hasidim. Once, during my first few days at the Skverer yeshiva, I stood in the hallway speaking to my friend Chaim Elya when our first-year instructor passed, then stopped in his tracks and looked me up and down.

"Why are you dressed like a *shaygetz*?" he asked.

I stared at him, frozen. To dress like a shaygetz was to dress like a goy: blue jeans, T-shirts, bare head. But I was dressed in my beaver hat and long coat, the same as everyone else.

Our instructor shook his head, annoyed. "Where's your gartel?" he asked, and I realized that my coat was unbuttoned and my gartel, the thin waistband worn during prayer, was in my pocket instead of around my waist. Skverers, I would later learn, wore their gartels at all times; to be gartel-less was to be vulgar, and to be vulgar was to be a shaygetz, which was only one step away from being a goy.

◆◆

The afternoon after we issued our warnings to our friends and ransacked Mendy Klein's room, an assembly of all the students was called. The dean condemned our actions. "Students should not take such matters into their own hands," he said.

"He had to say that," Avremel would tell us later, emphasizing that we'd done the right thing. We'd suffered no consequences, no suspensions, nothing even like the fifty-dollar penalty for failing an exam or the twenty-dollar penalty for missing a study session.

Still I felt shame, although I was not sure why. As the weeks and months passed, I tried to erase the memory of that day. I had been part of it, had volunteered to speak before those we had summoned, had taken part in the smashing and the stomping and the ransacking. I had felt during those moments like an insignificant part of a larger unit, my individuality swallowed by the collective. For the first time, I understood the power of a mob.

Nuta Margulis had been a good friend. Yossi Rosen had been my study partner. Mendy Klein had been my roommate. Each Friday afternoon, I would come by the dormitory with a pan of kugel for Mendy; it was common practice for married students to drop off homemade food for their former roommates until the latter, too, were married and would bring food to those who remained after them. The Friday after the incident, I brought the usual pan of potato kugel, and handed it to a resident outside the door to pass to Mendy. As I left, I wondered what Mendy would think of me, ransacking his room on Sunday and bringing him kugel on Friday. But Mendy said nothing about the event in the days and weeks that followed, and no one else spoke of it. If our friends bore us any grudges, they never expressed it. Yet, in the silence, in the unspokenness of it all, lay shame, thick as the densely woven prayer shawls over our backs, heavy as the braided silver adornments over our heads.

Chapter Six

Six months had passed since we were married. "Is there any news yet?" the rebbe would ask when Gitty and I went for one of the sixty-second audiences granted village residents in the days before Rosh Hashanah and during the nights of Chanukah. Gitty would watch from the far wall as I would shake my head, no news, and the rebbe would say, "*Nu*, may God help, it should be soon."

We had settled into a routine. In the mornings, I would go off to the yeshiva and Gitty to her job at the offices of the Monsey Trails bus company, where her father was the general manager. From a window in her office, above the bustling garage at the entrance to the village, Gitty could see down to where mechanics worked on buses raised onto enormous lifts. I didn't think it an appropriate place for a woman to work, with exhaust fumes and grime everywhere, a male world. But Gitty enjoyed being out of the house, along with the light secretarial work she was given.

Over dinner, we would sit mostly in silence, punctuated with polite inquiries about each other's day. I did most of the talking, with Gitty listening carefully and only very occasionally offering words of her own. When she did, it came first in a whisper, and then, after clearing her throat, a croak. Her face would flush, and I would look away as she battled her anxiety within the strangeness of this new relationship.

Our interactions felt dictated, most of all, by the laws of family purity, the fear of forbidden contact hovering over us at all times. Once every month, I would come home to find that Gitty had moved the small bouquet of silk flowers from the kitchen counter to the table—this was the agreed-upon sign: it was that time of the month. During the two weeks that followed, the small space of our home would be overwhelmed by the presence of something invisible to me yet mysterious and forbidding, a spiritual bacterium more noxious than any physical substance. A single moment of carelessness could lead not only to great sin but generations of tainted souls.

"Can you take something to the dayan?" Gitty would ask at times during the Seven Clean Days, during which she did her twice-daily inspections. The blood would rise to her face as our eyes met, her expression at once determined and tortured, and as much as I hated these requests, I had no doubt that she hated them more. On the bedroom dresser she would lay a small plastic bag, inside of which was a two-inch square of inspection cloth, or occasionally an undergarment, which I would place inside my coat pocket and hope to find the dayan in his office on the first try.

"Let's take a look at this, shall we?" the dayan would say, always too loudly, clearly audible to passersby behind me. At the window, he would hold up the item for examination by sunlight, while I looked away, anxious to be done with it all before the next man came knocking. Would his ruling be "kosher," or "not kosher"? For those extended seconds, I felt like a patient dreading a physician's diagnosis. If "not kosher," I would have to tell Gitty to begin counting her seven days all over again, which she would accept in silence, although her expression of dismay would be hard not to notice.

A woman's hair is nakedness, says the Talmud, and so, once married, she must never expose any of it. According to the Zohar, the primary text of the kabbalists, this applies even in her own home. During the last of her seven clean days, Gitty would take the set of electric clippers from above our bathroom sink and shear her entire head, leaving only several millimeters of growth, though even I, her husband, would rarely see those; a head-covering was required at all times. Indoors, or for casual visits and quick errands, a turban, green or blue or purple on weekdays and pristine white on the Sabbath. Outdoors, a short wig of synthetic hair covered with a hat—a pillbox during those early years of our marriage, though this would change with the fashions of the times.

After the seven clean days, Gitty would head to the ritual bath at the edge of the village, and return with her face glowing and her manner unusually serene. It was in those hours, between her return and the stroke of midnight, when we would retire for the special mitzvah of that night, that I would feel the first charges of eroticism, and an occasional spark of passion, so very distinct from the primal lust of previous years, though not yet fully recognizable. Over the next weeks, Gitty would be considered clean, and slowly we would get to know each other, though these early progressions felt infinitesimal.

Sometimes, Gitty would withdraw into herself for reasons I could not discern. "Are you upset about something?" I would ask, stiffly, and she would look away and say nothing.

"It is improper to call your wife by her name," Avremel had warned during one of his sessions, and I was careful to follow his guidance. To get Gitty's attention, I would clear my throat and say, "Um," or "You hear?" Among friends, we referred to our wives using only coy and oblique euphemisms. "The *household* informed me of a wedding next week," my study partner said, when notifying me of a pending absence. Yitzchok Schwartz was fond of speaking of his *yiddene*, his "Jewess," causing heads to turn at such bold language.

"Is there any news yet?" Avremel asked when I ran into him one day outside the study hall. When I told Avremel that there was no news, he fixed me a look with his dark, scolding eyes. "There should be news by now," he said. "Why is there no news?"

I didn't know why there was no news, although Avremel came up with a reason soon enough.

"You must be doing it wrong," he said.

He asked for details, and I gave him the rundown of our routine, parroting the directions I'd been given: We performed the mitzvah every Tuesday and Friday night after midnight, exactly as I'd been taught, always with "holiness and purity" at the forefront of our minds. We said the necessary prayers. We covered the windows with a quilt. We told stories of righteous men. We kissed twice. And then we did it quickly. *As if forced by a demon*—the vividness of those words proved extraordinarily effective in keeping the act sacred and devoid of pleasure.

Avremel looked confused, and then angry. "If that's the way you do it, then a slice of noodle kugel is more pleasurable!"

I remember feeling confused. Wasn't that the point, *not* to experience pleasure? "No," Avremel said. That was the point but also not quite the point, because if there was no pleasure, it wasn't the real thing. I was still confused, as he stood there making wild, wordless gestures and shook his head in exasperation. When he spoke again, it was with palpable irritation.

"For a woman's body to respond," he said, bringing his five fingers together opposite his nose, "in order for her to create a child, there must be *liebshaft*." *Liebshaft* is the Yiddish word for love, and it was a strange word to hear, applied to a woman, from a man who was otherwise obsessed with guiding me on the path to holiness and purity. I did not know how Avremel knew this medical fact, but I had no reason to doubt him. Yet the idea made me angry.

"*Love* her?" I asked. The notion seemed ludicrous. "How?"

"If the love isn't there," Avremel said, "then you have to create it." He shook his head and closed his eyes, as if thinking through a complex problem, and then opened them again. "You just have to find a way."

Later that evening, as we ate our dinner of roast chicken and breaded egg noodles and spoke quietly about the things we'd done that day, I looked at Gitty and wondered if I could love her. When she stood up to clear our dishes, I noticed the curve of her hips as they swayed gently when she walked. As she stood at the sink and washed the dishes, I leaned on the counter nearby, and noticed the color in her cheeks, the gentle way she looked at me when she spoke, the softness of her voice when she asked what to prepare for lunch the next day.

The next evening, after my last study session, I made my way to the Mazel Tov Gift Shop, a small basement store that sold everything from Rachel's Tomb needlecraft kits to sterling-silver menorahs to diamond rings. One night a week, after ten, the shop was open for one hour, for men only. The proprietor, Reb Moshe Hersh, a stocky man in a yellowed and grease-stained *tallis katan*, laid several trays of rings and earrings on the counter. I looked at the selection, and then looked at Moshe Hersh, who stood with his hands resting on the counter, waiting for my decision.

"What do you think?" I asked. I had never bought a woman a gift before, and the selection in front of me was a baffling array of gold and silver and glittery gems, like a field of pebbles glittering in the sunlight.

Moshe Hersh shrugged. "You're the customer," he said.

I studied the items in front of me. As Moshe Hersh stood breathing heavily, I inspected the pieces one by one and slowly began to notice their differences: silver and gold, sleek and intricate, chunky and subtle. I settled on a silver ring with a scalloped pattern and tiny diamonds inlaid across the top. I liked its understated elegance and hoped that Gitty's tastes weren't dissimilar.

I left the ring in a box on Gitty's pillow when I left for yeshiva the next morning. Under the box I placed a folded sheet of plain white paper on which I wrote what seemed like appropriate sentiments, using the same Hebrew script I used for jotting notes on the Talmud or for transcribing the rebbe's talks. *I hope that our love will grow and last forever.* As if the love was already there, and needed only to be tended and nurtured. As with faith, Avremel had declared it something one might will into existence.

When I returned home that evening, Gitty was at the kitchen counter, her back to me, putting our dinner onto plates. She said nothing, and so I thought perhaps she hadn't discovered my gift. I checked the bedroom, but the package was not on her pillow. "Did you find . . . the thing?" I asked when I returned to the kitchen.

She nodded without turning, and then, almost as an afterthought, said, "Thank you." She made no more mention of the gift, and neither did I, and I wondered if she liked it, if I was making any progress toward creating love.

Several days later, she turned to me bashfully as she laid our dinner plates on the table. "I'm two weeks late," she said, her face aglow with a brighter than usual smile. It was almost as if she were suppressing a giggle, embarrassed by her own giddiness. I wasn't sure what she meant, until she said, "I'm not certain about it yet. But I think there's a test I can take." The test could be purchased at the pharmacy. She was going to ask her sister, and if she was right, we would know tomorrow.

Later that night, as we prepared for bed, I noticed, on her left hand, the polished silver ring I had bought, with its scalloped patterns and tiny diamonds sparkling against the soft light of the bedside lamp.

Finally, there was news. There were so many questions and so many things to talk about—it was as if we were suddenly new people in an entirely new relationship. The reticence that had hovered for six months in the tiny apartment at the end of Roosevelt Avenue was now gone, almost as if it had never existed. We talked of baby names and upcoming doctor's visits. We also disclosed to each other how little we knew about what it meant to be parents.

One night, as we lay in our separate beds across the room, I turned to her. "Can I ask you a question?"

She propped herself up on one elbow.

"How does the baby come out?" I asked. I immediately thought, what a foolish question, and tried to explain. "I mean, where does it come out *from?*"

This was before Gitty had gone for her first doctor's appointment, before we'd had a chance to read any of the books and pamphlets she would bring home and point excitedly to charts and diagrams and drawings of ovaries and fallopian tubes, before I'd had a chance to go to our local bookstore and whisper to the cashier that I needed one of the books from beneath his counter, where they lay hidden from the prying eyes of teenage boys who made the bookstore their evening hangout.

"I don't know," Gitty said. "I wondered about it myself." She looked at me from across the room, a sliver of light from the edge of our window shades casting a thin white glow across her face, and in her expression I saw a touch of anxiety. "You don't think it requires surgery, do you?" she asked. I did not know what to say, because that was exactly what I had thought.

When I asked, hesitantly, before her first doctor's appointment whether we would see the doctor together, Gitty burst out laughing. It was a ludicrous thought, she said. Men did not accompany their wives to the doctor. "But I'll let you know what I learn," she said.

Gitty made an appointment at the Refuah Health Center, an imposing building with a beige art-deco facade at the entrance to the village. A five-doctor practice from Manhattan sent one doctor every Wednesday afternoon to attend to all the pregnant women of New Square. It was an arrangement worked out by the wizards of Hasidic politicking, through which patients on Medicaid were provided with world-class medical services. The exams typically lasted only a few minutes each, most of them for ordinary and uncomplicated pregnancies, so the doctor was able to see many women in a short time slot, for maximum efficiency.

"See the head here?" Gitty pointed breathlessly one day, showing me the photos of the first ultrasound scan. "See the hands? The feet?" I saw nothing but blurs of blacks and grays, and felt a distinct pang of envy for the attachment between mother and child, an attachment I realized that I could never fully share.

Gitty neared her due date toward the end of summer. The weeks were hectic with preparation for the seemingly endless procession of major and minor holidays squeezed into three and a half weeks: Selichos, Rosh Hashanah, Tzom Gedalya, Yom Kippur, Sukkos, Chol Hamo'ed, Hoshanah Rabbah, Shmini Atzeres, and Simchas Torah. Our baby's arrival was imminent, but in the frenzy of holiday preparations, it felt to me all but forgotten. Our refrigerator was stacked with aluminum pans of gefilte fish, roast chicken, farfel, kreplach, and jars of apple compote. In the freezer were a dozen containers of chicken noodle soup. While Gitty baked a surplus of challahs to last us the entire month, I climbed a ladder outside our small apartment, assembling wall panels, adjusting nuts and bolts, and putting up rafters on our eight-by-eight sukkah, the outdoor booth in which, during the Sukkos holiday, we would eat our meals, read, schmooze, and, along with the rest of the village, catch cold from sleeping seven nights under the cool autumn skies.

"Are you helping Gitty around the house?" my mother asked me several times. From the day we were first married, my mother had made it her business to offer tips for domestic bliss. "Marriage is not a give-and-take," she said to me the morning after our wedding. "It's a give-and-give." But Gitty would balk at my offers to help. "You can take out the garbage, maybe?" Even that seemed an acquiescence, a halfhearted nod toward my willingness to make myself useful.

"How is she feeling?" my mother would ask, and I would say, "I'm not sure." "Maybe you should ask her," my mother would say. I would ask in the silence between the half grapefruit and the split-pea soup at dinnertime, before we'd stumble yet again on possible baby names and occasional bits of gossip that Gitty gathered from the ladies' waiting room at Refuah, "And how are you feeling?" Gitty, with her near-permanent blush, would smile awkwardly, unaccustomed to so intimate a question. "I'm feeling fine," she would say, and when I would ask if she experienced morning sickness or headaches or fatigue— things my mother told me to ask—she would giggle demurely. "I don't have any of those."

"She says she's fine," I would tell my mother. "Are you sure?" my mother would ask. As if the varieties of ailments associated with preg- nancy were so many and varied that Gitty's claims were simply a medi- cal impossibility. "I feel normal," Gitty would insist when I'd ask her again, after which she'd suggest that she was fine to cook, fine to clean, fine to do laundry, and maybe my mother would, if it pleased her, stop minding our business.

Two days before Yom Kippur, I went to the village shopping cen- ter, outside of which stood a large open-air tent, with stacks of plastic crates filled with live chickens. Women and children stood around, many of them swinging the chickens over their heads in the traditional *kapparos* ritual. The ritual was meant to transfer the sins of the indi- vidual to the frightened bird, which would then be slaughtered and the sins of its owner atoned for. The chicken would end up boiled on some yeshiva student's plate sometime during the holidays.

The preferred time for *kapparos* was on the day before Yom Kippur at the crack of dawn, when, according to the kabbalists, a "thread of kindness" stretched across the cosmos and the heavens were in good spirits. So instead of performing the ritual on the spot, I paid for a chicken and had the vendor place it in a small cardboard box. I felt its weight shift into one corner of the box as I carried it. When I got home, I laid the box on the floor of my sukkah, opened the lid, and placed a slice of bread and a bowl of water inside.

My friend Yakov Yosef Freund was to give me a wake-up call at 4:30 the next morning, early enough to dress quickly, have a dunk in the mikveh, rush through the penitence prayers, and be primed for the thread of kindness that would hover over our village ahead of the ris- ing sun. Yakov Yosef and I would take our chickens, swing them over our heads in the prescribed ritual, and then rush to the garbage-strewn alley behind the shopping center to join the line of people waiting for the ritual slaughterer to run his knife over the chicken's throat at the back door to the butcher shop. By our calculations, that would leave us just enough time to head back to the rebbe's house and join the throngs squeezed into the dank basement to watch the rebbe swing his chicken over his head, weeping and chanting, "*Sons of man, sitting in darkness and the shadow of death.*"

Gitty and I went to bed at two in the morning. A short while later, I heard her calling my name. I thought it was a dream, until I heard her say, "Shulem, my water broke."

I shot up in an instant. The bedside clock read 4:00 AM. Gitty lay on her side with her eyes closed, and agony poured over her face. The only sound in the room was her slow and labored breathing. I sat on my bed and stared at her, unsure what to do next.

"Call the doctor," Gitty said, as soon as the contraction passed, efficient as ever. I called the number she pointed to in her little address book.

Mount Sinai was an hour away, and from the looks of it, it seemed as if Gitty would give birth momentarily. "Should we call an ambulance?" I asked the doctor. Gitty, wearily, rolled her eyes.

"It's a first baby," the doctor said. "It's not going to pop out."

Gitty stood up to get dressed while I had visions of the baby being born in the backseat of the taxi as the driver, apathetic, cruised down the Palisades Parkway.

"Call the rebbe," Gitty said.

It was shortly after four now, and I wondered if anyone would pick up, but the elderly gabbai, Reb Shia, answered as usual: "Yes?"

"I'm calling to inform about a birth. We're leaving for the hospital shortly."

"Name?" he asked.

"Shulem Deen."

"Not *your* name. *Her* name."

"Er—" My mind drew a blank. What was her name?

"What's *her* name?" the gabbai asked again impatiently.

"Er—Gittel. Gittel the daughter of Chaim."

"The *mother's* name!"

The mother's name? Wasn't Gitty the mother? But of course—Gitty's mother. "Gittel the daughter of Chava Leah." It all had to be conveyed just so if the rebbe's prayers were to be effective.

"I'll let the rebbe know," Reb Shia said. "Good tidings."

"Call the cab," Gitty said, as she struggled to adjust her wig at the vanity mirror.

While Gitty waited at the door, a small suitcase at her side, I grabbed some cash from an envelope in a drawer in our bedroom. As the car sped along the Palisades Parkway toward the George Washington Bridge, I held my small Psalms book, the same one the rebbe had used six years earlier during his visit to our Williamsburg yeshiva. Beside me, in a small plastic bag, lay *Reziel the Angel* and *The Sweetness of Elimelech*, sacred texts I was to place under Gitty's pillow, talismans for easy labor. Gitty sat in the back holding her own Book of Psalms, her maiden name embossed in gold Hebrew lettering on the white leather cover.

Psalms Chapter 20 is a wonderful aid for easing childbirth, I had read in a book of esoteric customs. Nine verses for the nine months of pregnancy. Seventy words for the seventy pangs of labor. The 310 letters for the 310 heavenly worlds of the righteous. It was tried and true, the book said. Very effective.

> *May the Lord answer thee in thy day of trouble.*
> *The name of the God of Jacob set thee upon high.*
> *May He send forth thy help from the sanctuary, and support thee*
>   *out of Zion.*

The taxi driver glanced at my Book of Psalms several times but said nothing. I looked back at Gitty periodically with what I hoped were appropriate expressions of concern. She would nod and mouth, *I'm OK,* alternating between her own recitations of Psalms and managing her breathing exercises.

> *May He receive the memorial of all thy meal-offerings, and accept*
> *the fat of thy burnt-sacrifice. May He bestow upon thee the desires*
> *of thy heart, and may He fulfill thy counsel.*

When I finished reciting Psalm 20 nine times, I recited it nine more times, and then nine more, until I had done nine times nine. We were barely past the mid-Parkway gas station and convenience shop.

Finally, we arrived at the Klingenstein Pavilion of Mount Sinai Hospital, and Gitty was shown to a room. I looked at her as she lay on the hospital bed, her face bathed in sweat, her turban askew and showing the edges of her close-cropped hair. She twisted from her back to a fetal position and back again as she tried to find a comfortable position. For the very first time, I wanted to reach out and hold her. I wanted to say something, if not quite that I loved her, then something very near to it. But I could not touch her or offer any words of affection. The law forbade it. And so, after bringing her several cups of ice chips from the visitors' lounge, I sat in a chair in the corner and turned back to Psalm 20, for another round of nine times nine.

"I think it's best if you stepped out," Gitty said a few minutes later, facing away from me. I would have to go soon, anyway—it was forbidden for me to remain present during the birth—so I left the room and paced the hallway, Book of Psalms in hand. A man emerged from the room next door, his face glowing, as if ready to burst into a grin. He looked at me for a moment and then looked away. I felt self-conscious in my Hasidic garb, alienating the strangers who might otherwise engage me in conversation, other men who had little to do but stand around and wait, grinning at strangers after their babies were delivered.

The doctor came out of the room and walked past me as if I weren't there.

"How is she?" I asked.

"Fine," he called from several paces away, without turning, as if I were some strange creature, my presence reluctantly tolerated, a tagalong with no purpose.

The father from the room next door came out again, and then went back into the room. "There's another one next door," I heard him say. "Is there screaming?" a woman's voice asked. I couldn't hear his response, and imagined him whispering: *It's one of those Hasidics.*

A nurse walked past me and entered the room. The doctor came a few minutes later. For a long time, I could hear the nurse counting to ten and shouting, "Push, push!" Then she would scold, "Not *now!* I told you *not* to push!" Occasionally, I heard soft moaning from Gitty, and wished I could be in the room with her, to hold her hand and wipe the sweat from her brow. After an excruciating thirty minutes, the nurse's yelling stopped and I heard the cry of an infant. I felt my throat tighten. The nurse said, "girl," then, "7:22," then, "six pounds, five ounces." I laid my forehead against the wall outside the door and let my tears flow.

Twenty minutes later, the doctor left the room and walked past me. When he neared the nurses' station, he paused, then turned back, as if trying to recall where he'd seen me. "Oh," he said finally. "It's a girl."

I was ravenously hungry when I left Gitty at around two in the afternoon. I remembered the words of the Talmud: *He who feasts on the Ninth, it is as if he fasted both the Ninth and the Tenth.* Yom Kippur itself, the tenth day of Tishrei, is for fasting and prayer, but before and after were times for rejoicing. Sins were going to be erased. Offenses written off. The balance sheet balanced once again, and all would be good in the great heavenly accounting. *If your sins are like scarlet, they shall be made as white as snow; if they are red as crimson, they shall be made like wool.*

I was all for feasting, except I had no idea where to get kosher food at the hospital. All I'd eaten that day was a small slice of honey cake in the morning, grabbed from a loaf on the kitchen counter just before Gitty and I had left for the hospital. A nurse told me that there was a kosher vending machine in the hospital cafeteria, but I found it with a large handwritten note saying, "Out of Service." The empty shelves inside the display windows—"Tuna Sandwich," "Strawberry Yogurt," "Cheese Blintz"—mocked me and my growling intestines.

The specter of Yom Kippur loomed large, and I was anxious not to have a two-day fast. I was also anxious to get back to New Square. The first of the penitence prayers was to be held at four. I wanted to tell the rebbe about my newborn child and to receive his blessings and his good wishes. I wanted to be back among family and friends, away from the alienating glances of Manhattanites. The last bus to New Square would be leaving at three, from midtown, several miles away. I had one hour, plenty of time to get there, I thought.

Just as I was about to hail a cab, I checked my wallet: I had no money.

I'd miscalculated. I'd brought cash for the taxi in the morning but had failed to take along enough to get home. I had a ticket for the Monsey Trails bus, courtesy of my father-in-law, but it would do me no good if I couldn't get to midtown within the hour. I owned no credit cards and carried no checkbook. I stood at the curb in front of the hospital, gripped with panic.

It was then that I noticed: *a Yid!* He was sitting in the driver's seat of a car parked several yards away. He appeared to be a Litvak, with his thick, short *payess* tucked behind his ears, white shirt with no *tallis katan* over it. Not a Hasid, but still, an Orthodox Jew. He was reading from what appeared to be a religious text, and he looked up as I approached.

I explained my situation. Could he possibly loan me a few dollars? I asked. I would send him payment as soon as I got home.

The man looked at me for a moment, expressionless. I had expected him to offer warm congratulations and best wishes for a meaningful Yom Kippur. I was certain that he'd help me out—it was inconceivable that a religious Jew would do otherwise.

Instead, he stuck his hand in his pants pocket and fished around for something.

"Take the bus," he said, and placed four quarters into my hand.

I looked at the coins in my hand, speechless. The man turned back to his book. What kind of Yid was this?

I thought of the words of the old rebbe, admonishing his Hasidim never to ride New York City's public transit system. *Be killed rather than transgress*, the old rebbe had said, declaring it a cardinal sin.

"Please," I said to the man in the car. "I can't." My tongue stuck in my mouth as I struggled to find the words, and then watched as the man reached with his index finger to the window button. He kept his eyes glued to his book as the window rolled up, as if my presence was just another noisy distraction in the bustling city.

"One glance where you shouldn't," the old rebbe had said, "and you lose an entire year of Torah study."

Protect your eyes. In the ritual bath. At the supermarket. On the streets. *He who gazes at the small finger of a woman, it is as though he has gazed at her place of immodesty.* How could I possibly ride the city bus, with so much immodesty on a hot summer day?

And yet, what choice did I have? Mournfully, I removed my thick plastic-framed eyeglasses, the world around me turning into a blur of indistinct shapes and colors, and stumbled onto a city bus, found a seat, and kept my eyes downcast.

The bus to Monsey and New Square, owned by Skverer Hasidim, would be different. It would have a curtain down the aisle to separate the sexes. Arriving just as the bus was about to leave, I rushed on and handed the driver my ticket, and then noticed that the curtain was gathered on its track toward the back of the bus. Surely, I thought, the other riders were simply too tired after a day's work to bother extending it. Surely, they would appreciate if someone would do it for them, so I laid my prayer shawl and my shtreimel on an empty seat, and set out to arrange the curtain properly.

"What's your problem?" A man shouted at me. "Isn't it hot enough in here?"

He, too, was a Litvak, and I remembered the words of one of my yeshiva teachers: "Litvaks don't care much for matters of holiness and purity."

Other riders joined in the chorus of complaints.

"Who cares about the curtain?"

"It's hot enough as it is. You want us to suffocate?"

"Why don't you just take a seat and close your eyes?"

I was startled, confused, and then angry. "Do you have no shame?" I shot back at one of the men. "No concern for protecting your eyes? The day before Yom Kippur, no less?"

By the time the bus reached the corner of Truman and Washington Avenues in New Square, it was four-thirty. The prayers had just ended, and I watched the swarm of worshipers exit the shul. I rushed inside to wait for the rebbe. He soon made his way out from his little room up front, and I stepped into the middle of the parted crowd.

"My wife had a baby," I said. "A girl."

The rebbe slowed as he extended his hand and shook mine with his fingertips, limp, as if my message carried no more significance than the arrival of the day's mail. "Mazel tov," he said, his expression unchanged.

I stepped aside and watched as the parted crowds closed behind him.

Our joyous occasions bring the rebbe more joy than they bring ourselves, Avremel had said over and over during his many speeches. Now I wondered: Was it really so?

Slowly, I walked to my home on Roosevelt Avenue, feeling sleep-deprived, exhausted from the ride, overwhelmed with a combination of joy for the new baby and stress from the day's events, almost forgetting my hunger. All I wanted was to be home, and for the first time, I found myself missing Gitty, and also missing the child that was born to us that day, with her clear and alert eyes and the peachy fuzz on her soft head and the strawberry patch of skin on the back of her neck.

It was then that I remembered: I hadn't yet performed the *kapparos.* My atonement process was incomplete. The chicken was still outside in the cardboard box, in the heat of the sun, without food or water. As soon as I got home, I stepped into the sukkah. The chicken moved its head as I peered into the box. Relieved that it was still alive, I laid a slice of challah carefully inside the cardboard box and refilled the water bowl. Then I went into my bedroom and lay down on my bed, fully clothed. I was desperate for sleep, yet forced myself to remain awake. The day was not over: There was still one festive meal before the fast began, and afterward I would have to rush to the mikveh, then light a candle in the shul for my father's soul; soon after, the Kol Nidrei would begin. Prayers would go until long past midnight.

A half hour later, as I sat at the table in my in-laws' dining room, eating my mother-in-law's challah and gefilte fish and chicken soup, I thought back to the day's events: the doctor's brusque attitude, the man who shoved four quarters into my hand without even looking at me, the bus riders who scolded me for my pious intentions, the rebbe's indifference to my joy. Suddenly, Gitty's unpretentious family seemed the most beautiful thing in the world.

When Gitty brought our baby home a few days later, we settled into rooms prepared for us in her parents' home, as was the custom.

Mother and baby were in danger of being harmed by Lilith and her demons for thirty days and could not be left alone. On the four walls of our room hung laminated sheets of mystical texts, names of protecting angels and warnings to all the forces of evil to keep their distance.

Our baby was laid in a dresser drawer set upon two chairs—a cradle or crib was not to be used until thirty days after birth—and as we stood silently gazing at the steady and alert eyes of our infant daughter, I looked toward Gitty and she smiled at me. There was something between us that at first I could not identify, a calmness of sorts. Gone was the anxious tiptoeing around each other, and in its place came the feeling that something had changed.

Soon it was time for the baby's feeding, and Gitty sat down on the bed opposite me, covered her shoulder and chest with a small blanket, and undid the top buttons of her robe. As we chatted about breastfeeding and diapers and the relative merits of pacifiers of various kinds, I realized what it was that had changed.

We had created love.

Chapter Seven

It was the year of the photo op, hundreds of moments that seemed perfectly staged, waiting for the click of a camera shutter.

Here is Tziri dragging onions and potatoes out of kitchen cabinets.

Here is Tziri on the floor, in each hand a tomato, pilfered from unpacked supermarket bags nearby, her face and nose smeared in red goo and tiny tomato seeds.

Here is Tziri standing precariously with one hand on the trash can, peeking out from behind a small plastic bowl, nose, forehead, and cheeks smeared in chocolate pudding, eyes frozen wide with guilt.

Here she is studiously ripping pages from books she'd emptied off the lower shelves of our dining-room bookcase; here she is on Gitty's bed, reaching for the cordless telephone on the pillow or scribbling furiously with a fat red crayon over the "Instruction for Brides" pamphlet that Gitty kept on the nightstand.

It was a blessed year. Gone was the angst that had accompanied me through my adolescence and the awkwardness of adjusting to married life. Yet to come were the full burdens of raising a family and its attendant anxieties, the pressures of health and finance, negotiating sibling disputes and wardrobe mutinies, overseeing school projects and homework assignments. Also yet to come were the torrents of doubt about my faith and the anxiety over how to deal with them. Even the nights passed unmemorably; a calm child, Tziri was sleeping through the night by the age of four months.

There were occasional frustrations. When I held Tziri in my arms, I felt as though I'd borrowed her, as if Gitty, generous with the precious thing, was allowing me, under her careful observation, to be a vice-parent of sorts. Springtime came, and Gitty and I would sit on patio chairs outside our door with Tziri in our laps. Sometimes I'd notice tiny goose bumps on Tziri's arms and say, "I think maybe she can use a sweater." Gitty would look away, annoyed. It was she who determined whether the baby was too cold or too warm, whether she was hungry or gassy, or whether, as Gitty would sometimes say, "She's just a bad baby today." When I offered once to change Tziri's diaper, Gitty looked at me as if the notion were too absurd for words. I, a young man barely out of yeshiva, still consumed with Torah study and prayer and all those things that were the opposite of domesticity, surely would know nothing of changing diapers.

It stung, the notion that my child belonged more to her mother than to me, but I learned to accept it. I allowed the love for my daughter to wash over me and felt the indescribable, almost painful, joy over her existence. At times, I would not understand where those feelings came from; they were there when I watched her sleep, when I watched her feed, even when she cried, her face scrunched up with wrinkles so fine, her whimpers like a sweet melody.

There would be more babies through the years, all of whom Gitty and I would love deeply, but what I felt with Tziri's birth would not repeat itself with the others. It was as if Tziri had come to repair something broken, and then it was fixed and the others had lesser roles to play. With my marriage to Gitty, I felt as if I had embarked not on my own journey but someone else's, living not my own passions but those assigned to me by a world and a community that wanted for me something I had not fully chosen but had broken my will for. In Tziri, I found my consolation. At the end of a day of study, I would return home, and Gitty and Tziri would be out together on the patio. Gitty would be feeding Tziri baby food, applesauce, or mashed-up peas and carrots, and they would both look at me, Gitty with a gentle smile and Tziri with a reflexive wave of her arms and a stream of excited babbles.

I remember holding her at sixteen months, in January 1996, when I brought her home from Gitty's parents to greet her new sibling, Freidy, our second child. I remember that she had something in her hand—in my memory it is an oblong object, vaguely threatening, like a soup ladle or a rolling pin, although it was more likely a toy of some sort—when she spotted the brand-new infant dozing in the portable crib between our beds. Still in my arms, Tziri looked at the bundle in the crib and then to me and Gitty, and then laughed a nervous adult-like laugh. *Tell me this is a joke*, she seemed to say, and she waved the object in Freidy's direction, as if wanting to strike it, that *thing* that dared usurp her pride of place. Gitty and I laughed, nervous, but oh, so charmed.

It was Freidy whose birth would make us realize how unprepared we were. Plump-cheeked and colicky, she screamed through her first twelve months. Gitty had her hands full while I was studying and praying and attending the rebbe's tischen. Gitty and I were both now twenty-one, with two children; before long, we realized that we were into something we hadn't prepared for.

"Rent is due tomorrow," Gitty reminded me one morning, and that same evening she waved a pile of bills in front of me. "FINAL TERMINATION NOTICE," read a letter from O&R Utilities in oversize bold red letters. There was a bill from the phone company and another from a mail-order catalog from which we'd purchased a state-of-the-art toaster oven for three easy monthly payments of $39.99. We owed money at the supermarket, at the fish store, and at the butcher's. "Mr. Greenberg said we need to pay off something on the account," Gitty said, and I grew furious at Mr. Greenberg for not realizing that a three-hundred-dollar credit limit on groceries was not enough for a family of four whose head of household was studying Torah for a living.

At first, raising and providing for a family had seemed simple enough. Everyone did it, more or less, and so I imagined there must be a formula, the specifics of which I would learn in due time. The important thing was to start the process. I assumed that the "system," the birth-to-death cocoon of institutions and support networks available for every Hasidic person, would take care of the rest. There were parents and in-laws to provide a year of dinners and Sabbath meals and a first baby's needs. There were Sabbath food pantries for the hungry, free loan societies for home buyers, free roadside assistance for car owners, cadres of Hasidic EMT personnel to tend to emergency medical needs. There were grants for marrying off children, a co-op grocery store with discounted prices for school employees and others with large families. Any man could take his meals free in the yeshiva dining room if he chose. There was free coffee in the shul each morning and a shower and bath in the mikveh, with a reasonably clean towel and a shard of flaky soap.

For other expenses—rent and utilities and the odd pair of pants or the occasional wig styling—there was a stipend from the *kollel*, the rabbinical-studies institution that extended from the yeshiva system, in which every young married male, by community ordinance, was to spend the first two years of marriage. I had little budgetary sense of my own but was certain that the kollel had calculated the proper formula and provided accordingly.

A week after our wedding, I headed to the kollel's administrative offices to enroll. The main kollel building was a drab edifice with a gray-and-pink stucco facade that formed one side of a quad in the village center, between the main synagogue and the rebbe's home and opposite the elongated, limestone-covered structure of the Great Yeshiva. The elderly kollel administrator handed me a pile of documents to sign as he entered my name and Social Security number into an ancient computer. He then rattled off the rules in a drawling unpunctuated monotone: "Four hundred thirty a month always be on time five minutes late one dollar penalty miss a session twenty dollars two exams per week fifty dollars penalty for missing an exam thank you and be well."

It seemed plenty: $430 a month. The ordinance required only two years of study, but I would stay for many years, I was certain. Oh, it will be challenging, my friends and I would say to one another, but that would only prove how worthy the endeavor. In the great hall of the kollel, at any given time, one could see men of all ages sparring over nuances of the law: from just-married young men, with peachy wisps of facial hair, to wizened scholars who shuffled on their walkers and canes to the senior-citizens' restroom just outside the main door.

There were, of course, those disinclined toward a lifetime of study; the weak-willed, the impious, those lacking the passion or discipline for sacred ideals. Those unfortunate souls who, as soon as the two years were up, left the kollel to take jobs as supermarket cashiers, deliverymen for the butcher or the fish store, plumbers, electricians, do-it-all handymen. A few started businesses: selling children's clothes out of converted basements or setting up child day-care centers in their living rooms. One enterprising friend started a small sandwich shop at the village's tiny shopping mall, where men would stop for a bagel and egg salad after morning prayers. Another opened a craft store, only to close it several months later when he realized that, really, how many needlepoint and hook-rug kits did each family in the village need?

If I had given any thought to what I would do past the kollel years, earning money was never part of it. My occupation would be of the *klei kodesh* sort, sacred vessels through which holiness passed: cantors, ritual slaughterers, scribes of sacred texts, teachers at the cheder or the yeshiva. I'd always assumed that I would end up among the last category, or perhaps teaching adults—the daily page of Talmud, or an evening lecture on Bible commentaries—perhaps even a scholar of note, teaching other learned men.

Now I realized that something didn't compute. After the babies arrived, there were new expenses I hadn't considered. Our in-laws bought us a baby crib, but we also needed a buggy, a stroller, a bureau, baby clothes—never-ending streams of soft pink ruffles, Onesies embroidered with befuddled-looking teddy bears, stretchies with colorful ABC pyramids. There were plush cloth books with images of friendly-looking tigers and giraffes, intended to plant the seeds of literary appreciation. There were rattles and baby bottles and pacifiers and more rattles and all kinds of other noisemaking devices that mothers and grandmothers assured us were necessary for raising healthy babies.

Baby diapers were being expended with alarming frequency. Gitty, blessedly frugal by nature, would purchase only no-name brands. "Look at this," she would point with disdain at packages of Luvs stacked above the fruits and vegetables at Braun's Supermarket. "Nine dollars a pack. Thievery." She'd cluck her tongue and roll her eyes and turn the aisle to reach for one of the generic brands.

"Maybe," Gitty said one morning, as she stirred a pot of farina with Freidy on her arm, "you want to look for a job of some kind?"

"A job?" The suggestion sounded offensively common.

"It's just a thought," Gitty said.

I knew she was right, though, and so when a notice appeared on the kollel door one day, I took note: *EXCELLENT JOB OPPOR-TUNITIES. Office work in New Jersey. Training provided. No experience necessary. Suitable for kollel men seeking work for the first time.*

It seemed absurd that I would, overnight, go from kollel student to office worker. But as I mulled it over, I wondered what it would be like to have material comforts, a steady paycheck, a car someday, maybe even a home of our own. Perhaps those things would provide consolation for having abandoned my aspirations. I ripped off a hangtag and stuffed it into my pocket.

"There will be a meeting in the kollel basement tomorrow at seven thirty," a young woman said when I called the number.

If I had been worried that forsaking the study hall was a betrayal of my pious aspirations, at least I was not alone. In the corridor between the administrative offices and the large library—the Vault of Sacred Books—a group of men stood around waiting. Bentzion Grunwald was there, a prodigy who had completed the entire Talmud before his marriage, finishing the very last page right before he was led to the chuppah. Chaim Yidel Gold was there, who would be seen in the yeshiva study hall until past midnight and back again at four in the morning. They all smiled sheepishly, trying in vain to make light of it all.

"Office work, huh?" Chaim Yidel said, on his face a look of resignation.

Gavriel Blum, said to be "the cleverest man in the shtetl," soon came skipping down the stairs with a sprightly bop, winding and rewinding his sidelocks around his ears, which seemed squished and reddened and made him look anything but clever. He crooked his head toward the library door and we followed him, thirty or so men, and took seats around five long tables.

Gavriel laid it out for us: A telecommunications company in New Jersey, owned by Orthodox Jews, was willing to hire Hasidic men just entering the job market. All we needed, Gavriel said, was to fill out these sheets—"*rezemays,*" he called them—and he tossed a pile of forms onto each of the tables. My friend Zundel, sitting next to me, looked at the sheets like a child studying a tax form: "What is this, *rezemays?*"

Gavriel explained: In America, before you get a job, a company needs to know something about you. *Rezemays*, he said, save time for everyone involved. "The main thing," Gavriel said, "is to write down your skills." The English word "skills" bounced incongruously off his clipped Yiddish sentences, and the men stared back blankly.

"Skills?" Zundel asked finally. "Don't you need to go to college for that?"

Gavriel shook his head noncommittally. "Not necessarily. You can write if you've ever worked with computers. Or if you're good at math. Things like that." He looked around the room as the men looked timidly at the forms in front of them. "Don't be modest," Gavriel said. "This is the place to brag."

And so we sat and wondered what we might brag about. We knew a lot about commerce in first-century Palestine. We could write contracts on property sales that would be legally binding in fifth-century Babylonia. A handful of us knew exactly how to slaughter an ox in Jerusalem's ancient temple, skin it, clean it, and separate the priestly portions. But this was the first we'd heard of *rezemays*.

Slowly, we began to fill in our names, our addresses, and phone numbers and then tried to think of what we might consider a *skill*.

Excellent English reading and writing skills, I wrote down. That sentence alone looked skillful.

"Excellent English?" Gavriel asked with a scoff when I handed him my sheet.

"I'm from Borough Park," I said.

He laid a hand on my shoulder. "Tzaddik," he said, "you might be better than these guys." He cocked his head to the line of men behind me. "But compared to Yeshiva University boys, your English isn't worth a half-eaten radish."

I walked home with my ego bruised, wondering what it would be like to get a job, to wake up each morning and catch a commuter bus and spend the day in an office. I imagined the whir of a fax machine, incessant phone calls, dealing with irritable customers, and, of course, other employees of both sexes.

A few days later, I ran into Gavriel at the shul. He was rolling his gartel around his fingers after the conclusion of evening prayers.

"Whatever happened to the job thing?"

He looked away. "Plan fell through." He finished winding his gartel and placed it in his coat pocket. "Not enough skills."

Several weeks later, there was another note on the kollel door.

Substitute Teachers Needed. Call Mordche Goldhirsch.

Mordche was one of the principals at the cheder, the elementary school for boys, and I called the number as soon as I got home for lunch.

"Can you come in at two?" Mordche Goldhirsch asked. One of the sixth-grade teachers had a dentist appointment.

The kitchen clock said 1:15. I would have to miss the afternoon study session at the kollel and incur the twenty-dollar penalty. The three-hour substituting job would pay thirty dollars.

"I'll be there," I said to Mordche.

On his office door was a nameplate: *Rabbi Mordechai Goldhirsch, Principal, Grades 4, 5, & 6,* and I walked in to find Mordche standing with a thin wooden rod over a boy holding his palm out for a thwacking. Mordche told the terrified boy to wait, and then escorted me down the hallway.

"Look each of them in the eye. Don't let them scare you," he said, and I felt an instant flash of terror. I remembered how my friends and I had treated our own substitute teachers, how one of our teachers had said, right before he took his two-week summer vacation: "Substitutes are a time to take things easy." For the next two weeks, we took things easy by sticking pins up the underside of the substitute teacher's chair cushion, pouring salt into his coffee, and spilling bottles of Elmer's glue onto the vinyl tiles under his desk, then watching as he struggled to wipe the sticky mess from the soles of his shoes.

From a nearby classroom came the singsong of a Talmud lesson and from another the sound of boys reciting Bible verses. From a classroom at the end of the hall, I heard laughing and shouting and felt my heartbeat quicken. As Mordche's hand went for the doorknob, he paused and peered through the small square window. Inside, boys stood on tables, tugged one another's sidelocks, and chased one another around the room, until one boy noticed us and leaped into his seat, followed, like a set of dominoes, by the rest of the class. By the time Mordche turned the knob, every boy was in his place with his Bible reader open in front of him.

Mordche said nothing to the class. He stepped aside to allow me to enter, nodded curtly, and closed the door.

I sat down at the desk and looked around, my gaze lingering on each boy, as Mordche had instructed. I tried to mask the fear I felt as the two dozen pairs of eyes assessed me.

The afternoon passed quickly enough, with few disturbances. I gave a lesson on the weekly Bible portion, told a story of an ancient saint, stepped out twice to get coffee from the teachers' room down the hall, and three hours later it was over. In my pocket, as I walked home, I carried thirty dollars in school vouchers.

"*Vouchers!*" Gitty sputtered in disbelief when I walked into the house and waved them in front of her. "What are we going to do with *vouchers?*"

Vouchers were the local currency, printed by the school system, with which it paid the bulk of its employee salaries. Everyone in the village seemed to have a surplus of them. The vouchers were redeemable at local shops, whose owners were then paid in dollars by the school, at a steep discount.

There had been a time when schoolteachers had to wait weeks, sometimes months, for their pay. But that was no longer the case. The school had a makeshift treasury, a small office on the ground floor of the boys' school with a computer and an old inkjet printer, and could print all the vouchers it needed. Denominations of fives, tens, twenties, still wet from the sputtering wheel of the inkjet were packed into cabinets by a young female secretary.

The vouchers were a source of constant aggravation. Every day, it seemed, one store or another changed its voucher policy. When Pollack's Dry Goods Store announced that it would accept vouchers, there was a run for the small basement store on Lincoln Avenue, and its supplies of underwear, socks, and baby outfits quickly cleared off the shelves. Einhorn's Basics and Beyond was forced to follow suit, while Grossman's Books & Judaica announced that it would no longer accept vouchers.

I thought Gitty was overreacting. There was a lot we could do with vouchers. "We might be able to exchange them for food stamps," I said.

If vouchers were like a Third World currency, food stamps were as good as the U.S. dollar. Grossman's Books & Judaica accepted food stamps without question, as did both dry goods stores and the small silver shop in the Winklers' basement on Jackson Avenue. At the annual yeshiva fund-raising dinner, one man after another counted out food stamp checks for donations and received appreciative nods. Even the elderly itinerant vendor, who stood in the shul foyer every Wednesday evening with his refurbished Walkmans and alarm clocks, accepted food stamps gladly. Unlike the vouchers, a strictly local currency, food stamps could be taken to Monsey and Williamsburg and passed on further.

Soon I had other substituting jobs, often for several weeks, as the regular rebbes took their two-week summer vacations. The vouchers piled up in an envelope in a kitchen drawer, right next to the dairy cutlery. We could buy all the groceries we wanted, or another bundle of pink and yellow baby outfits, but we still had no way to pay our rent or the electric bill.

Chapter Eight

Teaching felt strange to me, vaguely fraudulent. It hadn't been long since my own days as a cheder boy, and it felt as if I was not old enough, wise enough, learned enough to be teaching my own group of cheder boys. Mostly, though, I was reliving the memories of my youth, this time from the other side of the rebbe's desk.

As a child, I had been a daydreamer—one of the worst offenses, to have your mind wander from your rebbe's lesson and your finger drift away from the text in front of you.

"SHULEM, *VIE HALT MEN?*"

It was the most common question of my childhood, always, when it came, jarring me out of a sweet daydream. From first grade through ninth, each rebbe in his own gruff voice, angry, impatient, or sighing in resignation: "SHULEM, WHERE ARE WE HOLDING?"

Where we were "holding" was the specific passage, line, and word in the text of our Talmuds, which we were to know at all times by keeping our forefingers pressed against the small square letters, moving along as the rebbe led us through the jungle of dense, unpunctuated Aramaic text, the digest of rabbinic discourse in the ancient Babylonian cities of Sura and Pumbeditha.

Whenever the question came, my mind, in a frenzy, would spin through the haze of my daydream as I tried to recall a passage, a phrase, or even a word. I would hear the faint echoes of fragmented clauses, *This passage is not according to Rav Sheshes,* or *Ravina put the query to Rav Ashi,* and I would search frantically through the text, until— wait, was the phrase in the Gemara or the Rashi? Or I would find not one but two instances—and which was it? Often I could not find the phrase at all and would wonder, gripped with panic: Was I even on the right page?

If I failed to know where we were holding, the rebbe would beckon silently with his forefinger. I would rise, arms and legs quivering, and head to his desk, where, at his nod toward my arm, I would extend my right hand. The rebbe would grab hold of my fingers, then reach for his rod—the dowel of an old wooden coat hanger—raise it high in the air, and bring it down on my palm. Whoosh. Thwack. At his signal, I would extend my other hand, and the thwacking would be repeated until, by some arbitrary measure, the rebbe was satisfied. With each thwack, my palm would burn and I'd pray for it all to end, for the rod to break, for my rebbe to have a heart attack.

The thwacking happened often, and it happened to each of us, but still there was the shame, walking back to my chair, rubbing my bright red palms against my blue or brown corduroy trousers. I never questioned the justice of it, though. If the shape of a fluffy white cloud outside the open window, or the tooting of an angry cabdriver's horn, or the passing siren of a fire engine induced a daydream, it only followed that I was to be punished for it. If Ravina had a query to Rav Ashi, it would behoove me to pay attention. Because Ravina had important questions, as did all the rabbis of the Talmud, and to be a pious Hasidic boy, to grow up to be a pious Hasidic man, a boy must pay attention to the questions posed by the rabbis, and so not have any questions of his own.

These are the laws you shall put before them. So said God to Moses, who then taught the children of Israel the proper way to bore holes in the ears of their slaves (drag them to a doorpost first), how to treat a slave-girl sold by her father (marry her or set her free after six years), the amount owed to a slaveholder if your ox gored his slave (thirty silver shekels).

Each week, another portion of the Bible: priestly vestments, the half-shekel census in the Sinai desert, the golden calf, the Sabbatical year for the fields, purities and impurities.

Eleven days from Horeb, via Mount Seir, to Kadesh Barnea. I was in the fifth grade, and the class was restless with thoughts of summer. At home, my mother packed my trunk: bathing suits, flashlight, laundry bag, cup and basin for *negel vasser*—the bedside washing ritual. Also, bags of pretzels and potato chips that would be crummy and stale one week later. In our classroom at the Krasna cheder in Borough Park, Moses was entering his final days; the forty years of wandering through the desert were almost over, and soon we would be off to summer camp, at the end of which Moses would die and we, the student campers, would take off in a caravan of yellow school buses to ride the roller coasters and bumper cars at a nearby amusement park.

At camp, there would be games and activities, field days and color wars, but only in the late afternoons. Until five o'clock, Moses's words would continue, and we would study them from our dog-eared volumes of Deuteronomy, with the same rebbes as all year round, with their harsh voices, their scoldings, and their rods. All summer, Moses would berate, chastise, and teach the great lessons about loving God with all your heart and all your soul and all your possessions because those who ceased to love God were punished by war and famine and pestilence until the love of God was restored, and then we would go swimming or play kickball out on the grassy field.

Now, however, we were still in Brooklyn, still in the first week of Deuteronomy, and Moses was giving the children of Israel a talking-to about their bad behavior of the past forty years.

"Chaim Burich," the rebbe called, "what is the meaning of *Eleven Days?*"

Chaim Burich blinked, looked at the rebbe, then at the rod on the rebbe's desk. But Chaim Burich did not know the answer.

"Shea! What is the meaning of *Eleven Days?*"

Shea, too, stared back at the rebbe blankly.

"Shulem! What is the meaning of *Eleven Days?*"

I did not know the answer, but there was comfort in knowing that I was not alone. One by one, the rebbe's question went around the classroom, and each boy, in turn, remained silent.

Finally, the rebbe turned to Nusi, the smartest boy in the class.

"A *distance* of eleven days," Nusi's voice rang through the classroom, his tone unbearably smug.

"Nusi, read to us from Rashi!"

Nusi placed his index finger on the small rounded letters on the lower half of the page: "Says the holy Rashi," Nusi sang as the rest of us fidgeted in our seats, "*The presence of the* Shechina *was so great that you traveled in three days a distance of eleven days. And then you sinned, and you wandered for forty years.*"

The rebbe reached for his rod and walked over to Chaim Burich. Chaim Burich extended his palm, the rebbe grabbed his fingers, and Chaim Burich's mouth formed a sudden O as the rod met his palm and he let out a breathy, muffled shriek. The rebbe let go of Chaim Burich's hand and moved on to Shea, then to me, then to Srul Yosef, then to Motty, Berry, Shloimy. Twenty-four boys got their palms thwacked, twenty-four boys rubbed their sore palms on their trousers for forgetting Rashi's commentary on *Eleven Days*. All except Nusi, who sat with a half smile, his chin resting on his arm, while the rest of us struggled to hold back our tears.

Cheder wasn't all palm thwacking. Aside from Talmud and Bible studies, the Krasna cheder had a proper "English department." From four to six in the afternoon, four days a week, we were taught to read and write English and elementary mathematics.

Most of the students scoffed at these studies, taking their cues from many of the adults, who considered it a waste of time and a distraction from Torah study. Even our rebbes, the religious-studies teachers who were with us from eight in the morning until four in the afternoon, showed disdain for "English" by explaining that it was a grudging concession to the secular government and its laws. Some boys routinely left school at four, saying that their parents forbade them to study English, while the rest of us looked on in envy, wishing that our parents, too, were so pious.

English studies began in third grade. My first English teacher, Mr. Bernstein, was a tall, thin man, perpetually red-faced from shouting, with a tiny yarmulke on his head. He would enter our classroom each day, carrying his shiny black briefcase in hand, promptly at 4:00 PM. He would nod cordially to the rebbe, who would nod back in his superior way. The small red-and-blue knitted yarmulke was no match for the rebbe's broad-brimmed black hat. It was one of our earliest lessons: smaller hats always showed deference to larger ones.

Over time, I came to enjoy those two hours. Daydreaming was little impediment to mastering the correct spelling of *cat* and *house*. Two plus two equaled four, there wasn't much to it. This wasn't some ancient rabbi asking another ancient rabbi how to explain an extra letter or word in the Bible, which, in my mind, seemed neither extraneous nor consequential.

English studies proved pleasant for another reason: There was no palm thwacking. English teachers could shout, stamp their feet, blow their cheeks into a bright purple sheen, but they could not lay a hand on us. Still, as was common knowledge among us students, English teachers were to be despised as purveyors of profanity—"*Aynglish, foy!*" went the refrain.

Once, during morning recess in the third grade, I had the notion to heap public scorn on Mr. Bernstein by drawing a picture of him sitting on the toilet. My fellow classmates stood around my desk observing my impromptu art performance. Mr. Bernstein's humiliation on the pages of my notebook felt righteous.

Our rebbe, a humorless Satmar Hasid from Williamsburg, thought differently. When he entered our classroom at the end of recess and found the class gathered around my desk, he approached and studied my drawing. As it turned out, I hadn't understood his priorities. It was not Mr. Bernstein's honor that offended our rebbe but the fact that I had dirty things on my mind. Bathrooms were *tumeh*, profane places, and the things done in bathrooms were also profane, and so they were not to be spoken about and certainly not to be illustrated in our notebooks.

The rebbe grabbed my upper arm with his hand, lifted me out of my seat, and, clasping my arm firmly, led me to his desk.

"*Halt arois di hant.*"

Whoosh, thwack. Other hand. Whoosh, thwack. Other hand. Whoosh, thwack. The rest of the class looked on with profound boredom as our rebbe, his arm cantilevered across the air from his shoulder, swung his wooden rod up and down in an almost robotic motion, the rod swishing through the air and breaking its course on my palm while the rebbe, keeping time with his swing, issued the plaintive admonition: You. Thwack. Shall. Thwack. Not. Thwack. Profane. Thwack. This classroom. Thwack. With dirty images. Thwack, thwack, thwack.

••

It was now fourteen years since my third-grade rebbe thwacked my palms for my profane drawing, eight years since my ninth-grade rebbe slapped me for eating a bag of potato chips during a lesson on liabilities for digging pits in public places. All that thwacking and slapping now came to mind as I tried to teach Srulik Schmeltzer's sixth-grade class the laws of discarding leavened bread on the day before Passover. The boys chatted throughout the lesson, as if I weren't there, some even getting out of their seats and strolling around.

"Chaim Nuchem Braun, can you please sit down and keep quiet?" I called to a skinny boy who had stood up to look out the window and shouted something to a friend across the room.

"Chaim Nuchem Braun, can you please sit down and keep quiet?" the boy mimicked, then grinned at his friends as he walked to his seat and the class burst into laughter. I could feel the blood rush to my head as my body froze. I could not process any thoughts beyond the feeling of humiliation. I felt a kind of physical weakness in my body, a tremor in my jaws, and I clenched my teeth to keep it from showing. It was the second day of a two-week job. I could not imagine how I would last two weeks. But how could I, a twenty-two-year-old man, be cowed by a class of ten-year-olds?

At 12:45, I walked the two blocks home for an hour of lunch, before I would return for the afternoon. Along Clinton Lane, near the site of a new home construction, I spotted a "wire" on the ground, at the side of the road. It looked almost exactly like the one my fourth-grade rebbe had used instead of a rod, a white length of round, hollow rubber. It was the perfect size, twice arm's-length, just right to fold in half and hold at one end.

Halt arois di hant. I remembered the hundreds of times I had heard it. Hold out your hand. Without thinking, I picked up the rubber cord, wrapped it around my fingers, and then placed it inside my coat pocket.

There were the usual bouts of shouting and laughter across the classroom that afternoon, and I began to grow accustomed to it. I would not use the wire in my pocket, I decided. I would deal with the boys as best I could and somehow get through it. The next day, however, the boys grew even rowdier; when I called to Berry Glancz to stop speaking to the boy sitting next to him, his response sent me over the edge.

"Ich feif dich uhn."

He muttered it under his breath, not brazen enough to say it out loud, but the words were unmistakable. The language of defiance in the schoolyard, or among siblings in their rivalries, a child's bluster. *Ich feif dich uhn.* I fife my horn at you. I do not care for you or for your orders or your requests or desires, and so I blow my whistle at you. I shoot a burst of hot air in your face. Because you are nothing to me.

But I was not nothing to this boy. I was his rebbe. I reached into the inside breast pocket of my coat, where the rubber cord lay coiled flat against my chest. In a flash, I stood over Berry. For a moment, I intended to order him to "hold out your hand." Instead, as if my body acted on its own, I delivered a strike to boy's upper left arm, a hissing *sshhwisscchh-thwack!* that frightened even me with its violence. Berry's hand flew up to cover the spot I had struck, his mouth forming a sudden, silent "AH!"

I could see the anger in his eyes but did not care. He could fife and fife, but I was the one with the authority to use force, to strike him, and I watched as this realization sunk in and he looked back at me, angry but silent. The rest of the class, too, was silent as I made my way back to my desk. They remained silent for the rest of the afternoon, and the day after and the day after that.

Silent and contemptuous. I had gained the boys' obedience but not their respect. I had demonstrated not strength but weakness, and I saw in their eyes that they knew it. They had broken me, and I hated them for it.

In the teachers' room down the hall, the rebbes would talk about changes. The rebbes in New Square were always more brutal than the rebbes in Borough Park. I had heard the stories. One rebbe beat a boy with his gartel mercilessly until the boy lay on the floor howling for hours. Another thwacked a boy's palms several hundred times, until his welts began to bleed. One of my friends told me of a first-grade rebbe who had spanked his backside so raw that he couldn't sit for days, all because the rebbe had accused him of taking a small bag of candies from his desk drawer, only to find the candies in a different drawer a few minutes later.

Now the punishments were more measured. Some only slapped the students, instead of using a rod. "Feel the sting in your hand," one fifth-grade rebbe said to me earnestly. "If it hurts the child, it should hurt you, too." Others thought the rod was acceptable but that strikes must be meted out judiciously. Whipping a boy until he howled for hours was no longer advisable. Berel Eisenman, a teacher for nearly two decades who was once known to be the most brutal of all rebbes, had done a complete turnabout. "I no longer use a rod. Now I use ice cream pops." Instead of punishing for bad behavior, he rewarded for good. The other rebbes thought his approach too lenient. Even the principal shook his head. "Children need to be hit sometimes. That's never going to change."

Walking home from school, I thought about Berel Eisenman's words. Ice cream pops, there was an idea. I did not want to hit students. I wanted them to like me. I wanted to be a "good rebbe," and so, when I finished the two weeks with Srulik Schmeltzer's sixth-graders, I took on Reuven Mashinsky's seventh-graders, and had a new method.

"We'll do things differently here," I said before I opened the volume of Kiddushin on Mashinsky's desk. I told them I was splitting the class into two teams. I would pit half the class against the other and make them each accountable to their teammates. I would award points for good behavior and subtract points for bad. "The winning team," I said, "gets ice cream pops."

The boys regarded me warily, as if assessing whether this plan was for their benefit or mine. They were used to being scolded and slapped and thwacked, not awarded points.

For the next two weeks, I held not a rod or a wire but a little green-and-yellow notepad, in which I marked down which student earned points for his team or incurred a penalty. In class, during prayer time, for passing the exams, for showing up on time—everything mattered. Instead of scolding or thwacking, all I had to do was get my notepad out. When Chaim Greenfeld whispered something to Shea Goldstein during *mincha* prayers, I could see Shea's eyeballs bulging and his words hissing from between clenched teeth, "Shh, the rebbe is marking points!" Chaim Greenfeld quickly set his eyes back on his prayer book.

Mordche Goldhirsch was pleased. "I don't know what you're doing, but you clearly know how to hold a classroom," he said. He knew from looking through the small window in the classroom door that the boys were uncharacteristically well behaved for a substitute. And so he offered me a regular position, teaching Mishna to fifth-graders from four to five each afternoon.

This was unlike the Gemara, the elaboration on the Mishna, which could go on for pages about why a certain law was the way it was and how it was known. The Mishna was both easy and dull, a straightforward compendium of laws.

> *Two men clutch a cloak. Each one claims, "It is all mine." The cloak must be split.*

> *An egg that was laid on the holiday: the school of Shammai says, it may be eaten; the school of Hillel says, it must not be eaten.*

> *An ox gores a cow, and the cow is discovered with its fetus at its side; the ox's owner must pay for half the cow and a quarter of the fetus.*

That summer, we studied the laws of Yom Kippur as they were practiced in Jerusalem's ancient temple. The children learned that not only must the high priest have a deputy on call in case he becomes disqualified ("In case he's had an impure incident") but, according to Rabbi Judah, he was also given an extra wife, in case his wife died, and he needed a backup to fulfill the commandment: "He must atone for himself and his household."

I gave quizzes of multiple-choice answers, with the wrong ones playful and silly and obviously wrong, and the boys loved them. When they studied well, I took them on "hikes," strolls in the nearby woods until we came to a clearing, where we'd sit in a semicircle and I would hand out half-melted ice cream pops and tell them stories of rabbis who healed the sick, spoke with the dead, powwowed with angels, and battled demons, often all at once. On occasion, I'd split the class into teams for an impromptu "Mishna Bee," and toss candies for correct answers. Soon the children were paying attention. Sometimes too much attention.

> *Yom ha-kippurim ossur. On Yom Kippur, the following are forbidden:*
> *Be-achileh u-veshtiyeh. Eating and drinking.*
> *U-virchitzeh. Bathing.*
> *U-vesicheh. Applying ointments.*
> *U-vene'ilas ha-sandal. Wearing shoes.*
> *U-vetashmish ha-mitteh.*

I hadn't prepared for this last one. How was I to explain "service of the bed" to ten-year-olds?

I moved on to the next passage: *A king and a bride may wash their faces—*

"You skipped one!" Berri Neuberger cried.

"What?"

"You skipped one. You didn't explain *tashmish hamitah.*"

I pretended not to understand what he meant, but he persisted. "There are supposed to be five things. You explained only four."

"That last one isn't important," I said. "It won't be on the exam."

Berri narrowed his eyes, as if he were the teacher and I were the student, and he was calling me out for bad behavior.

Later, after the bell rang and the boys grabbed their bags and ran noisily to join the throngs of students crowding the corridor, I ran into Mordche Goldhirsch.

"Berri Neuberger wanted to know the meaning of *tashmish hamitah.*"

"*Nu?*"

"I was evasive. Told him it won't be on the exam."

Mordche thought for a moment. "Next time, just give him a really stern look, like this." He narrowed his eyes, exactly as Berri had done to me in class. "You give him the kind of look that says, 'Don't *ever* ask a question like that again.'"

I looked at Mordche skeptically, but he gave me a knowing look and nodded gravely.

"He'll know. He'll understand. You understand?"

Substituting and teaching Mishna in afternoons wasn't what I had in mind when I'd thought of teaching, but there seemed to be no opening for a full-time position. Every few weeks, I'd stop by Mordche's office to inquire.

"Which grade did you want to teach again?" he would ask, as if he hadn't asked the same just last week and I hadn't told him that any grade was fine. I had no preference. I wanted a steady position, a paycheck, even the despised vouchers. We were still behind on our rent, still getting termination notices from the gas company. Freidy was beginning to walk and needed shoes. Even the vouchers eventually found their uses, and now we owed hundreds more at the grocer's.

"Nothing yet," Mordche would shake his head, shuffling papers on his desk or fiddling with the photocopy machine. "I'll let you know if something changes."

Mordche met me in the hallway one day after my Mishna class. He wanted to know if I was interested in attending a meeting.

"A meeting about what?"

He seemed surprised by the question, as if meetings were to be attended for their own sake. He waved his hand dismissively. "Just a meeting. Gavriel Blum has some ideas."

The meeting was held on the first floor of the school, in a room that served as a conference room for village officials and, each Wednesday morning, as "village court," where a judge ruled on traffic violations—rolling through stop signs, or parking overnight on snow days, or driving down Washington Avenue at seventy-five miles per hour to get a last-minute mikveh dip before the siren announced the start of the Sabbath.

Now we sat seven men in the room, six Mishna teachers along with Gavriel Blum, the same one who'd had us fill out *rezemays* a few months earlier.

"The government," he said, "has a program for tutoring students." Title something or other. "They'll pay thirteen dollars an hour."

"Thirteen dollars an hour?" all except me asked in unison. The others seemed to think the amount was pitiful. I thought it sounded just fine. We were getting only nine for our Mishna classes.

"Thirteen dollars an hour is what the government pays. You can set your own rate and get the rest from the parents."

In the corner, a large American flag hung on a pole, incongruous behind this assemblage of black hats and long coats.

"Is this a scam?" I asked.

Gavriel gave me a wary glance. "Not at all," he said. "The rebbe doesn't allow any more scams."

There'd been problems in the past, with fraudulent use of government programs. Four men, including Gavriel himself, were given prison sentences, ranging from several months to six years. Three other men had fled the country to avoid prosecution. We'd learned our lessons.

Gavriel looked around to make sure we all understood.

"Because this is a government program, you'll have to fill out progress reports," he went on, looking around at our bemused faces. "For each student, you fill out a sheet describing how the student is doing. You'll need to be creative. Write how the student is doing in math, or in English, or social studies—"

"We're tutoring math and English and social studies?"

Gavriel looked at me as if I were a child. "Of course not," he said. "But the government doesn't pay for religious studies."

I looked at the other men sitting around the table, but none of them seemed concerned. I was terrified. In my mind, I could see it all unfold. A knock on the door at dawn. Handcuffs. An ill-fitting prison jumpsuit.

My options, however, were few, so I signed up for the program. Five boys each day, all between the ages of nine and thirteen. Laws of returning lost objects. Laws of oxen falling into pits in the roadway. Laws of the Sabbath. Laws of oxen goring cows. Laws of prayer. Laws of oxen goring cows fallen into pits during prayer.

And then I wrote the progress reports:

Mendy is improving his multiplication but still has trouble with division.
Chezky's spelling seems to have worsened.
Yanky's penmanship has vastly improved due to the practice worksheets.

There were no multiplication tables, no practice worksheets, and no improvement or deterioration in any of those subjects. I was handing in phony progress reports, with my signature, getting paid for something I wasn't doing.

"How can we be doing this and not be concerned?" I asked my friend Chaim Nuchem, who occupied the tutoring room next to mine with his own rotation of students. But Chaim Nuchem only shrugged.

"You think they'll come looking?" he asked.

I looked at him dumbfounded. Hadn't we learned? People were going to prison. Others were fleeing. Families had been destroyed. The community shamed in the papers. Clearly, someone came looking.

Chaim Nuchem laughed. "Those guys took millions. We're making thirteen dollars an hour. You think the government cares?"

Still, I hated it. I hated that we relied on the government for so much. I hated that we skirted, just barely, the edges of legality. That we made sure never to report earning one cent more than the official poverty level so that we could keep our food stamps and our Section 8 and our WIC checks. I hated that the economics of our village were such that all matters of finance were bound up in deception. "On the books or off the books?" was the big question for every new job.

And still, the money was never enough.

Chapter Nine

It was a balmy night in mid-autumn, the night of Shmini Atzeres, at the end of the Sukkos holiday. It was nearing midnight, and the streets were empty. I was on my way to the rebbe's Great Sukkah. The last tisch of the holiday was to begin in one hour and would go until morning. Gitty and I had finished our dinner early, and since there was time, I took a stroll down Washington Avenue. The words "Yeshiva Avir Yakov," in gold Hebrew letters across the front of the yeshiva building, glittered against the moonlight, and I thought I'd drop in at the sukkah behind the yeshiva, where students and guests would be having their dinner. I would find a friend for a chat until the tisch began.

I heard the rush of a car in the distance. I wondered who might be driving at this time, an act forbidden on the holiday. Perhaps it was one of the Hatzoloh volunteers, rushing to tend to a heart-attack victim, a child burned from a pot of spilled chicken soup, or perhaps a woman in premature labor. Or maybe it was one of the Haitian taxi drivers from Spring Valley, come to drop off a hospice employee. Or, there was always the chance it was a driver lost among the winding suburban roads. That's probably it, I thought. They'll figure it out soon enough, when they head down Washington Avenue and reach the cul-de-sac at the end. Maybe the driver would need directions, I thought, and slowed my pace to look back. The car was out of sight, but I could hear it coming toward the bend in the road, and I stood still to watch for it.

When it appeared, it came zooming past the bend, heading straight toward me. Speeding was dangerous in the village: the roads were filled with children, mothers with strollers, and the elderly—especially during holidays, when people would stroll freely in the middle of the roadway.

I jumped to the curb and held out my arm, waving it slowly up and down.

"Slow down!" I shouted. But the car didn't slow down; it only sped up, and in a flash, as it passed, I heard shouts and saw the angry, hostile faces, through the windows. Then I heard it: "FUCKING JEWS!"

Wild laughter. And then they shouted again, even louder this time, now from several yards down.

"FUCKING HASIDICS!"

I froze. I'd heard tales of this. From the very beginning, when the village was founded, there were those who sought trouble, and cries would ring through the village: "Shkutzim!" Vermin. Non-Jewish hoodlums. There would be violence, lessons taught, fists and blows and broken bones, the meek sensibilities of our ancestors making way for a people who no longer looked away in the face of aggression. I had just such an incident before me now, and I stood facing it alone.

"Shkutzim!"

I tried to raise my voice to yell, but my lungs betrayed me, as if insisting that they would not rise to the occasion. My heart pounding, I looked to the windows of the yeshiva, but they were dark, no sign of life at this late hour. From the homes across the street, I could hear fathers and sons singing, up-tempo melodies. *And thou shalt be joyful within thy festival.* Booming masculine voices mingling with young sopranos. Hands clapping vigorously, the sounds of cutlery banging against a table in rhythm.

I took a quick deep breath.

"SHKUTZIM!"

It came out louder this time but still felt ineffectual. I'd never before had to yell loud enough for my voice to reach inside people's homes, through closed windows and locked doors.

"SHKUTZIM!" This time, heads appeared in windows and doorways. Several people came running from the yeshiva's sukkah. The car was now almost at the end of Washington Avenue, its taillights still visible in the distance.

"SHKUTZIM!" I was no longer alone. My shouts were echoed by the dozen or so men who had gathered, and others were now running from each direction. Within moments, the call reverberated through the streets, and I no longer needed to shout. Other men now cried, angrily, hysterically, faces red and eyeballs bulging, as more and more men came running, some with their shtreimels and their *bekishes*, others in their shirtsleeves and yellowed *tallis katans*, miniature prayer shawls flapping vigorously in the night. Women and girls appeared in the windows and doorways all around. Here and there, an intrepid girl ventured to the edge of a lawn.

The car turned from Washington Avenue onto Wilson, out of sight. But Wilson Avenue was a dead end. This car had no escape. A sizable crowd had formed by now, and people pointed excitedly down Washington Avenue.

"Shkutzim! Shkutzim!" The chorus of shouts now came from all directions, in a deafening clamor.

"There they are!" someone shouted, and the crowd tensed up as we watched the headlights appear. The car turned, coming full speed, back onto Washington Avenue. As we bent to grab large rocks and other items to throw, the car, still several hundred yards away, rolled to a stop, like an animal cornered. Those within had seen the mob and were weighing their options.

For a moment, we all stood frozen. Then, like a charging bull, the car accelerated with a roar. The mob of men scattered to the sides of the road, and in a flash the car was between us. A deafening shout went up and a barrage of rocks pounded the car. We heard the shattering of glass, and as the car sped away, we saw it covered with pockmarks, both taillights smashed. As it sped past the yeshiva building, a wrought-iron bench, well worn from years of use in the study hall, came hurtling off the roof and landed right on top of the car, leaving a deep dent on impact, then falling behind and landing with a thud on the cracked asphalt.

The crowd charged. A cluster of men stood at the intersection of Jefferson Avenue, and as we ran, yelling obscenities, we watched a lone figure sprint toward the car. It was my friend Mechy Rosen, and in his hand, high above his shoulder, was a long steel pole. With perfect timing, Mechy smashed the pole through the front passenger window, like a savage aiming a spear at a wild animal. The sound of shattering glass mixed with the high-pitched wailing of a woman inside the car.

The car skidded around a bend in the road. The crowd pursued from behind, the clamor reaching a battle-cry pitch. We could not keep up with the car, but still we ran in pursuit. From all directions, more men came running from their homes and joined the growing stampede of black and white.

The crowd kept pursuing the car, even as its taillights dimmed, even when we could no longer see it past the final bend of Washington Avenue. We ran and ran, even as we knew we would never catch up.

As we turned that final curve—with the main road, Route 45, in view—we saw the car at the end, standing still. Then we heard shouts and screams. As we neared, we saw that the car had failed to make the turn onto Route 45 and had crashed at high speed into an enormous oak tree that stood facing the village entrance.

Traffic on Route 45 was beginning to back up, and drivers were emerging from their cars to inspect the wreckage, just as our mob, now several hundred men, came rushing toward the intersection. The first thing I heard was a man shouting obscenities, and then I got a good look at the car, smashed up against the tree. A teenage girl, one side of her face smeared with blood, sat on the ground, wailing near the open driver-side door. A teenage boy stumbled out of the back, then limped around to the other side of the car, in a daze. The shouting came from another man, who stood near the passenger side of the car, making wild gestures, pointing at us, the mob, now lined up on the other side of the road. He didn't look injured, only angry. And all I could think was: *He* is mad at *us?* Our furies had dissipated in the face of this just punishment, and I stood struck by the man's rage. Soon came the flashing lights of police cars and ambulance sirens, with traffic on the road backed up as far as we could see. The teenagers were taken away in ambulances, and our attitudes were gleeful. We'd taught them not to mess with us.

"The rebbe will be in to the tisch in five minutes!" someone called, and the crowd headed back down Washington Avenue. A short while later, we stood, a thousand men or more, on rows and rows of bleachers, the shtreimels of the uppermost row of men brushing against the rafters of the rebbe's Great Sukkah. As the rebbe recited the kiddush, my mind raced. *He who has chosen us from among all people, and exalted us from every tongue, and has sanctified us with His commandments.* Chosen. Exalted. Sanctified. What did it mean?

I thought of the difference between us and those who despised us. Those teenagers in the car, I had taken for granted, were common anti-Semites, Hitler's spiritual progeny. They would've caused us bodily harm if they'd been able to, I was certain of it. And yet, what *really* differentiated us? What made us so quick to rally a mob and pursue a group of young people for what really were, in this incident, no more than harmless insults?

And if we had caught up with the car, what would we have done to them?

Several months later, I visited a body shop in Monsey, where a young mechanic named Matt worked on my car. As I stood near him, we found ourselves chatting.

"You from New Square?" Matt asked, reading the address on the work order form.

I nodded.

"I was there last night," he said. He was a volunteer firefighter, and there'd been a fire emergency that night. "Real interesting place."

"How so?"

He looked up from fiddling with something under the hood. "Well. You know. I wouldn't be allowed in New Square otherwise, so it was just interesting."

"What do you mean?" There were always people in New Square who didn't live there: construction workers, janitors, taxi drivers, supermarket employees. I'd never heard of anyone being denied entry. By communal ordinance, it was forbidden to sell property to anyone outside the community, but New Square was a public village, a legal municipality. Anyone could enter its streets.

Matt turned to look at me again, as if he were teaching me something elementary about the world. "You can't go into New Square if you don't live there. You'll get beat up."

"That's not true," I said, a touch defensively.

Matt straightened up and leaned a hand on the hood's latch. In the other hand, he held a rag, black with grease, which he held out as he pointed to my chest. "You," he said, waving the greasy rag up and down to indicate my Hasidic garb, "can go in there. But if I go in there without having any business there, I'll get beat up."

I must've laughed, because I remember Matt saying, "You think it's funny? They've got their own laws, their own rules. You go into New Square and you don't belong there, you're in trouble."

He turned back to his work, then looked up at me again. "Don't get me wrong. I respect all people." He took his rag and wiped something under the hood of the car. "But if you don't belong in New Square, you just stay out. That's just how it is."

PART II

Chapter Ten

Kol bo'eho lo yeshuvun.
All who go to her do not return.

So says the Bible regarding a woman of loose morals. So said the rabbis of the Talmud regarding heresy.

Heretics, the rabbis said, can never repent. "We do not accept their return, ever," wrote Maimonides, the twelfth-century sage known for his rationalist approach to faith. "We do not accept the repentance of heretics because we do not believe them. If they appear to have repented, we maintain they have done so fraudulently."

Others say that heretics cannot repent because heresy is a force so potent that an individual is powerless to combat it, an insidious trap from which there is no escape. One never knows where heresy lurks. It can lie in the seemingly innocent words of a stranger, in knowledge outside the Torah, or in the writings of anyone who has not been vetted by the sages of his generation. It can lie in a seemingly innocent tale, when told in the wrong language, by the wrong person, or through the wrong medium, its nefarious intent so subtle as to pass almost unnoticed.

I was thirteen, during my year at the Dzibeau yeshiva in Montreal, when I learned a lesson about this danger. It was evening, after a full day of study, nearing bedtime. Yeedel Israel stood at one end of our dorm room polishing his shoes, and Sender Davidovitch sat on his bed clipping his toenails. Moshe Friedman, who occupied the bunk beneath mine, stepped out to the bathroom to brush his teeth. I, too, should've been preparing for bed; instead, I lay on my top bunk reading an English-language book, *Akiba*, a fictional reimagining of the life of the second-century sage Rabbi Akiva, by the German Jewish author Marcus Lehmann.

The Talmud tells the story of Rabbi Akiva in brief. Until the age of forty, Akiva was unlearned, a poor and ignorant shepherd, who tended the flock of the Jerusalem aristocrat Kalba Savua. When Akiva fell in love with Rachel, Kalba Savua's daughter, she insisted that she would not marry him unless he promised to devote his life to Torah study. Akiva promised, and the couple was married. Soon after, Akiva left home to study Torah with the sages Nachum Ish Gamzu, Eliezer ben Hyrcanus, and Joshua ben Hanania, the great masters at the academies of Lod and Yabneh.

For twenty-four years, Akiva remained in the house of study while his wife was home alone. After twenty-four years, Akiva returned to his wife, accompanied now by twenty-four thousand students. Now he was *Rabbi* Akiva, the greatest rabbi in all of Israel, in all of Jewish history, perhaps. Rachel, living in poverty and solitude all these years, received word of her husband's return, and set out to greet him. Upon seeing him, she fell to her knees and bent to kiss the hem of his cloak.

"Get away!" Rabbi Akiva's students shouted to the woman kneeling before the great master. But Rabbi Akiva recognized her. "Let her be," he said to his students. "For all that is yours, and all that is mine, belongs to her."

"Why aren't you undressed yet?" an angry voice bellowed.

In the doorway stood Reb Hillel, his unkempt jet-black mustache growing over his lips into his sprawling black beard, ferocious-looking despite his slight frame. Reb Hillel was one of the most feared rabbis at the yeshivas. His slaps were legend—they always came twice in succession in one fluid motion, palm striking left cheek, then returning sharply for a backhanded strike to the right. Until that night, I had studiously avoided him.

"And *what* do we have *here?*" Reb Hillel asked, pointing his beard at my book.

Outside I could hear students rushing about, the bathroom door in the hallway being opened and banged shut as my dorm mates prepared for bed.

"It's—a *biechel*," I said. A book. A *little* book. Not a book of Torah or its commentaries but of general knowledge. A storybook.

"A *BIECHEL!*" Reb Hillel cried. "Don't you know what the Chasam Sofer said about a *biechel?*"

I didn't know what the Chasam Sofer had said about a *biechel*, although I knew other things the Chasam Sofer had said, chiefly this: "All that is new is forbidden by the Torah." *All that is new* covered many things, including modern dress, modern speech, modern names, modern ideas.

"*Biechel*, the holy Chasam Sofer says, stands for '*Kol bo'eha lo yeshuvun.*'"

Biechel. Beis, yud, kof, lamed. B-Y-K-L. *Kol B'o'eho Lo Yeshuvun.*

All who go to her do not return.

So said the Bible regarding a woman of loose morals. So said the rabbis of the Talmud regarding heretical ideas. So said the Chasam Sofer regarding *little books*—which I imagined meant *little books of a certain kind*, books of unknown provenance, written in strange languages by strange people. The book I now held, because it was in English, not Yiddish or Hebrew, looked suspicious to Reb Hillel.

But the book I was reading was kosher.

"It's a *ma'aseh biechel*," I said. "It's about Rabbi Akiva." The tale of a sage. Not Torah, but close enough.

Reb Hillel stood very near my bed, his flared nostrils right up against my face as I lay with my head glued to my pillow. Reb Hillel raised his hand and I flinched, but he only reached to take the book. I watched as he studied the front cover, then the back, then flipped through the pages. I realized then that he could not read it.

After a few moments, he tossed the book back onto my bed. He turned briefly to stare at Sender and Yeedel, who sat frozen on their beds, and turned back to me: "You couldn't find a book about Rabbi Akiva in Yiddish?"

If my little book contained no heresy, Reb Hillel's point was well taken. Foreign reading brought foreign ideas and foreign influences, and before you knew it, you were speaking ill of God and His anointed one.

All that is new is forbidden by the Torah, said the Chasam Sofer, an Austrian rabbi far from Hasidism's Polish and Ukrainian origins. His principles had no connection to Hasidic teachings and, in a sense, ran counter to them. Hasidism, when first formed in the mid-eighteenth century, had come to liberate the Jewish people from a worldview ossified under centuries of legalistic arcana. Hasidism came to eschew the artificial and the pretentious and the formulaic. To raise the spirit of the law over the letter of it and to find infinite layers of that spirit. To celebrate the mystical experience over scholarly wrangling. It declared matters of the heart and mind superior to pietistic excess.

Yet the principles of the Chasam Sofer rather than the Baal Shem Tov came to characterize the modern Hasidic worldview. With the spread of the Haskalah, the Jewish Enlightenment movement in the eighteenth and nineteenth centuries, new challenges created new priorities for observant Jews. The teachings of Hasidism, many realized, were quickly becoming irrelevant in the face of the devastation wrought by the Enlightenment movement, and so Hasidim rallied around the Chasam Sofer's battle cry and rushed to carry his standard.

All that is new is forbidden by the Torah.

Years later, I would read the works of Martin Buber and Abraham Joshua Heschel and Elie Wiesel and wince at their romanticized portraits not only of Hasidism, the teachings, but also of Hasidim, the people, as if all those who bore the name surely lived by its principles. In fact, other than a small cadre of mystics and the remnants of early Hasidic practices—dedication to the rebbe and communal events with song and dance—Hasidim in the twentieth century seemed to know little of the mysticism, the ecstasy, the melancholy and the joy of the Baal Shem Tov and his disciples. Instead, it regressed to the heavy-handedness and the rigidity that Hasidism had come to eradicate.

Because of the merit of three things, Israel was delivered from Egypt: they did not alter their names, their language, or their dress. This is the midrashic dictum that encapsulates the ethos of the modern Hasidic world, a world characterized by the simple values of cultural fidelity. The objective is self-imposed ghettoization. Distinct language and dress keep interactions with outsiders to a minimum and help maintain separation from the wider world. Restrictions on secular education and outside knowledge keep foreign ideas at bay. Bans on media and popular entertainment keep away temptation. And so the Hasidim are spared the calamities of modernity.

"My father used to listen to the radio," my friend Motty confided in me one day.

Motty, a former classmate with whom I now had an evening study session, had recently bought a car, a used brown Dodge minivan. In his car, away from the meddling of his wife, he had begun to listen to the radio. He had been raised among Skverer Hasidim in Montreal, and had moved to New Square only for yeshiva studies and marriage, and now he was trying to explain to me that listening to the radio was not all that bad.

"Was my father not pious enough?" Motty flashed me a look, as if to say, how preposterous. His father, who woke each day at dawn to study Talmud for several hours before going off to his office, had been a close confidant of the old rebbe. He gave generously to charity and raised a dozen offspring, the majority of them scholars or married to them. "It's not the worst sin in the world," Motty said.

It was true. The prohibition against radio listening was not one of the 365 biblical prohibitions, for which the theoretical punishment ranged from lashes to the death penalty to extirpation. It was not even a truly rabbinic one, as it was not mentioned in the Talmud.

Motty gave me a sidelong glance. "I think you'd enjoy it too, by the way." He brought all five fingers together in front of his face, then sprang them apart theatrically. "Opens your mind." He described how captivating it all was, news reports flowing into traffic reports, flowing into commercial breaks and then weather and sports, every moment of airtime perfectly calibrated. "Modern technology. I'm telling you, you'd be amazed."

In truth, we already had some of that modern technology in our home. In our kitchen, right above the refrigerator, sat a sleek, silver double-deck Panasonic stereo cassette player.

When I had first brought it home, several weeks after our marriage, in the summer of 1993, Gitty had frowned.

"It has a radio," she said with an accusing glare.

The device, fresh out of the box, lay on the chintzy oilcloth on our kitchen table, and Gitty stuck her index finger at a spot on top, near the volume control. *Tape, AM, FM* were printed in tiny white letters along the ridge of the circular switch. There was no denying it.

"We'll do what everyone does," I had said then, annoyed at the suggestion of impiety. Many of my friends had cassette players, and when the device came with a built-in radio tuner, there was a standard procedure for it: Krazy Glue the switch into the tape-playing position, paste a strip of masking tape over the station indicators, and put the antenna out with the next day's trash. As Talmud students, we were nothing if not resourceful; loopholes and workarounds were our forte.

I assured Gitty that I would disable the radio, but she only shook her head and went back to her housework. The cassette player soon went on top of our refrigerator, where it would remain, through four different apartments and across the births of our five children, for the next decade or so.

But I never disabled the radio. I either procrastinated or I forgot or perhaps I thought it useful to have in case of emergency. Still, we never switched it on, allowing it to serve only as a phantom decadent presence in our otherwise pure and pious home. The tape player would serve mostly to entertain our children, who would haul their Legos, Tonka trucks, and American Girl dolls out onto the kitchen floor, and the cassette decks would spin an endless spool of musical tales featuring Yanky, Chaneleh, and Rivky, good Jewish children who spoke no lies, loved the Sabbath, and always, without fail, honored their parents.

Few radios were to be found when I was growing up, but I remember one incident when I was around ten. It was late on a Saturday night, and my father was being interviewed by a Jewish radio station about his work, teaching secular and unaffiliated Jews about our brand of Orthodoxy. My mother borrowed a radio from one of our non-Hasidic neighbors for the evening, and our family gathered around the table in our small kitchen while my father, in his study down the hall, gave his interview over the phone. I remember little of the interview itself, as I spent most of the thirty-minute segment marveling at the mystery of my father's voice being transported from the other end of our apartment to a studio in some unknown place and back to us in the kitchen. I remember also that it felt oddly aberrant. Secular influences were such anathema to our lives that the presence of the radio on the kitchen table, right next to the silver Sabbath candlesticks my mother had just cleared off the dining-room table, was jarring.

During my teenage years and the first few years after our marriage, there were no accessible radios nearby. Current events were learned about in old-fashioned ways. In the yeshiva dining room, news of the failed coup against Boris Yeltsin in Moscow and Saddam Hussein's invasion of Kuwait were passed along with plates of farfel and slippery noodle kugel. When Israeli prime minister Yitzhak Rabin shook the hand of Yasser Arafat on Bill Clinton's White House lawn, we looked up briefly from our Talmuds to listen to the student who claimed he had the news on good authority—probably from the school's non-Jewish janitor—and we promptly returned to our studies. Later we repeated the news at home to our wives, who carried it farther to their mothers, sisters, and neighbors.

Over time, however, I came to look up to the radio on the refrigerator with longing. By then, I had already learned two rules of radio. The FM dial, I knew, carried music—secular, vulgar, abhorrent, especially female voices. The sin was so great that I couldn't even be tempted. It was the AM dial that intrigued me. I learned from Motty that it carried news and opinions and all kinds of fascinating bits of information about the world. My curiosity grew nearly unbearable as I wondered about all that was available to me with only the flick of a switch.

The more I thought about it, the more the temptation grew. Motty was right, I thought. It wouldn't violate Jewish law but only the restrictions of our community. I would sit at our kitchen table eating the dinner that Gitty had prepared, and my eyes would wander to the red band on the station indicators on the device above the fridge. The dial seemed to hiss and beckon in a seductive whisper: *I've got news for you.* But I worried about Gitty. If she caught me, she would scold and sulk at the impurities I was allowing into my heart and, by extension, into hers and those of our children.

Finally, I could no longer resist. Late one night, Gitty and the children asleep in the bedrooms at the end of the hallway, my eyes wandered up to the stereo system. At first, I shoved the temptation aside, as I had done so many times before, but the more I tried to suppress it, the greater the urge became.

In one of our kitchen drawers, alongside utility bills and an assortment of multicolored rubber bands, I found an old pair of earphones. Careful not to make a sound, I moved one of the chairs near the refrigerator, stepped up onto it, and plugged the earphones into the tiny jack. I leaned my elbows on the dust-covered surface above the fridge and began twisting the dial slowly, listening with one ear to the cackle of static as the white indicator floated across the red band, while keeping my other ear tuned for noises from the bedrooms down the hallway.

I switched the dial from one station to another, commercials for medical malpractice attorneys, car dealerships, and department-store blowout sales filling me with forbidden pleasure. The strange jingles, the smooth transitions from traffic to news to commercials, captivated me; the fact that the sale was for *one week only*, or that I was not currently on the Brooklyn-Queens Expressway, which, I now heard, was backed up to the Brooklyn Bridge because of an accident in the right lane, mattered little. I was like a visitor from a different era encountering our modern one, captivated by its very mundaneness.

Eventually, I came upon a talk show. The host was angry, particularly miffed about the antics of someone he called "Alan Dirty-Shirts." After several minutes, I gathered that "Alan Dirty-Shirts" was a liberal, and liberals were bad. They were in favor of sinful things, such as abortions, and wacky ones, such as homosexuals getting married. I listened as caller after caller berated "Alan Dirty-Shirts" for intending to uproot conservative values from the American heartland. The *American heartland*, whatever and wherever that was, had my sympathy. "Alan Dirty-Shirts" was against people of faith, who, I was happy to learn, existed even outside my own Hasidic world.

"Were you listening to the radio last night?" Gitty asked the next morning, while flipping a slice of French toast in the pan. I stood dumbfounded by her mysterious intuition. I tried to deny it, but she wasn't fooled.

"You promised you'd disable it," she said. "It starts with radio, and the next thing you know, you're eating *trayf* and driving on Shabbos."

I gave my halfhearted assurance that I would now disable it. Days passed, however, and I knew that I would not do so. I wanted to listen again to that talk-show host. I wanted to hear more news, more traffic reports about cars stalled in the left lane of the BQE, and how we were doing on the Hudson River crossings. More commercials for car dealerships in Lodi or mattress stores in Paramus.

Several nights later, the volume near mute, I spent another hour on the chair near the fridge, earphones pressed tightly against my ears. Once again, Gitty confronted me the next morning. She wouldn't tell me how she knew. In fact, she wouldn't say much at all, but the fury in her expression suggested that she was just about ready to toss the device off our second-floor balcony.

But I would not cave. I would be a dutiful Hasid in all respects except this one. Gitty would have to accept me the way I was.

Gitty was right, though. The radio was just the beginning.

One day, I noticed an ad in the local community bulletin: *Used car. Excellent condition. $1,500.*

Owning a car was unbecoming for a young Skverer Hasid, especially one with pietistic aspirations. The old rebbe had warned that cars led to bad things. "One press with your foot, and you can be anywhere," he had said. But I was now out of the study hall, concerned less with being a good and pious Hasid and curious to explore what the world had to offer. If I had a car, I could run errands for Gitty, or take her shopping on occasion. I could get a job outside the village. I could be going places.

It was a gray 1985 Oldsmobile sedan, with unfashionably sharp edges, boxy and long. The air conditioning didn't work, and the turn signals didn't light up on the dashboard, but it was otherwise in good working order. After haggling with the owner, a Yemenite Israeli car mechanic, I got the price down to $750 and drove the car home.

The next afternoon, I took the car out again. I had a destination in mind but knew that I should resist the temptation. I thought about the old rebbe's words. *One press with your foot, and you can be anywhere.* But I could not resist. Still wrestling with the idea, I drove the three miles to the Finkelstein Memorial Library, in nearby Spring Valley, and turned into the underground parking garage, out of sight of Hasidim passing on the busy roadway nearby.

The library was housed in a red-and-white building on a hilltop along Route 59, the county's main road, halfway between New Square and Monsey. I had passed the building many times before and, through the tall windows across the library's two-story facade, had seen the many rows of bookshelves within. Stepping inside now, I felt overwhelmed. What did one read first?

"You can borrow up to five books from each section," one of the librarians told me.

The librarian showed me the list of sections—history, science, philosophy, politics—and with some quick math, I realized I could borrow several dozen books at once. This was like being told you could have all the doughnuts in the doughnut shop, and suddenly you don't know what to do with so many doughnuts, or if you did, you had no way to carry them home, or a cupboard large enough to store them. The prospect of having so many books was strangely paralyzing.

I lingered for a few minutes around the new releases, and then wandered into the children's section, near the library entrance. In front of me sat a group of tots reading *Curious George* and *Amelia Bedelia*. *Nothing to see here*, I thought, ready to move on, and then I noticed, behind the children, along a low shelf, a twenty-volume set of *World Book* encyclopedias.

For the next three hours, I sat on a tiny orange chair at a low green-and-yellow table as the pile of volumes grew beside me. Alongside a little boy paging furiously through *The Berenstain Bears*, I read about Archimedes and Einstein, about Elvis Presley and Egyptian hieroglyphics, about electromagnetism and the history of the printing press and the production of avocados in central Mexico.

In later years, I would think back to the heady delight of those first days at the library. In a world of Google and Wikipedia, the simple pleasures of a basic encyclopedia can be hard to fathom, but the experience at the time was intoxicating. Suddenly, it seemed as if all my curiosity about the world could be satisfied in that little children's section of the library.

It had been years since I had read a book of secular knowledge. I had always been a reader, but most of my childhood reading was about tales of ancient sages, the tannaim and the amoraim, the Baal Shem Tov and the Gaon of Vilna, scholars and saints who battled the forces of evil, physical and spiritual, and helped their brethren with their wisdom and scholarship and the occasional wondrous miracle.

Occasionally, secular books were to be found by accident. When I was eleven, I discovered an abandoned pile of Hardy Boys mysteries in the back of a dusty and cluttered variety shop two blocks from my school. The books had been tossed into a large black trash bag that lay behind a stack of boxes of other useless merchandise. This was Borough Park, and the owner must've realized that those books weren't going to be sold anytime soon. For several weeks, I returned to the store each day after school and stood in the back, in a hollow space in the corner between the shelves lining the two adjoining walls, and went through the entire pile until there was nothing left to read.

We also had a small number of secular books in our home, most of them belonging to my sister Chani. Girls did not have the obligation of dawn-to-dusk Torah study, and so she was allowed a limited amount of secular reading material, mostly books considered to be from a more wholesome era. Often, I would sneak into her room and take books from the small white-and-pink bookcase near her door—*Pippi Longstocking, The Little Princess, Little House on the Prairie*—and hide them between my bed and the pine wainscoting of my bedroom wall, and then read them until late at night with a small flashlight.

I'd also stumbled upon books at the homes of more worldly neighbors, families who lived with fewer restrictions, whose children played sports and watched an occasional Disney movie. Often, after an afternoon visit, when a neighbor family would be eating dinner, I would be hiding in one of their bedrooms, deeply engrossed in *The Wind in the Willows* or *My Side of the Mountain*.

Soon, however, I would turn thirteen, and all of that would end. For a boy past thirteen, anything other than our holy texts was frivolous, at best.

I returned several times to that set of encyclopedias, and the children's librarian, a pleasant middle-aged woman, began to notice me and smile when I entered. Suddenly, I felt self-conscious: a grown Hasidic man sitting each day on the tiny orange chair at the green-and-yellow tables. So I moved on, hesitantly, to the adult sections upstairs, where the encyclopedias were heavier and denser, with fewer illustrations, the different sections like a maze in which the purpose was not to find the way out but to linger and stroll into each dead end and to gather as many treasures as possible along the way.

I do not remember the first books I brought home from the library, but I remember the disquieting silence from Gitty whenever I brought something home, the countless times she would finally, after holding it in for hours or days, burst out: "I don't want these trayf, goyish books in my home!"

Sometimes she'd say it angrily, and sometimes with sadness; sometimes she'd be nearly convulsing with fury, and sometimes with deep but gentle anguish. The words, though, were always the same: "I don't want these trayf, goyish books in my home!"

There was nothing particularly dangerous about what I was reading. They were mostly books about politics or history or science or of the various religions and cultures of the world. I would plead with Gitty to understand that I was doing nothing truly wrong, and if I was, my religious failings were on my own account, not hers. But Gitty would not be appeased.

"If you don't approve of it, don't read it," I would tell her, and she'd grow angrier and angrier, more entrenched in her belief that I was corrupting not only myself but the purity of our home.

Books would soon be the least of it. Newspapers and magazines followed shortly after. To Gitty, they were an even greater offense. When we'd first married, it was I who had declared the evils of newspapers. I had refused to read even the *Monsey Advocate*, which came free in the mail, half English and half Yiddish, published by Hasidim in Monsey. "If it's written on 'newspaper sheets,' it's bad news," the old rebbe had said. Even *Der Yid* and *Di Tzeitung*, Yiddish weeklies published by the Satmar Hasidim in Brooklyn, were not sold in New Square.

Now, with my battered gray Oldsmobile, I'd drive each Thursday night to a nearby gas station for a copy of the *Jerusalem Post* and the *Jewish Daily Forward* and an occasional *New York Times*. In the begin-

ALL WHO GO DO NOT RETURN : 127

ning, I would read them in my car, sitting for hours in the parking lot outside the Refuah Health Center near the entrance to the village. After a while, I decided that it was unfair for me to be banished from my own home. At first, I would hide the newspapers in a bag in one of my bedroom drawers, and read them only in the bathroom or behind the closed door of our dining room. It wasn't long before Gitty discovered them, and as she did, I grew bolder and began to read them openly. We fought constantly over the books and the newspapers and the radio. When I accidentally left a newspaper on the kitchen table, Gitty would reach for it with her fingertips, disgust all over her face, and toss it into the trash.

The radio and books and newspapers were just the beginning. At the home of a friend who owned a computer, I found myself browsing through a computer mail-order catalog, and discovered a sudden urge to buy a computer myself. I was still working with students at the time, and thought that I could use it to create educational worksheets, using word processing and desktop publishing software.

Several weeks later, I placed the order, and the computer arrived several days later in a great big box. Gitty and the girls stood in the doorway of the dining room as I set it all up on a small desk in the corner.

In the package of bundled software was a 3.5-inch floppy disk with a label: *America Online. 30-Day Free Trial.*

"What's that?" Gitty asked.

I was as clueless as she was, but the instructions said to connect a cord to the phone line and install the software. Curious, I did as instructed, and the four of us listened to the wheezy, whiny tones of the dial-up modem.

"Welcome!" a female voice announced.

"You've got mail!" said a male voice.

Colorful icons and graphics appeared on the screen, a dizzying array of links, each of which opened up a whole new world: News. Shopping. Chat rooms. It was all so bright and inviting, I could only marvel at the world that opened up before me.

"Look at this!" I called to Gitty a few days later. "I'm having a conversation!"

Gitty came and glanced at the screen.

"Watch," I said. "I type something, then this guy types something, then I type something, and so on. And it shows up instantly!" I couldn't contain my excitement, but Gitty looked confused.

"So . . . it's like a phone, except you type instead of speak?" she asked.

Like a phone? For a second, I wondered: Was that all it was? But of course it wasn't.

"This is a stranger! A random person!"

"Why would you want to speak to a random person?"

There was no way that Gitty would understand. She did not share my curiosity, did not care to learn about the world the way I did. All of a sudden, I was connected to millions with whom I could interact, and soon I discovered a world of people entirely different from anyone I knew. I encountered Jews who ate pork and drove on the Sabbath, Christians who did not appear to be anti-Semitic, Muslims who weren't terrorists.

One conversation stood out for me. A Jewish man living somewhere in the Midwest, whom I encountered in AOL's "Jewish Community" chat room, shared with me his passion for Jewish learning. He told me of his regular study sessions in Talmud and Maimonides with his local Conservative rabbi.

He was not Orthodox. He kept the Sabbath sometimes, he said, when he was able, although to him, keeping the Sabbath meant not so much living by the rules but something about "reflection" and "refraining from creative activity." Sometimes the man kept kosher but often did not. His comments were infuriating to me.

"You're not making any sense!" I typed furiously. If the rules were not fixed, then what determined our obligations? "Do you just pick and choose the things you like? That's not Judaism."

"Perhaps not to you," he said. "But there are other ways to look at it."

I could not understand it. Here was a man who shattered the narrative I had been given. I knew that non-Orthodox Jews existed, but I had assumed that they were unlearned, and so they didn't know any better. If only they studied the Talmud and Maimonides and all the other works of the great Torah sages, they would see that there was only one way to live a Jewish life. Here, however, was a man who studied it all; yet his practice was so different.

"How can you study the Talmud and not keep Shabbos?" I asked him. "How can you eat trayf if you know it's forbidden?"

The man was patient. "There is more than one way to live a Jewish life. I do not think of the Torah as the literal word of God but only as a man-made document of divine inspiration."

Maybe Gitty was right, I thought. Speaking to people outside our world made me think too much, and, as we all knew, too much thinking led to problems.

Yet I could not resist. Every night, for hours, I would log on to America Online and strike up conversations with people from outside our world, always wanting to prove to them that their way of life was wrong, but also madly curious about their views and the worlds that they lived in.

When I first purchased the computer, in the spring of 1996, it was a piece of office equipment, considered no more a threat to anyone's faith than a water cooler with a stack of pointy paper cups. Certainly no worse than a photocopier or a fax machine. As the years passed, however, word got around. DVD drives would soon come standard. That and a Netflix subscription were all a Hasid would need to access a world of popular culture that had once been entirely out of reach. With the Internet, a Hasid could go even further—not only observe and consume but also interact.

This was no longer a piece of office equipment. It was a mind corrupter, fast catching up with the reigning champion for the "Vessel of Profanity" title—the television set.

Gitty, as was to be expected, was growing displeased about the Internet in our home.

"The rabbis have banned it," she took to reminding me.

It was true. The rabbis had banned it just that month, after they'd banned it the previous month and the month before that. Banned and banned and banned, and still, it was said, Internet usage among us was only increasing, as if with each new ban posted on the synagogue door, scores of Hasidim rushed to the nearest computer store to see what the fuss was about.

Gitty agreed with the rabbis, even as she herself was not immune to the Internet's allure. While I was away during the day, she would log on to AOL, search for shopping coupons, for discounts on shoes, diapers. One day, she mentioned something she'd read in a chat room.

"In a *chat room? You?*" I could not have been more surprised.

"I only pop in to see what people are saying," she said, defensively, as if the fact that she did not herself interact with anyone mitigated the sin.

Yet she found much to disparage. When, in 1997, we learned about Princess Diana's death, I showed Gitty the reports on the Internet. Neither of us had heard of Diana before, but as we looked at the images that would become so ubiquitous over the next week or so, Gitty sputtered with indignation.

"What a disgusting person!"

All she saw were naked arms and bare shoulders and a bold, shameless clavicle.

"It's all *shmutz*. The entire Internet—filth, filth, and more filth."

"Why do you use it, then?"

"Only because you do. If you stop, I will."

But neither of us stopped, and soon we had corresponding screen names, area codes tacked on as surnames: Shulem914 and Gitty914. One day, she told me of a man who chatted her up via AOL's Instant Message, a man I had encountered before in the "Jewish Community" chat room. He claimed to be a Hasid from Brooklyn. "Are you Shulem914's wife?" he asked when he saw her screen name. When she said that she was, he referenced the few facts he knew about me, and drew her into conversation.

Later that evening, she told me about the encounter. "He ended the conversation with 'Kiss,'" she said, and pursed her lips to stifle a giggle.

I laughed. "Clearly, you liked that."

She turned a deep shade of crimson. "*That's* why the Internet is so bad!"

"Why must you do these things?" Gitty asked one Friday night, when we sat alone talking after our Shabbos dinner. The children were asleep. The candles flickered at the end of the table, almost burned down, flames dancing over wide pools of molten wax in our tall silver candlesticks. Behind them stood the computer cabinet, its doors now closed and the computer hidden, locked so that a child would not accidentally pull the door open and spoil the Shabbos atmosphere.

I didn't know why I did these things. I didn't know why I could not resist listening to the radio or reading newspapers or visiting the library or interacting with strangers on the Internet.

"What would happen if you stopped?"

Gitty was a practical person with practical questions. Couldn't I make a list of pros and cons, and see, as she did, that I would lose nothing?

"Maybe you need to study more," Gitty said.

My interest in religious texts was waning, and I grew lax with my evening study sessions with Motty. At first, I'd begun showing up ten minutes late, then twenty. Some days, I wouldn't make it at all. Soon Motty, too, would show up late or not at all.

Still, every so often, Motty and I would recommit, tell each other we had to take our studies more seriously. I would make a renewed effort to attend prayer services more diligently, instead of rushing through them like a chore. And as I'd sway over my Talmud, or during prayers, or on the bleachers during the rebbe's tischen, I would think about the fact that I was allowing new ideas into my head.

Biechel. Kol bo'eho lo yeshuvun. All who go to her do not return.

I would remember the words of Reb Hillel, and wonder if indeed something was changing, and I would realize that Gitty was right. Something was being lost, an innocence slipping away while I stood and watched, one moment reaching out to hold on to it and the next moment letting go, only to reach out again for a final futile grasp.

Chapter Eleven

It was a week before Passover when I noticed Chezky Blum in an alcove in the shul, surrounded by floor-to-ceiling bookcases. He stood facing a wall, his open prayer book resting on the ledge of a shelf. It was nearly midnight, and the last prayer group was now ending, the mourners' kaddish recited by a lone figure at the far end of the sanctuary, the sibilant sounds half-echoing softly in the cavernous, near-empty hall: . . . yiss-*borach, ve*-yish-*tabach, ve*-yiss-*po'er, v*-yiss-*romem, ve*-yiss-*naseh,* praised, glorified, and exalted be the name of *kudsha brich hu.*

Chezky swayed gently, his string-thin gartel around his waist, repeatedly bowing and rising, faintly tipping his heels each time he straightened up. Bow, rise, bop, bow, rise, bop. Behind him were two large double doors leading to the foyer, where I was headed. As I passed him, Chezky turned slightly and our eyes met. His eyebrows rose faintly in greeting, not a full nod but a subtle acknowledgment, the easy glance between acquaintances during unexpected encounters.

Something made me stop, and for years I would think back to that moment. I did not know him well, and could've simply moved on, with no undue violation of courtesy. Instead, I offered him a handshake.

"*Shulem aleichem,*" I said. "Haven't seen you in a while."

He closed his prayer book and brushed it against his lips. "Just got back from Israel. I'm here for the holiday, then heading back." He said it with pride, as if our village had little to offer him, a place to which he returned only for brief visits, obliging family and old friends but eager to be done with it all.

Chezky had been an acquaintance back in yeshiva. He was two years younger than I and had been known as a troublesome student. He asked too many questions, they said. He challenged the rabbis and made them uncomfortable. I remembered seeing him often in conversation with the red-bearded Reb Anshel, spiritual counselor for second-year students. I'd never spoken to Reb Anshel myself back then, but it was said that he was a Deep Thinker, the one to talk to when students had Deep Questions. For hours, Chezky and Reb Anshel would stand in the study hall corner, with Chezky doing the talking, his gestures animated, his speech, even when observed from afar, seeming well articulated. Reb Anshel would tug on his long ginger-colored mustache, mostly silent.

It wasn't long before I stopped seeing Chezky around the yeshiva. From what I'd heard, he'd been expelled, although the details were murky. Too smart for our rabbis, people said. Too smart for his own good. Later I would hear that he had been sent to study in Israel.

"What have you been up to?" I asked as we headed out of the shul.

His initial responses were vague, as if it were all too complicated to explain. Instead, he asked, "Heading up Washington?"

We were going in the same direction, and as we strode together across the shul parking lot, he became more talkative. "I've become involved in *kiruv*," he said.

I was struck by that phrase. *Involved in kiruv.* There was pride in those words, an air of sophistication and worldliness. Kiruv—"bringing near"—was a noble enterprise, the process of encouraging secular and unaffiliated Jews to adopt Orthodox observance. Kiruv workers elicited admiration and respect. They were saving souls, rescuing captive children.

We Skverers were not involved in kiruv. Teaching those unlike us meant engaging the outside world, acknowledging questions best left unasked, lifestyles best left unobserved. Kiruv required an understanding of outside ways and the blasphemy of nonbelievers in order to mount a response, and we did not want to understand anything about them. Yet we couldn't help but admire those who undertook the task.

As we walked, Chezky described a revolution. In Israel, auditoriums were being filled with thousands of secular Jews, who, after listening to several hours of speeches, streamed forward to don yarmulkes, kerchiefs, and small prayer shawls. Men cut off their ponytails and dropped their gold earrings into large piles that would later be

fashioned into Torah crowns. Women stepped forward to don headscarves and vowed to observe the laws of family purity. Institutions were
being set up where the newly observant could study all the Torah they
had missed in their youth. Former movie stars and pop-culture heroes now sported full beards and spent hours on hard yeshiva benches
studying Talmud and Jewish law.

All this, Chezky claimed, was due to the reinvigoration of an old
school of thought: rationalist Judaism.

"Heard of Gerald Schroeder? The nuclear physicist? He wrote this
book, *Genesis and the Big Bang?*"

He looked at me, as if expecting a knowing glance, but I only shook
my head.

"Or Dovid Gottlieb? The Bostoner Hasid who was once a philosophy professor at Johns Hopkins?"

These people, Chezky said, were figuring out ways to synthesize faith
and modernity, although I'd never heard of any of them—John Gottlieb
or Dovid Hopkins or Schroeder or Schrodinger or Shroedowitz. But
I had known people who worked in kiruv.

"My father was involved in kiruv," I said.

Chezky gave me a look, as if appraising me with newfound respect.
"Seriously?"

I told him briefly about my father's work, his organization that spon-
sored classes in Judaism and Hasidism, and I could tell that Chezky
was intrigued. "I have some of his lectures on tape. You're welcome to
borrow them."

Chezky walked home with me, and stood near the kitchen door
while Gitty, blushing at the sight of a strange male, looked up from the
kitchen table. Chezky, now the modern sophisticate, affected an air of
courtliness and nodded to her. Gitty, flustered, looked away quickly.

I climbed a ladder through a trapdoor to the attic. Boxes of cassettes were piled haphazardly alongside sukkah panels and boxes of
Passover dishes. I grabbed a handful of cassettes from one of the boxes,
headed back down the ladder, and handed them to Chezky.

As soon as he left, Gitty threw me a look: who was *that?*

"Chezky Blum," I said. "Meilich Blum's grandson."

"Oh, that one," she said, and thought for a while. "Still unmarried?"

I nodded, and we shared a knowing glance. Chezky was a cautionary tale. This was what happened when one was too different, too smart, too independent-minded. Prolonged bachelorhood was what happened.

Not many in our community would've appreciated my father's lectures, so I felt pleased watching Chezky take the tapes. When I was a child, my father would leave our home each Tuesday and Thursday evening. "I'm going to the 'center,'" he'd tell my mother, and she would nod and say, *Hatzlocho*, may you have success.

The "center" was a mysterious place I had never visited but where I knew that my father spoke to people from outside our world. Later, I would learn that it was a synagogue basement somewhere in Manhattan, a "Center for Jewish Studies," where my father would give classes in Judaism. People who had first heard my father teach at the center would often come to our home for a Shabbos meal or to attend the more advanced classes that my father gave in the synagogue basement. On the men's heads were stiffly perched yarmulkes, which they would pat to check that they were still there. The women wore their hair uncovered.

They would tell me that my father was brilliant.

"I don't understand all that he says," one man told me. "But he says it so beautifully!"

"I don't even understand many of his *words!*" another man said. "He's like a walking Oxford dictionary!"

I knew what the Oxford dictionary was. My father owned a set— not the full eleven-volume edition but a two-volume box set, each page laid out with four pages of the original, the letters reduced to a size so small that they could barely be read without the magnifying glass that came in a small built-in drawer at the top. The dictionary was kept in a special room in our home, the "little study," which, in contrast to the "big study," was a room that my father preferred I did not enter.

Both studies had shelves filled with books lining all the walls, but each had books of a different kind. In the "big study," my father had sacred texts; the Talmud figured prominently, as did the *Shulchan Aruch* and the Rambam, Judaism's primary law codes. Also in that room were many volumes on Jewish mysticism, including the Zohar and the Writings of the Ari. A ten-volume red-and-gold set of *The Words of Joel*, the magnum opus of the late rebbe of Satmar, rested prominently on the shelf above his desk.

The "little study" had an air of mystery around it. The books in it were mostly in English; from their titles, I could tell that they were books about other faiths, philosophical works, containing ideas from outside our traditions. Once, my father caught me in the "little study," browsing a book that had caught my eye. The title, I remember, had the words "Judaism and Christianity," the latter a faith I knew nothing about, except that for centuries it represented the persecution of Jews. As I flipped through the pages, I was stunned to read a passage in which it was claimed that early Christians were Sabbath-observant Jews. Just then, my father walked in.

"I don't want you reading that," my father said, and he took the book from my hand. "Please don't come in here when I'm not around." My father was a gentle man, so when he grew angry, I knew that something had really upset him. He took the book from my hand and returned it to its place on one of the shelves. He turned and patted me on the head, calling me *shayfele*—little lamb—a habit that he retained from when I was very little but that, by then, felt embarrassing. He said, "I know you're a curious boy. But if there's something in here you want to read, tell me, and we'll talk about it first."

I never did ask him about any of his books, but occasionally my father allowed me into his world for brief glimpses of his work. When I was twelve, he took me along to a conference he was attending at the United Nations headquarters. "It's what they call an 'interfaith conference,'" he said, as the taxi went over the Brooklyn Bridge into Manhattan. Rabbis, priests, imams, and ministers were coming together to speak of ideas that were common to people of all faiths. It was unusual for a Hasidic rabbi to be attending such an event, and I knew that my father was an unusual man. I knew also that I could not talk about his work to my friends or to others in our world. Engaging the outside world, at that time, was a new kind of enterprise, and they would not understand.

But Chezky would understand. Chezky, who was now himself engaging with outsiders, would appreciate a brilliant and unusual mind like my father's.

I looked for Chezky in shul the next evening, and we walked home again together.

"So what'd you think?" I asked.

He shook his head and pursed his lips, then looked away, uncomfortably. "I have a problem with some of the things your father says."

I was taken aback. I was certain that he, too, would say how brilliant, how inspiring, how erudite were my father's words, how beguiling his personality.

When I asked Chezky to elaborate, though, he turned evasive. "It's a long discussion," he said. It would take a lot of explaining. I wouldn't understand.

"Can you summarize it for me?"

He had to get home, he said. His mother needed him to kosher the sinks before Passover. His grandfather needed him to pick up several pounds of matzah. He'd promised his little brother he'd teach him a special song for the Four Questions. Around us, men and boys walked briskly, heading home from the shul and the yeshiva and the kollel, rushing to complete the Passover preparations. Across the street, a woman scurried past, as if rushing from her own self in the presence of so many men.

I could not let it go. My father was always spoken of admiringly by all who knew him, and I had to understand Chezky's objections.

"Just give me the gist of it. We don't have to get into it too deeply."

Chezky paused, bit his lower lip, then looked at me and nodded.

"OK. Your father says faith is beyond reason."

"And so?"

"I disagree," Chezky said. "Faith is fully within reason."

Chezky was right. It was a long discussion, one we did not have time for that night. He was also right that I wouldn't understand it. When over the next few days we resumed our conversation, Chezky not only declared that faith was fully within reason but also that a rational approach to faith was the only one that could work in the modern world. It was the reason that so many were returning to the faith.

"The people who are returning," Chezky said, "are educated. They live in the modern world. They don't understand the concept of blind faith. They don't care for *beautiful teachings*. They don't care for mysticism. They want to know the truth. They want facts." He tapped the back of one hand against the palm of the other. "They want data, and they want sound reasoning."

Chezky's people didn't tell Hasidic miracle tales. They didn't practice hocus-pocus rituals—swinging chickens around heads for atonement or grabbing leftovers from the rebbe's kugel or gefilte fish. Chezky's people were rational—university professors, philosophers, scientists, men and women of sound thinking—and they needed a different approach. Books were being written to explain how the wisdom of our sages was consistent with the latest advances in science. Statisticians were demonstrating how all events in the universe, past and present, were secretly encoded within the Bible text. Philosophers were presenting logical formulas to prove ancient dogmas. Chezky had met personally with many of them.

With as much enthusiasm as Chezky described this new world, I professed my disdain for it. What he described was at once foolish and dangerous. The sages warned against this: *Filozofia* led to heresy and wickedness. Even the scholarly and the saintly were wary. *Four have entered the garden*, the Talmud says. One died, one went astray, one went out of his mind, and only one, Rabbi Akiva, emerged with his faith, his life, and his sanity intact. The garden was a place of dangerous knowledge. Faith, to the ordinary person, was about discarding reason and trusting the transmission of our heritage. Faith meant not only to ignore but to actively suppress the niggling doubts and the persistent questions that called for understanding what was beyond human comprehension.

"Faith," said the master Reb Mendel of Vitebsk, "is to believe without reason whatsoever." Anything else leads to an erosion of our pure faith and, ultimately, to heresy.

Chezky ended up staying in New York. "There is kiruv work in the U.S., too," he said. He got a position on the faculty of Ohr Somayach, a kiruv yeshiva in Monsey. The yeshiva had been founded in the 1980s, in a few dilapidated buildings on a sprawling property at the corner of Route 306 and Viola Road in Monsey. Now, in the late 1990s, with the kiruv enterprise gaining popular support, it had upgraded to state-of-the-art facilities, with new, beautifully constructed study halls, dormitories, and library.

Through Chezky, I came to know more about this yeshiva. It targeted college kids of the MTV generation. The students were law- and med-school graduates from prestigious universities, with homes and two-car garages in the suburbs, content with their professional lives but looking to round them out with a bit of tradition.

This yeshiva was "open-minded," Chezky explained, and to describe just how open-minded it was, he told me of a student who was expelled for wearing a hat.

"There's a process," Chezky explained. "Not everyone's ready for a hat. You need the dean's permission."

This was not a Hasidic institution, and it didn't want students going off to explore streams of Orthodoxy that it had not itself advocated. All inquiry must be done just so.

Chezky and I soon became close friends, although it was not an easy friendship. Chezky's views threatened mine. In spite of myself, we would often circle back to discussions of faith, how best to maintain a religious worldview within a modern world.

"I'm afraid that he'll change you," Gitty would say, and I wondered whether she was right. There were days when I was determined to cut ties with him. There was something powerfully alluring about his views, and I worried that his arguments would cause my own convictions to falter. The very possibility that there existed a rational basis for our beliefs was intriguing, and I couldn't help but wonder: Can faith claims really be proved? Can one use logic to comprehend fundamentally incomprehensible notions? Could we really understand God's existence as a *scientific* or even a philosophical matter? Could one possibly provide evidence for the giving of the Torah at Mount Sinai? For the crossing of the Red Sea? I couldn't imagine it, but if it was possible, as Chezky claimed, then wouldn't it only strengthen my faith? A part of me felt a burning curiosity, but the Hasid in me knew that it was a muddy path to tread; I might come out with my faith intact but dirtied beyond real cleansing. My pure and simple beliefs, still sparkling and unsoiled, would suffer. I didn't want to go there.

I'd already had a faith crisis once. I was fifteen, at summer camp in the Catskill Mountains, in Swan Lake, New York, when I shared the crisis with my friend Menashe Einstein. Menashe and I were best friends, both of us brooding and dreamy adolescents, anxious about life and our futures. Often we would head into the woods behind the bunkhouses, past dense thickets of shrubs and tangles of brushwood, past discarded and rusting farm implements at least a century old, past steep hills and tall cliffs to a clearing of tall grass and bright sunshine. There, we'd sit on a large rock at the edge of the meadow, hoping to keep as far as we could from the camp's study hall for as long as possible.

One day, I told Menashe that I was having doubts. I wondered how we really knew the things we knew, whether heaven and hell really existed, whether the rebbe was truly saintly, whether Moses really split the Red Sea for the Israelites fleeing the Egyptians, and whether those Israelites and Egyptians and Moses ever existed at all.

Menashe looked thoughtful as he ran his fingers over a blade of grass rising from a patch of soil between the rocks. "I read somewhere," he said after a few moments of silence, "that doubts are a result of Strange Thoughts."

Strange Thoughts was how our books referred to forbidden lust, and I felt embarrassed during that moment because it meant that Menashe knew I was having Strange Thoughts, although Menashe had said it casually, as if he, too, were familiar with my dilemma. I wondered if he, too, had Strange Thoughts. Whether he, too, found the thoughts entering his mind during the silent portion of prayer, as he prayed for God to *grant us knowledge and wisdom. . . . Raise a cure for our maladies. . . . Return with mercy to Your city of Jerusalem* and in his mind would be images of Reb Chezkel's twin teenage daughters, their chestnut hair in tight ponytails, jumping rope outside the camp's dining hall. I wondered whether Menashe, too, had a sister, like mine, who brought friends home, and he would find himself thinking about them at night, when he lay in bed and tried to sleep.

After my conversation with Menashe, I tried hard not to have Strange Thoughts because if they led to doubts they weren't worth it. Strange Thoughts were bad, but doubts were more unsettling. If one doubted that the word of God was indeed the word of God, if none of it was true, then one would, logically, have to become *frei*, which was as bad as being a goy, and what kind of life would that be?

So I monitored my thoughts for signs of Strangeness. Mornings, when I walked the short distance between the bunkhouse and the ritual bath near the camp's parking lot, I took a circuitous route. Instead of taking the gravel road that passed along the camp's dining room, where women and teenage girls, wives and daughters of our teachers, would congregate for breakfast, I would edge along the side of the woods, behind the bunkhouses and the cluster of bungalows for the counselors and teachers, until I reached the mikveh. Afterward, I would return the same way, and remove my eyeglasses in case a girl or a woman appeared suddenly. At night, when I lay in bed, I'd catch a stray fantasy of my sister's friend Rachy worming into my semiconscious mind, a blurry image of a bouncing ponytail and a knee-length, pleated navy-blue skirt. I would slap my palm against the side of my head, remind myself that I'd gone a full week without waking to a wet reminder of a sinful dream, and that it would be a terrible thing if I let my guard down. I would think of a verse of Psalms or a passage of Mishna and hope that the Strange Thought would disappear. Above all, though, I would think of the creeping doubts and the weakness of my faith, and I knew that I must banish the Strange Thoughts if only to banish the doubts.

Strange Thoughts, however, kept up their ebb and flow throughout my adolescence, often appearing during the strangest times, creeping through the musty yellowed pages of old Talmud volumes, through evenings spent in song and Hasidic tales, through nights filled with dancing at the rebbe's tischen—always, in a weak moment, they appeared, thoughts of flesh and forbidden passions.

But I conquered the doubts. Apparently, they were unconnected.

He'emanti ki adaber. Avremel Shayevitz would later bang his fist on the table, repeating the words of Reb Mordche of Lechevitch: "*He'emanti,* I will believe! *Ki adaber,* when I speak words of faith! Speak words of faith, and your faith will be strong!"

And so each morning at the end of prayers, as I wrapped the black leather straps around my tefillin cases, the smell of French toast and scrambled eggs wafting up from the yeshiva dining room, I recited the Thirteen Principles of Faith, slowly and deliberately, hoping, praying for the conviction of the words:

> *Ani ma'amin*, I believe with perfect faith that the Creator, blessed be He, created and leads all of Creation. . . .

> *Ani ma'amin*, I believe with perfect faith that the prophecy of Moses our teacher is truthful . . . that all of the Torah now in our hands was given to him. . . .

> *Ani ma'amin*, I believe with perfect faith in the coming of the Messiah. And though he may tarry, still I await him.

Walking each morning from the dormitory building to the ritual bath to the yeshiva study hall, I would repeat to myself the words: *Ani ma'amin be'emunah sheleimah*. Over and over again, like a mantra, hundreds, thousands of times. "I believe with perfect faith. I believe with perfect faith." And then I would speak the words of the great master, Reb Mendel of Vitebsk: *To have faith is to believe blindly, to demand no proofs, no evidence, no logic. To have faith is to believe without reason whatsoever.*

More powerful than mantras, however, more powerful than the words of Avremel Shayevitz, or of Reb Mendel of Vitebsk, was simply this: If my faith fell apart, what was I to do then? If I stopped believing, did that mean I would stop keeping kosher? Stop keeping Shabbos? Waltz into shul without my hat? What, then, would the matchmakers say?

Chapter Twelve

My friendship with Chezky would eventually lead me back to questions of faith, but in the meantime, there were more immediate concerns. In November 1997, our daughter Chaya Suri was born. At twenty-four, with three children, five mouths to feed, and little by way of job security, I could think only about how to make ends meet.

One winter Friday, three months past due on rent, our landlord threatening eviction, Gitty and I pooled our personal valuables. I brought out the gold pocket watch that Gitty's father had given me after our engagement. Gitty brought out the gold bracelet and necklace she'd received from my mother. We estimated their total original value at about $3,000.

I gave her one last look before I stepped out. "You sure?"

Gitty was kneeling by the fridge, rummaging in the vegetable bins. Freidy, aged three, stood near her, staring into those bins as if they contained some plaything better than the secondhand, off-brand pink plastic kitchen set across the room.

"I'm sure," she said, without looking up. "When do I even wear them?"

"One day, I will buy you the most expensive pearl necklace money can buy."

Gitty looked up and smiled, a little sadly, I thought, as I headed out the door to a local pawnshop.

"What's it say?" the man at the pawnshop asked, as he inspected the engraved inscription on the back of my pocket watch.

"It's Hebrew. My name. And a blessing." It hadn't occurred to me that he'd care.

"What's the blessing?" he asked, fingering the rough texture of the engraved text.

I wasn't sure how to translate it. *"For an everlasting union . . . Sort of."*

The man grunted, and took the items to a back room. An elderly woman with a small dog walked in. I watched her go directly to the other side of the counter. For a moment, I thought she was a brazen burglar, until she continued to the back room, and I heard her say, "Did you have lunch, Mor?"

A few minutes later, the man returned.

"Four hundred," he said.

It was barely a half-month's rent, but I was desperate. The landlord wasn't very pleased, but I promised to have more soon, and we survived to worry another day, another week, another month. We never knew quite how we did it, but somehow we managed, always in the nick of time, barely avoiding the electricity being cut off or the phone line being disconnected.

Why did it have to be this way? I wondered. And how did others do it?

I knew how others did it: with difficulty. Most of my friends from yeshiva were living the same way, either still studying at the kollel, or teaching at the cheder, and struggling, making do with whatever they could—yeshiva vouchers, food stamps, Section 8. They went from one poor moneymaking idea to the next. One friend bought a popcorn machine, set it up in his basement, and offered home deliveries around the village. Another set up a table outside the shul, selling noise-conditioning devices for people with sleep problems.

My friend Yakov Mayer was the most ambitious of all. He was two years older than I and already had six children, including a set of triplets. He, too, was desperate for a way to feed them all, and his latest idea was selling life insurance.

"There's decent money in it," he said, as he tried to sell me a policy and, at the same time, to explain his choice of trade.

"*If* you can sell policies," I said. He hadn't sold a single one yet.

He nodded. "If I can sell policies." He looked at me keenly, as if pleading for my approval. "It's only been three months, though."

Yakov Mayer had found his idea, but I hadn't yet found mine. Teaching at the cheder hadn't turned into the career I thought it would. I had grown tired of writing fraudulent progress reports, tired of worrying that the government would come investigating, tired of running after parents for their share of the payment, and so, in July 1997, when my friend Motty proposed that we start a business together, I gave up my work at the cheder and decided to become a businessman.

Motty had the idea that we could package nuts and dried fruits and other healthful snacks and sell them to snack shops and convenience stores across the tristate area. I knew nothing about running a business, but I liked Motty's idea, and so I borrowed a few thousand dollars from several free loan societies around New Square and Monsey, and pinned our family's hopes on popular appetites for salted cashews and sugared pineapple chunks.

We kept the business running for about two years, and I would later marvel that we'd kept it that long. I was too timid to push our product on uninterested customers, too impulsive with purchasing new office equipment, too dreamy to pay much attention to the *business* of running a business and more interested in creating pretty-looking cash-flow reports using a secondhand, DOS-based computer, with its text-based interface and incessant, blinking command-line cursor. I also really enjoyed buying office supplies: desks and file cabinets and staplers that worked so well that you wanted to do nothing but staple all day until the stapler broke and you were forced to buy a new one—an electronic one this time, for double the stapling fun.

In April 1999, Motty and I faced the fact that our business had yet to turn a profit. We put an ad in one of the Yiddish newspapers, and sold it all—the account lists and the computer and our weighing and bagging equipment and our heat sealers and the Chevy cargo van with which we made our deliveries.

Afterward, I rotated through a number of odd jobs. One job, ostensibly as a bookkeeper, lasted three days, until the boss fired me for calling him crazy. He ran a multimillion-dollar operation, buying and selling photocopier and fax-machine toners on the gray market but refused to buy a computer for the office, preferring an old-fashioned double-entry system in an enormous, ancient ledger. I could do bookkeeping as long as I had a computer with a working copy of QuickBooks. But manual, double-entry ledgers? I thought that was crazy.

For some time, I manned the phone lines for a company that provided a telephone-directory service for Hasidic businesses. Callers interacted with voice prompts, unaware that a human—me—was listening on a headset, pushing buttons to deliver the audio listings. I fielded calls from housewives looking for clothing sales, men looking for Judaica bookstores, teenage boys asking about "lindjerie" shops—probably calling from yeshiva dorms, where the most titillating thing was an automated voice listing of local stores selling women's hosiery and Shabbos robes.

My passion for study, piety, and prayer was mostly forgotten. Now I wondered only how I was going to support my family. After rotating through a half-dozen jobs in as many months, I felt increasingly as if I were not a grown-up but a child. Somewhere, somehow, a decision had been made: Gitty and I were to playact as parents, she as homemaker, and I as provider. Except, while Gitty seemed a natural for her role, I was clearly a failure at mine. Gitty fed and clothed and bathed our little ones as if groomed for the task her entire life. I never saw her hold her head in despair over a burned pot of chulent. I, on the other hand, went from job to job, wondering about all those years I was taught the importance of Torah study and never a word about how to earn a paycheck.

In my spare time, I sat on the plastic-covered chairs at our faux-mahogany dining-room table, and studied computers—how to work with them but also how they worked on the inside. I was fascinated by their parts, how magnetic hard drives worked alongside RAM, connected via motherboard, input and output devices. But most of all, I was fascinated by software, the mind within all that metal and silicon.

"Why are you spending so much time on this?" Gitty would ask, as I brought home book after book from the library on the inner workings of hardware, writing computer code, setting up networks. Gitty thought that I should be doing more productive things, such as inquiring at the fish store about the "Cashiers Wanted" sign in the window. Or maybe selling life insurance. Or starting another business of some sort. "What's the point of all this computer stuff?"

I would shrug in response. I'd say it was just really fascinating and fun and interesting, and Gitty would roll her eyes. What I really thought—a fantasy I didn't dare voice out loud: I wonder if I might work as a computer programmer one day.

I didn't know how one became a computer programmer, but I could not quiet my fascination. The books would pile up around the house, on the kitchen counter, on the bedside nightstand, on the little window ledge in the bathroom. When reading about the binary number system, I was struck by the beauty of mathematics, the symmetry of numbers, concepts I had never thought about before—we'd studied no mathematics past seventh grade, which had pleased me perfectly at the time. But what I was reading now was fresh and exciting: machine language, overlaid with assembly language, overlaid with "high-level" languages—C++, SQL, Perl—nested levels of abstraction built on reusable modules. I was fascinated by the use of a machine to imitate a human brain, to break down human thought processes to their smallest parts and to mimic them through concise lines of computer instruction. Like a mechanical lever, but for the mind, computer code could make a machine outperform humans to near-limitless degrees—and I was learning exactly how it was done.

I would behold a page of code like a work of art. In mapping algorithms and routines, I found a kind of exhilaration that was similar to the logical processes of Talmud study, except these processes were not stretched over ancient rules of textual exegesis but strictly logical premises. At the most basic level, they were staggeringly simple: If balance is greater than zero, funds can be withdrawn. If time is past 6:30, sound the alarm. If snoozed, repeat until unsnoozed. Yet the possibilities, built only on ones and zeros, on and off, true and false, were literally limitless, allowing the creation of complex routines of both beauty and utility. Endless possibilities from one essential binary. In the Talmud, too, there was beauty, but here was a true amalgamation of the human and the divine. If the Talmud was built on the purported word of God, that *word* struck you as suspiciously human, with ambiguities and layers of meaning and all the arbitrariness of human language. The very idea of faith suggested something man-made—the idea that we must submit to conviction, rather than simply behold the universe in its natural order. In the principles of logic, however, which formed the basis of computer software, the premises were fixed. True was true. False was not. There was no gray, no middle ground, no room for ambiguities or contradiction or layers of interpretation. Precision and predictability were key. Prayer was of little help when your executable was stuck in an infinite loop.

Yakov Mayer, I soon learned, wasn't having much success selling life insurance. When he learned about my interest in computers, he, too, grew curious about them. Yakov Mayer, however, had never learned to read English well, and had a hard time studying on his own. The few books he acquired on the subject didn't feel sufficient, so he went to look for another way.

An Orthodox organization, Yakov Mayer told me excitedly over the phone one day, was offering courses in computer programming at its offices in lower Manhattan. The organization, Agudath Israel of America, was an advocacy group for Orthodox Jews, and it had set up a division called COPE Institute, to train men in "kosher" professions: accounting, computer programming, networking.

"How about we go for the programming course?" Yakov Mayer asked.

He thought we could become real programmers, but I laughed at the idea. I imagined that one could not become an actual computer programmer without going to college any more than one could become an astronaut or a brain surgeon. At the very least, I imagined that one needed a high school diploma. And really, what good was a course? I had taught myself enough computer programming to write decent code for at least a thousand different business uses. Learning the stuff wasn't the problem. Finding a way to get paid for it was.

"Well," Yakov Mayer said. "They've got a job placement program."

Several days later, Yakov Mayer and I sat in the very last row of the Monsey Trails commuter bus to Manhattan. It felt like a synagogue—the sights and sounds were the same: men in their prayer shawls and phylacteries, eyelids still heavy from sleep, mumbling prayers. The prayer leader stood in the center of the aisle, calling the ends and beginnings of chapters: *Halleluyah, halleluyah,* mumble mumble, *And David blessed the Lord,* mumble mumble, *On that day Moses sang with the children of Israel,* mumble mumble.

The men all sat on one side of the bus with a curtain drawn down the aisle, beneath which we got glimpses from the other side: gold-foil flats, fashionable heels, stockinged ankles.

For the Shmoneh Esreh, we rose and squeezed into the aisle, swaying along with the jerky motion of the bus as it cut between cars, tractor-trailers, and New Jersey Transit buses on their way to the Lincoln Tunnel. A man squeezed through the throng in the aisle, dangling a navy-blue velvet pouch between his thumb and forefinger: *Rabbi Mayer, Master of the Miracle* was embroidered on the pouch in gold thread. From within came the jingle of coins as men dropped nickels, dimes, quarters, to support the pious men of Jerusalem. For the Torah reading, a scroll was taken from a makeshift ark overhead. One man read aloud from it, his tinny voice losing strength as it traveled through the mass of bodies, sounding, to us in the rear, like an overseas phone call with a bad connection.

The men were Orthodox, and yet most of them were non-Hasidim, working professionals—attorneys, accountants, doctors, investment bankers. They wore starched button-down shirts and sharp suits and polished black shoes. A handful of Hasidic men, who worked mostly as diamond dealers in midtown or as salesmen for the Hasidic-owned B&H electronics store, huddled in the rear. Unlike the others, the Hasidic men looked shabby, in ill-fitting overcoats, beaver hats speckled with rain spots, unkempt beards. These were *my* people, and at first, the others filled me with disdain. Such vanity! Their shoes so polished, they sparkled. Their trousers so perfectly creased, it was as if they had pressed them just that morning. Who had time for such nonsense?

Yet they had something I wanted. I envied their sense of purpose, the vibes of success they emitted, electric charges of money and comfort zapping off their power ties and their shimmering gold metal cuff links. These men, I imagined, didn't pawn their wives' jewelry to make rent.

Could I be like them?

Only a few years earlier, the thought would've horrified me, but now, I wondered, why not? They, too, were Orthodox. They prayed, they kept kosher, they kept Shabbos, and yet they lived in the modern world, engaged with it, interacted with it, earned decent livings through hard work and honest professions, and then they came home to their families and lived fully religious lives. Couldn't one have it all?

Later that morning, in an office building on a narrow street in Manhattan's financial district, Yakov Mayer and I sat in a room filled with long tables as a nervous little man in a white shirt, his tangled tzitzis fringes hanging from his belt, handed us a pile of stapled sheets of paper. This was the course's entrance exam, an "aptitude test," and it had three sections: English, mathematics, and logic. We had thirty minutes for each, and I zipped through the questions with ease.

> *What comes next?* 16, 32, 64, 128, ?
> *Rewrite the sentence: Theirs a dog on the porch with a tale between it's legs.*
> *True or false? If all keneebels are gezeebels, then all gezeebels are keneebels.*

"Why would they give us such a difficult exam?" Yakov Mayer asked, as we headed to catch the bus back home. "What's English grammar got to with programming?"

He'd guessed his way through most of the questions, he said.

Clearly, we experienced the exam differently, and I wasn't surprised. All Hasidic boys' schools were substandard in their general-studies curricula, but in New Square, things were particularly bad. Yakov Mayer's "English" classes had consisted of little more than lessons in the English alphabet and basic arithmetic. His teachers were young men who had themselves been educated in New Square's cheder, and they didn't know much more than the students. *"Aynglish, foy!"* we had cried at the Krasna cheder in Borough Park, but now I felt thankful for those two hours we'd had in late afternoon. As disdainful as we were back then, it gave me a good enough foundation. Yakov Mayer hadn't been so lucky. In preparation for the exam, he had asked his wife to tutor him in English and math, but even so, he found it all too challenging.

Two days later, we got our test results. I passed, but Yakov Mayer failed.

"I still don't understand what English has to do with programming," he said to me over the phone. Yet he was not discouraged. "I can take the test again," he said. He'd already begun new tutoring sessions with his wife.

A couple of weeks later, he retook the test, and this time he passed—just barely. There was still a catch, though, for both of us. Neither of us had high school diplomas, and so we would have to take another exam that covered some of the basic high school subjects.

"You ready for the next exam?" I asked.

Yakov Mayer was silent for a moment. "I think not. I'll just have to make a diploma."

I was stunned. "Forge one?"

"What else can I do? There's no way I'll pass this exam."

A few days later, I took the bus to the city, alone this time, and took the second exam. It was more challenging than the first, especially the math questions. I found myself staring at problems involving x's and y's, and was stumped.

Simplify: $9x + 3y * 6 = 24x - 2$

How did *letters* get into a math problem? Baffled, I stared for a long time at the sheet in front of me. Was it A equals 1, B equals 2, and so on? I tried to remember back to my math lessons as a child. The last lessons we had were on fractions, and I vaguely recalled converting mixed numbers and finding common denominators, but nothing about the value of letters.

This time, it was my turn to guess my way through my responses. I answered the questions as best I could, and handed in my exam. I wondered if I should've just followed Yakov Mayer's lead and forged a high school diploma. But now it was too late. Perhaps my first instincts had been right. Maybe this course wasn't for people like me. Maybe it was meant only for non-Hasidim, those raised in less sheltered environments, who'd taken high school math and all kinds of other subjects that our Hasidic yeshivas did not bother with.

To my surprise, I passed this exam, too. Not with a perfect score, but good enough. Yakov Mayer, for his part, submitted his forged high school diploma, and on a scorching day in July 1999, we took the bus to downtown Manhattan for our first day of class.

Two months in, Yakov Mayer sat down next to me in the classroom.

"I've decided to drop out," he said. "I struggle to get through every page." He pointed to our textbook, *The C Programming Language*, which lay on the table in front of us. His tone was almost apologetic. The course had turned out to be more stimulating than I'd expected, and as much as I'd taught myself on my own, I quickly learned a lot more. Yakov Mayer was a bright fellow and was quick to grasp the concepts when they were explained to him. He had been a good student in yeshiva. He was disciplined and determined and conscientious about the reading and the lab assignments. But his English skills were too weak. Even with his wife's help, he had trouble reading and understanding the material.

Optimistic as usual, he assured me that it was for the best. Programming just wasn't for him.

Yakov Mayer's departure from the class left me anxious—for his sake but also for that of my own family. It was he who had encouraged me to pursue this course seriously; yet his own handicaps, a result of the educational neglect of our world, kept him from pursuing his own career aspirations. Even if I myself had been more fortunate, was this to be my children's fate, to be raised not only with rigidly defined roles but deprived of any ability to step out of them?

It was early January 2000, and the course was winding down. It was a new millennium. The Y2K bug brought no catastrophes. Hundreds of Internet-based companies were going public. The national economy was in better shape than it had ever been—in less than a year's time, outgoing president Clinton would announce that the federal government had an unprecedented $230 billion budget surplus, with projections of paying off the national debt within the decade.

Hope and optimism could not have been more infectious, and it seemed apropos of these good times that I received a phone call one day from a woman about a job. I was in the computer lab, finishing our final class project, when the call came. I'd e-mailed my résumé to a number of listings on several job websites—Monster, Dice, Jobs.com—and now a recruiter was calling in response.

"I was wondering if you would like to take this interview," she said.

The name of the company was Bloomberg. "They're a media company. They provide news and analysis on the financial markets."

"*Bloomberg?*" She couldn't really mean—

"Yes, Bloomberg. They're a company in midtown."

"*The* Bloomberg?"

"Yes," she said with a chuckle. "*The* Bloomberg."

It felt surreal. Only a few years earlier, I had been a kollel student. A cheder teacher. A Hasidic young man who knew so little about the world that I had to sneak behind my wife's back to listen to the radio or read books at the library. Now I faced the prospect of working for an iconic New York corporation.

A job interview at an iconic New York corporation was different from an interview at one of our Hasidic-owned businesses. The portly fellow who sat two rows behind me in shul, or the fellow who, like me, soaked a little too long in the hot mikveh on late Friday afternoons: they weren't intimidating as interviewers, but an interview at a major New York corporation required preparation. And so on my way home that day, I drove to Barnes and Noble and purchased a yellow handbook: *Job Interviews for Dummies.*

On the bus ride home, I felt a wave of anxiety. There were Hasidim who interacted with outsiders with confidence, even arrogance, never pausing to consider their handicaps—of education, of language, of their essential alienness from the surrounding culture. But I had never been that way. Just walking down a Manhattan street in my Hasidic garb made me uncomfortably self-conscious, as did my Yiddish accent. I was suddenly anxious that I, a former aspiring Torah scholar, would never fit into a secular office environment. I would say the wrong thing, or look the wrong way, and it would only confirm what everyone knew: just another Hasid, freakishly stuck in a medieval world, unable or unwilling to make the necessary accommodations to modern living.

At home that evening, I stood in front of the vanity mirror and assessed my appearance. I looked at my close-cropped hair, my untrimmed beard, the tangled knot of *payess* over my ears. I stared at my large boxy plastic-framed eyeglasses, black on top and blending into clear on the bottom, and saw for the first time how remarkably ugly they were. I had first begun to wear those glasses as a teenager, when paying attention to one's appearance was considered unseemly. At the yeshiva, there hadn't been a single mirror on the premises. *It is forbidden for a man to gaze into a mirror,* we studied, *as he must not act in the manner of a woman.*

Now, however, I needed to make some adjustments. Later that evening, I drove to an eyeglass store in Monsey. The middle-aged Hasid behind the counter grinned widely when I pointed to the display case with its selection of stylish pairs of glasses.

"Time for an upgrade, eh?" He nodded approvingly when I pointed to a gold-wire frame. "Givenchy," he said, removing it from the display case and laying it on the counter.

"What?"

"Givenchy," he said again, with an excited nod. "A brand name."

I had never heard of the brand, but I liked the style, and walked out of the store with a new burst of confidence.

The day before my interview, I stopped into Men's Wearhouse, down Route 59. I had never before been to a non-Hasidic clothing store, but I was now out for a special purchase. I had been reading through the various sections of *Job Interviews for Dummies,* and I came to notes on attire. Men, the book said, were to wear a suit and tie to all job interviews.

I had a suit but had never worn a tie. No one I knew had worn a tie. Hasidim simply didn't wear them, and yet, there was no rule against it—and that's when it struck me: a tie! The perfect touch to transform me from slovenly Hasid to modern gentleman.

After purchasing what I thought was a suitable style, I brought the tie home and called to Gitty to have a look. I removed it ceremoniously from the store's plastic bag, and unfolded it. It was resplendent in its gradations of soft blue and gray.

"You bought a tie just to wear it once?"

"Maybe I'll have more than one interview," I said hopefully, forgetting for a moment that the objective was fewer interviews, not more.

It wasn't only the tie that Gitty was skeptical about. She hadn't been taken with the whole programming idea. "Who's going to hire you?" she had asked throughout the six-month course. When I told her about the interview at Bloomberg, she only shook her head in exasperation. "Has it not occurred to you that we'll lose our food stamps?"

Gitty intuited another problem as well. "Do you even know how to wear it?" she asked. Before I could respond, she turned back to the full-color brochure of prizes for some local organization's Chinese auction, leaving me to wonder on my own.

I took the tie to the vanity mirror, turned up my shirt collar, and placed the tie around my neck. I wrapped it first one way and then another. I flipped and pulled and twisted and wrapped it around in every conceivable way until I'd nearly strangled myself, but all I got was a sloppy bulge at the base of my throat, which promptly undid itself as soon as I removed my hand.

I was nearly ready to concede that the tie was a foolish idea, when, thirty minutes later, I had the answer. "God bless the Internet!" I shouted to Gitty as I ran from the computer in the dining room to the vanity mirror. In my hand, I held printouts of all the tie-knotting instructions I would ever need, courtesy of howtotieatie.com.

I chose a full Windsor, practiced in front of the mirror for half an hour or so, and then placed the printouts carefully in my coat pocket. I might need the instructions again when I got off the bus the next day. I would find a corner somewhere on the streets of Manhattan, and fasten the tie under my collar before heading to the interview. For a moment, I considered fastening the tie before I left home, but quickly gave up the idea. I couldn't possibly wear a tie on the bus. I imagined men staring, women casting nervous glances, children pointing and laughing: *Look! A Hasid wearing a tie!*

But the Bloomberg people wouldn't laugh. They would be impressed. *Look! A Hasid wearing a tie! How uncanny—just what we were looking for!*

Around noon the next day, I stood at the corner of Park Avenue and Fifty-Eighth Street, my shirt collar up, staring at my reflection in the glass wall of an office building. Around me, men in smart suits and women in tight skirts and fashionable heels strode purposefully between buildings, a corporate sheen reflecting off the many revolving doors. Stern, uniformed men looked out from behind security desks, guarding the entrances to these palaces of capitalism.

It took several tries, until the tie finally felt right, more or less. The knot felt a little too wide and a little too loose, and I wasn't sure that I got it the correct length down to my belt but decided that it would do. I couldn't be late for the interview.

In the waiting area of Bloomberg's headquarters, I sat with my beaver hat on my lap and stared at giant yellow-and-orange iridescent fish in floor-to-ceiling aquariums. Employees came and went from a nearby room filled with snacks and drinks—I remember a retail-store-style refrigerator filled entirely with Coke cans—and bantered with one another in a way that I knew I never could. Their speech sounded like a foreign language. I tried to sit tall, purse my lips into the polite-but-not-too-expressive smile that everyone else appeared to be wearing, but I knew that I was putting up a facade.

Tie or no tie, I was a Hasid from New Square, and this was too strange a world for me. When I was finally summoned for my interview, the interviewers were cordial and businesslike, but I wasn't surprised when the recruiter told me the next day that I didn't get the job. Still, just the fact that I'd managed the interview made me feel proud. I was certain that I was the first Hasid from New Square to be interviewed at Bloomberg. That had to count for something.

A month later, I took the bus into midtown for another interview, this time at the offices of a trade magazine for the diamond and jewelry industry. I didn't bother with the tie. The business was owned by an American-Israeli businessman who was used to hiring Hasidim. The owner himself was Modern Orthodox, and he admired those who'd honed their analytical skills on years of Talmud study. Some of his clients were Hasidim, too, longtime diamond and jewelry dealers, and I felt right at home.

On a Monday in February 2000, I rode the 7:15 bus from Monsey to my first day of work. It was an entry-level position, creating custom software applications for the staff of a dozen or so employees. Still, my salary was greater than anything I'd previously earned. Three weeks into the job, I received my first paycheck. Soon after, as Gitty predicted, we lost our food stamps. And for the very first time in my life, I felt like a man.

••

The next time I saw Yakov Mayer, he was trying his luck again with life insurance. He'd sold a couple of policies, he said. "With God's help, it'll all work out."

I wished him well.

"Maybe we can sit down some time, talk a little about finances and stuff?"

"About finances?"

"Some life-insurance policies can be attractive investments. And also, you know, if something should happen, God forbid—"

I shook my head sadly. I was in no position to buy life insurance. I was only now finding my footing in life. Matters of death would have to wait. As it was, our expenses were up. Just a few months earlier, we'd welcomed the newest member of our family. In September 1999, Gitty gave birth to our fourth child, our first boy: Akiva.

Chapter Thirteen

It was the day of my son's bris. The tables across the south section of the shul were covered in white tablecloths and laid out with small challah rolls and perfectly sliced portions of gefilte fish swimming in sweet sauce. Off to the side, the caterer was preparing servings of roast chicken, potato kugel, glazed carrots, and the most delectable rolls of apple strudel. My sister and her husband and their three children were here from Borough Park. My brothers, with their wives and children, were assembled nearby, as were Gitty's parents and siblings, along with an assortment of aunts, uncles, cousins, and some family friends. My mother stood in a nearby doorway, in her arms my infant son, swathed in layers of white ruffles and lace under the gold-embroidered inscription: *Elijah, angel of the covenant, behold, yours has come before you.*

The rebbe had just finished the morning prayers, and now there would be a five-minute break, after which the bris would commence. The rebbe would serve as *sandek*: he would hold the child in his lap as the circumcision was performed, recite the necessary prayers, and announce my new son's name.

My mother smiled at me from afar. Gitty, per custom, was at home, a coterie of women keeping her company until our newborn would be returned to her, duly admitted to the covenant. After the ceremony, the men would remain in shul for the celebratory feast, presided over by the rebbe, while the women would join Gitty for a separate celebration in the dining room of her parents' home.

Zisha Schnitzler, fundraiser-slash-panhandler for the yeshiva, approached me. "Reb Shulem, how about a donation, in honor of your celebration?"

I withdrew a five-dollar bill from my wallet. Zisha looked at the bill, and pulled back, as if in horror.

"Five—*for a bris?*" He shook his head resolutely. "No one gives less than fifty-four—three times *chai*." He held up his palms, in a gesture of apology. "Tell you what. Give me thirty-six and I'll give you a blessing, my best wishes for a prosperous future, and to take great pride in your newborn son. And you *know*," Zisha shook his head and spread his arms wide, as if it were all so tedious to repeat, but some people were just impossible, "you *know* my blessings are effective."

Just as I was contemplating a counteroffer—a half blessing for eighteen, maybe?—the shul doors opened wide, and dozens of men and teenage boys burst through the doors. Behind them soon came scores more, streaming through each of the three large entrances, until there were several hundred men coming toward the front of the shul. The sudden presence and the attendant cacophony of so many men were disorienting, and it took me a moment to realize that they had come not to celebrate my son's circumcision.

I had nearly forgotten. This day was not only the day of my son's bris. It was also the anniversary of the death of one of the rebbe's many illustrious ancestors, a rather obscure sage who lived during the nineteenth century in the town of Skvyra, Ukraine. As custom dictated, the rebbe would be handing out cake and wine after prayers. The crowd, the entire student bodies of both the yeshiva and the kollel, were here for the cake. My own family celebration, elaborate with culinary delights as it would be, was subordinate to the greater, more significant event: commemorating the death of the old sage Reb Hershele of Skvyra.

I had never liked the fact that private family celebrations were public events. I did not enjoy being at the center of a crowd, especially when well-wishers were, as often as not, people I barely knew. The running around beforehand, arranging the space and the caterer and notifying the rebbe and the gabbai and the shul caretaker and all the other people who had to be notified, turned it from a celebration into a burdensome obligation.

"Why can't we just celebrate at home, as a family?" I asked Gitty once. "You, me, our parents, our siblings, a few cousins. Who needs more?"

Gitty scowled. "Why can't you do what everyone does and stop being so contrarian?"

In truth, our past celebrations hadn't been so bad. Our three eldest were girls, and so the ceremonies were limited to three events each: receiving an apple from the rebbe's hand at the Friday night tisch; being called for a reading of the Torah on Shabbos morning, followed by a rather unceremonious baby-naming by the gabbai; and then the kiddush—a celebration with wine and pastries in a corner of the shul following Shabbos morning prayers. Three modest ceremonies to mark the birth of a female child, and no further celebrations until the girl was engaged to be married. It wasn't too much to handle.

But a boy child—ah, what good fortune! It was as if the celebrations never ended—and it was not a proper celebration until all and sundry had taken part.

It began with the *shulem zucher* on Friday night, when men gathered to eat fruits and boiled chickpeas and great quantities of roasted peanuts in their shells, which they would crack open and pile high on the table, on the chairs, on the floor, and drag fistfuls stuck to their shoes as they went back out into the night, tipsy on too many Heinekens.

The *vach nacht* followed, during which the father stayed up all night and studied Torah, while men—friends, strangers, all were welcome—sat around eating gefilte fish and kugel and drinking great quantities of Old Williamsburg whiskey and leaving even greater piles of peanut shells for the women to clean up after.

Then, of course, came the bris—morning prayers, the ceremony, the celebratory feast.

Three days after the bris was the *shlishi lemilah*, a feast to commemorate the day our forefather Abraham was healed from his circumcision wound. More gefilte fish and kugel. Maybe not as many peanuts.

If the infant boy was a firstborn, there was the *pidyon haben* three weeks later. Bedecked in gold jewels, sugar cubes, and garlic cloves, the infant was laid on a sterling-silver tray, as if he were a roasted fowl stuffed into a light-blue Snuggie with a matching pacifier, while the father and a *kohen*, a descendant of the priestly class, playacted an ancient negotiation ritual: the father offered the *kohen* five silver shekels in return for which the *kohen* would spare the child from a lifetime of priesthood. Afterward, more gefilte fish and kugel.

Further celebrations ensued: for the child's first haircut (age two), first day in cheder (age three), first Bible lesson (age five). And at thirteen, of course, the bar mitzvah—which came with its own set of pre- and post-events.

All these events were held communally. Among Skverers, that meant the rebbe participated in at least some of them, and when he did, he took pride of place. Before and after a birth, the rebbe was to be notified. The rebbe was to be consulted before the child's name was decided upon. And while the rebbe might skip out on the *vach nacht* or the *shulem zucher*, under no circumstances would he miss a bris. It was said that from the day the rebbe became rebbe, in March 1968, at the age of twenty-eight, he attended nearly every bris in the village, unless he was away on vacation, and even then, as often as not, the proud parents would travel with the infant and hold the ceremony at the rebbe's vacation home in the Catskill Mountains.

Now, I found myself not only at the center of a public ceremony but a far greater one than what I had prepared for. In addition to family and friends, there was the usual assortment of those who came to the shul each morning looking for a free meal and a glass of schnapps, along with the entire yeshiva and kollel assemblies. They stood around, chatting, shouting, shoving, waiting for it all to begin.

"When's the rebbe coming out?" I overheard two boys talking. They couldn't have been older than fourteen.

"There's a bris first," the other said.

"Ugh," said the first, as if he had somewhere to be and it was all throwing off his schedule.

Soon enough, the rebbe emerged and took his seat on the Throne of Elijah.

"*Kvatter!*" the gabbai cried. At the doorway in the corner, I watched as my mother handed the baby to my brother Mendy, who then brought the bundled package to the cleared space in front of the Holy Ark.

"Reb Chaim Goldstein!" the gabbai cried, and Mendy handed the baby to my father-in-law, who then handed it to his own father-in-law, who had traveled from Williamsburg for the occasion and who then handed the baby to a series of uncles and great-uncles and brothers-in-law and even some of the older cousins. The gabbai rattled off their names, giving each the honor of holding the infant for barely a second before it was dropped into the arms of another. Finally, the last of the male relatives had their turn, and the baby, still contentedly sucking his pacifier, was laid to rest on the rebbe's knees.

I couldn't watch. Off to the side, my prayer shawl pulled heavily over my head, I would let the professionals handle it. All I had to do was listen for my cue—my child's scream—after which I would recite the circumcision blessing with great joy.

There was no scream.

"How could there be no scream?" I would later ask Gitty. "Are you sure they did it properly?" She would assure me that they did. "But he didn't scream," I would say. "He didn't even cry. Maybe a whimper. *Maybe.*"

My mind must've strayed to the wafting aromas of apple strudel, when the shouts came from all around: *"Nu! Nu! De brucha! De brucha!"* How on earth—? *"Nu! Nu! The blessing!"* Flustered, I fumbled for my prayer book. *Recite with joy!* said the little instruction above the recitation, and I looked at all the impatient men around me and mustered all the joy I could: *Blessed are You, Lord . . . who has commanded us to bring him into the covenant of our father Abraham.*

The circumcised infant was reswaddled in his blanket, and the rebbe stood from the chair and raised a silver goblet of wine: *O Lord, God of our forefathers. Give life to this child . . . Akiva the son of Shulem! Let the father rejoice with the emission of his loins. Let his mother be gladdened with the fruit of her womb. . . . As it is written: By your blood, you shall live.*

The ceremony complete, Mendy carried Akiva back to my mother, who still stood in the little doorway in the corner. Men of all ages came to shake my hand, offer best wishes for raising my newborn son to be a pious Torah Jew. Some of the more eager uncles were already sitting at the prepared tables, breaking open challah rolls and helping themselves to cucumber salads and gefilte fish and dollops of shredded beets and horseradish. I folded my tallis, placed it inside the velvet pouch, and headed to the sink just outside the door to wash before the meal. Around me, some men called, "Mazel tov, Reb Shulem, mazel tov!" I smiled in return, wished them *mertzeshem bei dir*—your own celebrations, too, if God wills it. Maybe this wasn't all so bad.

I filled a large stainless-steel washing cup with water. Just as I was about to pour the water over my right hand, I heard a commotion from inside the sanctuary. A moment later, a gaggle of young men burst through the door.

"*Nu! Nu!*" they shouted. "Shulem! The rebbe's waiting!"

I had forgotten. It was not my day alone. I rushed back inside. The rebbe now sat at the head of a large arrangement of tables, before him a dozen or so enormous trays piled high with slices of honey cake. As the celebrant of a new birth, I was to be the first to receive one of the rebbe's blessed pastries, and because I was not there, the crowd of men stood pressed tightly against one another and gazed in silence at the rebbe, who now sat motionless, casting a peevish pall over the room.

I hurried across to the front of the shul, pushing my way through the crowd up front in order to reach the rebbe, when I felt a violent shove from behind. I turned to see Yossi Fried, the gabbai Reb Shia's grandson, behind me, his outstretched arm receding from my shoulder. "Making the rebbe wait!" he hissed.

A few moments later, the honey-brown slice of pastry in my hand, I stood feeling crushed as men around me pushed forward to receive their own portions. As I jostled my way through the crowd surging against me, I wondered to myself: Why, for heaven's sakes, did I need the rebbe at my son's bris?

"That's your friendship with Chezky talking," Gitty would say afterward. "I knew he'd be a bad influence."

"Tell me," Chezky had asked me a few days earlier. "What is so great about this man?"

This man. As if the rebbe was just *some guy*.

I didn't like Chezky's sneering. If some of our practices had begun to feel inconvenient to me, it was a failing on my part, I was sure. I liked the rebbe, for the most part, even if I was no longer as great a believer as I once was. Sometimes I even loved him. I remembered the days when I had idolized him, watched intently as he ate from the dishes placed in front of him at the Friday night tisch, or on Shabbos afternoon, always the exact same routine. For over three decades now, fifty-two weeks a year, the rebbe performed every single tisch according to script: nine spoonfuls of soup, three bites of onion kugel, seven forkfuls of chicken, two slices of sweet carrot. Each tisch lasted between one and three hours, sometimes longer. He never stood up in the middle for a break or to use the bathroom, never skipped out because of illness or fatigue. For years, I stood on those bleachers, listening to the tremors in the rebbe's voice as he prayed and chanted and sang, exactly the same as the previous week, the previous month, the previous year. We were attuned to the subtlest deviations—a smile, a laugh, an unexpected gesture. On Passover, at the seder, when the rebbe reached the passage *"until now, You have stood to our aid, and may You not abandon us with Your mercy forever,"* those very same words, each and every year, catching in his throat, the same spell of hysterical weeping, except—that was just it, it was *always the same.* And still, we spoke about the smallest signs of spontaneity. "The rebbe wept this year more than last year," one Hasid might say, and the other would agree. "But not as much as the year before." Then they would compare the number of seconds. Last year, the rebbe wept for seven seconds, then after a pause, wept for thirteen seconds more. This year, he wept only once, but for a twenty-three-second stretch.

Until one day, I began to wonder. Where, exactly, lay the rebbe's greatness? Was he a scholar? Was he a saint? Had he ever shown anyone any exceptional kindness? How would one even know it, considering that he was barely accessible to his followers, his acts so meticulously scripted, his public utterances limited to carefully prepared thoughts of little consequence, private audiences always brief and perfunctory, five-minute consultations after a five-hour wait?

I thought about the rebbes of other sects—so many of them, of late, consumed with squabbles. Many of the major sects were being split into factions. The once-mighty Satmars were splitting into the Aronites and the Zalmenites. In Vizhnitz, Mendel and Srultche had battled over their father's throne, even though he wasn't to die for another twelve years. In Bobov, there would soon be the Forty-Fivers and the Forty-Eighters, each gearing up to grab the greatest portion of the great Bobov empire after the death of their very beloved old rebbe, Reb Shloime. The squabbles were often coated in veneers of piety, but the differences were rarely matters of principle or ideology. They were about power and control. And real estate. Millions of dollars in properties and institutions and the great communal wealth amassed by each sect.

"Are any of these rebbes examples for their followers?" I fumed to Gitty.

But Gitty had little interest in the politics of Hasidic courts. "I don't know anything about them, and I don't care to." Our rebbe, she insisted, was not to be questioned. "I was taught to have *faith in the righteous*," she said.

But what did it mean to have faith in the righteous? Was it to have faith in their very righteousness? There was something maddeningly circular about that—how did one know if they were righteous enough to have faith in? By faith?

"Next bris," I said to Gitty, "is without the rebbe." I'd had enough.

One Saturday night, several weeks later, Gitty and I were in the kitchen together. She was dumping leftover chulent in the trash, while I was sorting through the day's mail. It was past midnight. The kids were long tucked into bed, and I, too, had begun to yawn.

"I think I'm going to bed," I said, my eyes tearing up as they did when I felt sleepy.

"What was that?" Gitty asked, cocking her head.

"I said, I think I'm going to bed."

Gitty held up an index finger. "No—listen. What was *that?*"

"What was what?"

All we heard was the hum of the refrigerator.

"I thought I heard something."

"It's in your head." I stood up and stretched.

"Wait! Listen!"

This time I heard it, too. A shout. Then came crashing sounds, like breaking glass, then more shouting. Then the sound of boots pounding the pavement. The pounding came nearer, until it was right beneath our window, and then quickly faded away.

We rushed to the window, but saw nothing, and so I stepped out the kitchen door to the side porch. Across the alleyway, one of the blinds in a neighbor's window was spread apart, a face peering out. A moment later, the blind fell back, and everything was as before. Across the road, insects swarmed a streetlamp. A yellow-and-red tricycle lay forgotten at the side of the road. A curbside trash can stood with its cover balanced precariously over an oversize load of white trash bags. Nothing out of the ordinary.

Gitty joined me on the porch. "See anything?"

"No. Must've been a few bored *bucherim* doing something harmless." Yeshiva students were often up late on Saturday nights, after napping for hours during the day.

Gitty and I went to bed. In the morning, when I awoke, Gitty was not in her bed, but I could hear her voice from the kitchen. "*Meshiguim! Chayess!*" she cried. "Morons! Animals!"

I headed to the kitchen, where Tziri and Freidy sat at the yellow Little Tikes table in the corner, empty bowls in front of them, waiting quietly for someone to pour their cereal and milk. Gitty sat at the kitchen table, the phone to her ear and an incredulous look on her face. I could hear through the receiver the excited voice of one of her sisters—from the faint pitch, I could tell it was Bashie, the family's most reliable source of village gossip.

"Who? What?" I mouthed.

Gitty held up an index finger. I tried to pick up the conversation from the fragments but couldn't glean much. In the meantime, I got a box of Cheerios from the pantry and poured them into the girls' bowls. Tziri put her hand over her bowl as I was about to pour the milk. "Only till the middle," she said. She didn't like her Cheerios too soggy.

Finally, Gitty hung up the phone, still shaking her head. "Remember those sounds last night?" she asked. "They slashed Amrom Pollack's tires and smashed his car windows."

I could tell from her voice that she was angry but also reticent, as if knowing we would end up arguing. Amrom Pollack was a quiet man from across the street, several years younger than I. I didn't know much about him, except that, like me, he was originally from Brooklyn, and that his father was the rabbi of a small Borough Park shul. Amrom and his wife had had their first baby boy a week ago, and the rumors had begun to spread soon after.

"He's holding the bris in Borough Park," people said. "At his father's shul."

Some said it sadly, a lament—what had we done to deserve this? Others reacted with anger. "The insolence of him!" Avrumi Gold shouted in the mikveh on Friday afternoon.

Others said it with disbelief, shaking their heads. "I don't envy him," Chezky said to me as we drank our coffee from Styrofoam cups before services on Shabbos morning. "Hard to believe he'll get away with it."

Later that morning, I saw the damaged car, parked right at the entrance to Amrom's apartment. A burgundy Toyota Corolla, likely purchased secondhand, all but one of the tires flattened, and all four windows smashed. Glass shards were spread across the pavement, and a handful of young boys were circling, inspecting the damage.

"This is insane!" I fumed to Gitty later that day. "We're no better than the Taliban!"

But Gitty didn't like that kind of talk. Earlier, she had been out-raged, but now she said that maybe the Pollacks had brought it upon themselves. "They don't have to live here," she said. "If you don't want to go by the rules, you can live somewhere else."

The perpetrators' names were well known, three men in their early twenties. Some hailed them as heroes. Others thought they'd been rash. "I don't hold from doing things this way," said Shia Einhorn, the leader of the a cappella group that performed each week at the Friday night tisch. "It's not the Skverer way," he said. "It's the Skverer way when there is no other way," shot back Levi Green, the mikveh caretaker. But there was no question of making any of the young men suffer any consequences. Even Amrom Pollack knew not to involve the secular authorities. This was an internal matter.

Later, the question would be fiercely debated among some of my friends: Had the incident been ordered by the rebbe himself? Chezky would argue that it must have been. Or at the very least, by the rebbe's sons. "And even if none of them ordered it," Chezky said, "they were definitely pleased."

I did not think then, nor do I think now, that the rebbe ordered a man's property damaged for dishonoring him. He didn't have to—

plenty among us were willing to act on their own. But I had to admit, I imagined the rebbe was pleased, proud of the men who would take up the spear of Phineas to fight for his honor. God was a jealous god, and so perhaps in that way, the rebbe and God were similar. Yet it gave me no comfort to realize that, possibly, just as I had misjudged the rebbe, I had misjudged God, too. What did I know of God? Had I seen Him? Heard Him speak? And what else was I taught to believe, without pausing to question it, to ask for its source, to examine its logic?

Chapter Fourteen

It was two in the morning, on the second night of Passover, and I stood at the far edge of the rebbe's seder table. Hundreds of men in white *kittels* watched as the rebbe rose from his seder couch and lifted his gold cup to welcome the prophet Elijah. The oversize front doors of the shul were dragged open by a pair of preadolescent boys in black *kasketels*, and a gust of wind blew into the shul.

Spill Your wrath upon the nations, the rebbe cried, and the men on the bleachers swayed vigorously in agreement.

I felt a tap on my shoulder, and turned to see Chezky, his arm reaching between the heads of men behind me. "I have to tell you something," he whispered. As the rebbe chanted on, I slipped away from the crowd, and we retreated to a corner.

"A friend of mine loaned me a couple of movies," he said. "I thought you might be interested in seeing them."

Chezky had been working for a year now at the Monsey yeshiva, where he continued his kiruv work. He had new friends now, who didn't think movies were so bad, and one of them had loaned him a handful of videocassettes. Chezky had watched them and found them so delightful that he could not help but want to share them. He burst into fits of laughter as he described a scene of two thieves taking off with a milk truck full of puppies stolen from a pet shop.

"You just *have* to see this. It's hysterical."

"Shh!" Someone hissed from the bleachers.

For they have destroyed Jacob, and defiled his temple, the rebbe cried.

Chezky lowered his voice. "It's called *Beethoven*."

"It's about music?"

"No, no, no, it's about a dog. The dog's name is Beethoven. This family adopts him, after a bunch of puppies get stolen—it's hard to explain, you have to see it yourself."

Spill upon them Your fury, the rebbe cried.

"I have another movie, too. An action movie—although I have to warn you: there's a naked woman in one of the scenes."

"Oh," I said.

"She comes out of a birthday cake. You probably don't want to see that. We can fast-forward through that part—it's not important to the story."

Pursue them with a vengeance, the rebbe cried. *Obliterate them from beneath the heavens!*

"Come by tomorrow night," Chezky said.

Chezky had left our world in many ways but still had the outward appearance of a Hasid, and we were in many ways alike, Hasidim, or quasi-Hasidim, questioning everything, fascinated by the most ordinary aspects of the outside world. Chezky, too, listened to the radio, read books from the library, and cherished every opportunity to discover something new.

Chezky's movies wouldn't be the first for me. At age ten, I had seen *Dumbo* at a friend's home in Borough Park, projected from an old-fashioned projector onto a white basement wall. My friend's parents were more lax with such things and allowed an animated Disney film on occasion. I remember being so moved that I cried through much of it.

When I was fourteen, soon after my father died, my sixteen-year-old sister Chani went out and rented a VCR with a television monitor for a day. My father was no longer around to forbid it, and my mother's protestations fell on my sister's apathetic adolescent ears. She locked herself in her room with a handful of videocassettes she'd rented from VideoRama around the corner—a store I had passed hundreds of times, never imagining I could enjoy its offerings—and allowed me into her room to watch *The Chosen* and selected parts of *Ferris Bueller's Day Off.* Every now and then, she would shoo me out, declaring particular segments "not for boys."

I had seen just enough to whet my appetite for more, and I now accepted Chezky's invitation eagerly. The next night, after the first days of Passover had ended, I picked up Chezky from his parents' home and we drove to his place. The yeshiva where he worked had given him a room in the dormitory, a long and narrow two-story building surrounded by immaculate lawns and well-maintained shrubbery—a far cry from the dorms we had in New Square. His room was on the second floor, and the corridor had a faint odor of moldy rugs, the décor resembling that of a low-grade chain motel. Chezky's twin-size bed was neatly made. A low bookcase stood against the wall, and in the corner, sitting atop a compact desk, was a small television monitor.

"They let you have a TV?" A television in a yeshiva struck me like a pirate in a rabbi's caftan, but Chezky just shrugged.

"It's not mine," he said. "I borrowed it from the office." He had already explained that this yeshiva was different, but I hadn't realized just how different.

Chezky slipped a videocassette into the VCR slot, and for the next ninety minutes I sat, riveted, from the first frame of the FBI warning until the very last of the credits. *Beethoven* was a comedy about puppies and goofy dog thieves (later I would know them as Stanley Tucci and Oliver Platt) and an all-American family with handsome parents who slept in one bed and kissed good night before snuggling in each other's arms. Chezky and I laughed and cried, and when it was done, we rewound the tape and watched it all over again.

Afterward, Chezky slipped in the second tape, an action thriller called *Under Siege*. This one made me feel as if the world had turned dizzyingly, terrifyingly intense, with a ship carrying nuclear missiles hijacked by a band of terrorists for reasons I could not quite make out but that didn't seem to matter much. I had yet to learn the term "escapist entertainment," but never before had I felt so transported from reality.

Sometime during that second movie came the scene with the birthday cake. I didn't get to see much of it. As soon as Chezky saw the giant cake, he grabbed the remote and pressed a button. This was, ostensibly, for my sake, the still-semi-pious Hasid. The tape screeched faintly as the images swished on the screen in a half blur. It was like viewing something underwater through leaky goggles but in fast motion, although I could easily make out the nearly naked blond woman who popped out jerkily from the top of the cake. I turned my head to look away, but the corner of my eye remained fixed on the screen, wanting desperately for Chezky to let go of the fast-forward button but too embarrassed to say anything.

After the movie, Chezky and I sat in his room and talked, snacking on potato chips and Fresca. We discussed plot points and memorable quotes with the kind of enthusiasm we usually reserved for talmudic texts. Soon, however, we grew tired. It was three in the morning. I had told Gitty that I was going to Chezky's place, without elaborating, and I knew that if I didn't get home soon, things would get unpleasant.

I wasn't ready to leave, though. When I had first entered Chezky's room, I had noticed his small bookcase in the corner, and glanced at the book's titles. They, too, beckoned, like the movies—except these books felt dangerous. They were books about faith. Not my kind of faith, but Chezky's kind. The rational kind. The wrong kind.

As I was getting ready to leave, I noticed those books again.

Chezky excused himself to use the bathroom out in the hallway, and in the meantime I put on my coat and shtreimel. A moment later, I heard voices out in the hallway, a conversation between Chezky and one of his dorm mates about a leaky faucet or a clogged toilet. The voices went on for a while, and now, with silence in the room, the night's featured amusements finished, I looked over to Chezky's bookshelf. As with the naked woman in the movie, I knew I should look away, and yet I couldn't.

I stepped closer to the bookshelf. A set of volumes caught my eye. They were titled *Permission to Believe* and *Permission to Receive*. Two slim volumes, one blue and one red, by the same author. I read their jacket covers.

Rational approaches to God's existence. Rational approaches to the Torah's divine origin.

"You want to borrow those?" Chezky was back in the room, looking over my shoulder.

I shook my head. "Nah. This doesn't make any sense to me."

"Why do you say that?"

I sighed. "We've been over this already."

I'd made this point to him many times. The things we believed could be sustained only by suspending our normal faculties of reason. We believed in a God we could not see or hear. We believed that this God showed up one fine day in a Middle Eastern desert and said to our forefathers: *Here are the rules you must live by, forever and ever.* We believed in an afterlife, in the resurrection of the dead. We believed in the most fantastical occurrences as part of our history. God's voice from a burning bush. The waters of an entire land turning into a sticky soup of blood. The sudden deaths of every male firstborn Egyptian, at the stroke of midnight, without so much as a sneezing spell beforehand. These things could not be believed rationally, and thinking too much about them could do no one much good.

"Read the books," Chezky said. "Maybe they'll change your mind."

I wanted to. In fact, I was burning with curiosity, but to read these books felt treacherous, like stepping onto a tightrope across rocky river rapids with no tightrope-walking skills. This was exactly what the rabbis had warned about. *Chakirah,* they called it. Rational inquiry. And it led, they warned, to bad things.

Rational inquiry increases vanity and leads to sin, said Jacob Emden, an eighteenth-century German rabbi.

The Greeks, wrote Reb Elimelech Shapira of Munkatch, *invented rational thought. And what did they bring to the world? Darkness! Heresy!*

God forbid—I should be like the Greeks?

"No, thanks," I said. "And you probably shouldn't be reading them, either."

Chezky shrugged. "Just remember this: when blind faith is all you have, you end up slashing people's car tires for not inviting the rebbe to a bris."

"Tell me," Chezky said, a few days later in the foyer of the shul, where we met each week before Friday night prayers. "Has it occurred to you that it is simply an accident that you were raised with your beliefs? That if you were born Christian or Muslim you'd be just as convinced about those faiths being true? If blind faith is all you have, doesn't it make it all so arbitrary?"

It was a simple question, but I had always assumed that such a question needed no answer. The many great thinkers of the Jewish tradition had already figured it out, I was sure. Who was I to start asking the obvious?

I walked home from shul with a mild feeling of resentment toward Chezky. Why was he so insistent? Why did he keep asking these questions? Yet the question unsettled me, like a scab you know not to scratch and yet you can't help it. Indeed, what *was* the answer? In spite of myself, I began to wonder: If I hadn't been born and raised into Judaism, would I have chosen it? If I had not been taught to recite the Shema at age two, Torah Tziva at three, prayers and Psalms at four, the Bible at five, and Talmud at eight, would I have believed in it all as I did now?

Later that evening, while I recited the kiddush before our Shabbos dinner, sang the Sabbath hymns with my two young daughters, and mumbled my way through *bentchen*, Chezky's question continued to bother me. Afterward, as I sat with friends and studied *Ohr haChaim*, the classic Bible commentary by the Moroccan Jewish scholar Chaim ibn Atar, I continued to wonder: Would I have chosen this, if I had had a choice? Would I have accepted the existence of God, if I hadn't been raised with it? Would I have believed in the Torah as His word? Would I have chosen to be Orthodox? To be Hasidic? To be Skver?

Chezky and I soon made a habit of going out on Saturday nights. Often we'd head to Jerusalem Pizza on Route 59, where Chezky liked his slices burned to a crisp, and the owner, a genial Vizhnitz Hasid with a silvery beard and wire-rimmed glasses, would come by and chat for a few minutes. Occasionally, we'd drive to Blockbuster afterward, and Chezky would head inside and rent us a movie, which we would take back to his room and watch on the small television monitor he kept borrowing from the office. I would never go into Blockbuster with him, though. New Square's Vaad Hatznius, the Modesty Committee, was known to come after individuals for lesser offenses.

One Saturday night, we sat in my car talking, cracking sunflower seeds between our teeth and filling an empty coffee cup with their shells. Again, as so often happened, we came to questions of faith. And this time, finally worn down by Chezky's insistence on his superior approach, my resistance dissolved. "Fine," I said to Chezky. "Give me your proofs."

He looked at me, startled. I'd given no warning that I was about to change my position, but I'd been thinking about it over the previous days, and decided that I would hear him out.

"Give me the proof that God showed up on a mountain and gave the Torah to the children of Israel. Give me the *rational* view."

Chezky appeared to be softly biting the inside of his lower lip, as if gathering his thoughts. "You really want to hear it?"

"I do."

"OK," he nodded, silent for a moment. He then fixed his gaze on me intently. "It's simple. You can't invent a historically memorable event, unless it really happened."

I shook my head, confused. "What does that mean?"

"The giving of the Torah was a mass revelation. No other religion claims that, and that's what makes Judaism different. You simply can't get people to believe in an event of historical significance if the event didn't actually take place."

"Why not?"

"Because no one can stand up and tell an entire people: Your grandparents once stood at a mountain and saw God and heard His voice. The people would turn right around and say: I think our grandparents would've mentioned it."

There was something strange about the logic he was positing, as if the clarity of it lay just beyond reach, attainable with only a little hard thinking. It didn't make perfect sense, but I was intrigued enough to want to hear more.

"Think of Jesus," Chezky said. I knew almost nothing about Jesus, but Chezky claimed to have read the New Testament, and was familiar with Jesus's miracles. He was unimpressed. "There's a reason why Jesus's miracles were claimed to have been witnessed only by small numbers." He waved his hand dismissively, as if curing lepers and healing the blind were things he did routinely himself.

"Same thing with Islam," Chezky said. "Muhammad claimed that he was visited by the angel Gabriel. So? You either believe it or you don't. It's not a very bold claim."

But the Jewish claim was bold. It took chutzpah to tell an entire nation that 3 million of their ancestors were witness to the most astonishing event in human history. It took such chutzpah, in fact, that it could not be done, Chezky said, unless the event in question had actually occurred.

I offered the obvious responses. Every people, every faith, had its founding myths. I was not an expert in the perpetuation of legend, but I was pretty sure that humans were gullible enough to be convinced of anything if the circumstances were right. And so, I told Chezky, his logic failed. As I had predicted it would.

It was one of those nights when the hours flew by without our realizing it and still we sat in my car, talking, arguing, shouting, pleading for the other to just shut up and listen. Twice we left the car to stroll up and down the parking lot outside Chezky's dorm, and twice we had returned to the car after an hour in the predawn chill. Soon the sun began to peek through the leaves of Ohr Somayach's pastoral grounds, and Chezky and I were still arguing. To me, it was clear: It was all precisely as I had predicted. Logic will get you nowhere if it's faith you're after.

Except, now I couldn't help but wonder: What if, in fact, we all *were* fooled? After all, I'd just spent seven hours arguing that it was possible.

Chezky told me later that the "proof" he presented was an argument known as the Kuzari principle, formulated by the twelfth-century Iberian Jewish poet and philosopher Judah Halevi, and now that I'd heard it, I began to look up books on the subject. The more I read, the more I wanted the argument to work, and the more I wanted it to work, the more its flaws became apparent. I went back and forth between thinking that the Kuzari principle was the most ingenious argument I'd ever heard to being dismayed by its apparent sophistry. It wasn't long before I realized that, whatever its merits, it was not straightforward, and so it was hard to know whether its complexity was that of an elaborate mathematical equation or of an optical illusion, fooling the observer into seeing something that was not there.

Soon I was creeping into related subjects: arguments for God's existence, reconciling talmudic assertions with modern science, responses to the claims of Bible criticism. These were subjects that had never bothered me before, but once I started, I couldn't stop.

At Itzik's, a Judaica shop on Route 59, I would browse the shelves to find more books on these subjects and others. This was a shop unlike the other Judaica stores in Monsey. It carried books and audiotapes and videos not sold elsewhere, many of them on controversial topics: books about evolution and the big bang and Bible criticism and biographies of sages and saints in which the subjects were treated as human, rather than the superhuman legends produced by Orthodox publishing houses.

Itzik himself, the store's middle-aged proprietor, was a blithesome fellow whose love of books was matched only by his irreverence. Alongside Aleph-Bet jigsaw puzzles and silver-plated menorahs was a wall of baseball caps with Yiddish-peppered, subtly subversive slogans, which Itzik himself had designed:

> *Official Litvak shtreimel.*
> *I wish I could afford a Borsalino like my son-in-law in kollel.*
> *I'm stringent about things you never heard of.*

One day, I went to look for a particular book on modern scholarship on the Bible. I had seen mention of it on the Internet and thought that perhaps Itzik's might have it, but when I didn't see it on any of the shelves, I turned to Itzik himself, who stood at the cash register adding up figures in a dog-eared notebook. When I mentioned the name of the book, Itzik looked up and fixed me with a stare I could not immediately decipher.

"Who *are* you?" he asked.

"My name, you mean?"

"No," he said, and shook his head. "Never mind." He asked me to wait while he headed to his office in the back. Five minutes later, he was back with the book.

"Yeah," he said, as he swiped my Visa card. "What's your name?"

When I told him, he nodded, and I could see that he was storing something, my identity, perhaps—my face, my name, the book I purchased—into some mental repository. I had been to his store many times, for yarmulkes, Hebrew calendars, religious texts, Jewish musical albums, and novels from Orthodox publishing houses, but I realized that until that day, Itzik hadn't seen me. His was a popular store, and I was one of a great mass of customers. He was usually too busy shouting instructions to an employee, or answering the phone, or helping some elderly lady find a bar mitzvah gift for her grandson.

Now, clearly, he'd taken note of me.

I headed out the door, the plastic bag under my arm, with the friendly "Itzik's" logo—the image of a bearded man in a golf cap and tzitzis, underneath the store's slogan: "Because Itzik's has it all!"

Soon I would return for other books, and I would learn more about Itzik. The rabbis in our world were fond of book bans, but Itzik was not. In back, he kept a closet in which he stored items too sensitive for public display, which he kept for special customers.

It appeared that I had joined the ranks of his special customers, which felt like a small consolation for the troubled, feverish inquiry that I had embarked on. What I really wanted was something else. *Itzik, give me the book that will make the questions go away,* I wanted to plead. Yet in my heart, I knew there was no such one book. There could be no authoritative response, no single all-encompassing theory that would explain it all. I was beginning to realize that every book I read set off a tempest of conflicting thoughts and ideas, and this was not something I could find answers to from outside myself. The answers were not in a book but within. I was on my own.

Soon I began to spend hours at Chezky's place, reading his books, listening to his cassettes, watching his videos. Chezky wouldn't know it until years later, but what I was doing then was hoping for something to get my faith back—and now any kind of faith, blind or rational, would do. A strange thing had happened: once Chezky began to present rational arguments for faith, I tried to disprove them, and yet I found that I was rooting not for my side but for his. I could feel the faith that I had clung to blindly for so many years slowly slipping away, and it was then that I realized that I wanted my faith to be rational. I *needed* it to be rational. As if a switch had been flipped, I realized that I had lost the ability to simply accept what I had believed for so long. I needed Chezky's approach to work.

I came to know a handful of Chezky's dorm mates, students from Long Island and St. Louis and Los Angeles, born and raised in secular homes, with maybe a spot of Hebrew school, a lavish bar mitzvah, but with otherwise little attachment to Judaism. Only now were they coming to Orthodox observance, through the very books I was reading and the tapes I was listening to. As they moved toward deeper religiosity, I was moving away. The same books, the same lectures, the same video presentations by philosopher-rabbis—the very things that were drawing them close were having the opposite effect on me.

On Saturday mornings, instead of heading to the seat in shul that I'd purchased for $2,500—and was still making payments on—I would stand with Chezky in the foyer, and we would talk about the books we were reading. I would argue their flaws, no longer because I thought my faith superior but because his kind of faith was quickly becoming the only kind that held any hope for me. I needed for him to defend them. I needed for him to prove my own arguments wrong. As much as Chezky tried, though, I remained unconvinced.

After shul, we would walk home together, and Chezky and I would stand in front of my home on Bush Lane, with Gitty looking out from the side porch. Unable to let go, we would still be arguing long after the neighbors could be heard singing the Sabbath hymns through their wide-open windows, eating their sautéed liver and p'tcha, their chulent and kishke, and then retiring for their Sabbath afternoon naps. Tziri and Freidy would come walking down the pathway from the side steps of our apartment. "Tatti, Mommy is waiting." But Chezky and I could find no resolution. The questions had become too urgent, the flaws in the answers too gaping wide. Eventually, we would reluctantly agree to take it up again in the evening, when we would meet at the shul for the afternoon prayers and the rebbe's final tisch of the day.

Chapter Fifteen

Among people who lose faith, I would later learn, many point to scientific knowledge as the catalyst for their changed worldviews. I, too, found much of what I learned troubling. Wherever I turned, I discovered that ideas I had once taken for granted, trusting in rabbis and sacred texts to convey absolute truths, were dubious at best. The universe was not six thousand years old but closer to 14 billion. Humans shared a common ancestor with apes—and all living things, for that matter—and were not the exalted species created by God's hand out of clay of the earth on the sixth day of Creation. The sages of the Talmud, by our traditions infallible, were demonstrably wrong in their understanding of the natural world.

Two great balls of fire descended from heaven, and their names were Abaya and Rava, said the old rebbe of Ruzhin. The two great masters of the Talmud, their names occurring at least once every three pages, were not humans but chunks of divinity. Balls of fire.

Reading the Talmud anew, however, I discovered that the sages were as flawed as could be expected of any ancient people. They were mired in superstition and misogyny and xenophobia, which did not necessarily mark them as villains but offered troubling indications of ordinary humanness.

Nothing, however, had a more shattering impact on my faith than the realization that, stripped of religious exegesis, our primary religious text, the Hebrew Bible, had the markings of human rather than divine authorship; it was beautiful, intricate, layered in poetry and metaphor and heart-stopping drama, but human nonetheless.

According to the Zohar, the eleventh-century work that forms the basic text for the Judaic mystical tradition, *God gazed upon the Torah and created the universe.* The Torah, divine and eternal, was the blueprint for all existence.

Now, however, I could no longer see it that way. The very essence of our faith, passed down, it was believed, from generation to generation over 3,300 years without change, was most likely a collection of ancient documents authored and compiled and redacted over many centuries. This was the view of all modern Bible scholars. I didn't have to take their word for it, but the evidence for their view was compelling. Suddenly, all the strangeness of this text, the contradictions and anachronisms and troubling tales of fratricide and genocide and great family dramas and tales of wondrous miracles, all of it now made sense—but in an entirely new way. Seen through the prism of history and anthropology, buttressed by studies in archaeology and laid side by side with other texts from the ancient peoples of the Near East, the Bible was an endlessly fascinating window into the world of our ancestors. But as a basis for theology, to me, it simply fell short.

Chezky and I began to drift apart after several years, when it became clear that he was not troubled by these matters as I was. He had the answers, he said, and his faith, rational and sound, was strong. But when I sought that same level of certainty, I could not find it.

At one point, Chezky gave me the name of a Monsey rabbi to speak to. An unusual Hasid, this rabbi was said to have read all the great philosophers. He knew of all the challenges to faith, and he knew the answers, too, Chezky said. When I went to speak to this rabbi, though, in the book-lined study of his Monsey home, he could offer me little.

"Oh, it's all been written about," the rabbi said, when I asked how a merciful God could order the genocide of entire nations and how the essential command of our faith—you must believe in the Torah because the Torah declares that you must—could be so maddeningly circular.

How is it, I asked the rabbi, that our understanding of God—benevolent and all-powerful and lovingly, unfailingly attentive to our needs—so conveniently mirrors the ideal qualities we seek in humans? How is it that we attribute to God feelings such as sadness and joy and pleasure, and even want for our love, when one would expect an omnipotent and omniscient being to be far removed from the qualities that signify the frailty of humans?

"Asked and answered," the rabbi said, as if, once again, I was meddling in the affairs of greater minds than mine. "It's a little bit . . . childish," he added, pausing before issuing his insult, "to think that your questions are anything new." I could see his patronizing gaze through the veil of his benign smile. "Go learn. Study. And then, if you look inside your heart, you'll find the truth."

But that was precisely it. My questions did not strike me as novel or profound, but basic and elementary. The evasiveness that characterized so many of the responses, from this rabbi and others, suggested that the answers were a tangled spaghetti of sophistry meant to obfuscate rather than illuminate. And always, there were instructions to look further, elsewhere. I hadn't read the right books. I hadn't spoken to the right people. I was asked to place my trust in authorities who had not earned such trust—who had, in fact, declared demonstrable falsehoods as truth, distorted ancient texts to mean things they clearly did not, and recast historical events and figures to align with current ideologies.

If you look inside your heart, you'll find the truth, that rabbi said, and I looked inside my heart and discovered that there was no truth, anywhere, not inside my heart and not outside it, only the scalding furnace in which my beliefs were now smoldering embers.

"What happened?"

This would be asked years later by strangers, who, for one reason or another, would ask to see my photo ID. Bank tellers. Bartenders. The lady at the Rite Aid store where I'd buy my Marlboro Lights. Even a policeman who stopped me for a routine speeding ticket on the Palisades Parkway. The photo on my driver's license would be of a Hasid, but before them would be a bareheaded, beardless man in secular garb. Usually, I could tell it was coming. They would look at the photo, then at me, then back at the photo. "That you?"

I would nod, and they would look at the photo again, then ask, casually, the way you notice a stain on someone's shirt, or a bruised chin, or a bad haircut: "What happened?" Did you spill your coffee? Did you have a shaving accident? Did you forget to instruct the barber, walked in a Hasid and came out a shaygetz?

I would offer a curt smile. "Life." Or, "Long story." What else could I say?

Sometimes I would imagine the conversations. I would tell the bank teller everything I learned about the ancient Israelites, about the migration from Egypt that probably never happened, about the walls of Jericho that existed, according to archaeologists, centuries after the Bible declares that they had fallen. I would tell the cop about the United Kingdom of Israel—from the Mediterranean to the Euphrates—that never was. About King Josiah, in the seventh century BC, who cemented the faith of the ancient Judaeans from Canaanite idolatry to Judaic monotheism.

"You want to know what *happened?*" I would imagine telling the bartender with the gauged earlobe and the tattoo in the shape of California on her neck. I'd be sitting in a grungy dive in Bushwick and nursing a Pabst, considering whether to tell her about Wellhausen and the documentary hypothesis. About Genesis and all the duplicate narratives; two creation stories, two Adams, two flood narratives, and how Occam's Razor teaches us to seek simplicity—multiple human authors is more plausible than a divine one who lacked basic editing skills.

I would imagine these conversations, but I would not have them. *That's not what they want to hear,* I would say to myself. They want to hear what *happened.* What was the incident? The moment that changed it all. But there was no moment, no solid line across time to which I could point and say: *That's* when I became a nonbeliever.

I often think back to particular times—a conversation with a fellow commuter about local elections, an argument with my boss about a work project, the first time I visited a barbershop—and wonder: Was I still a believer then?

In my memory, it is a blur. I had first become friends with Chezky in the spring of 1996, when I was twenty-two. By 2002, I no longer thought myself a believer. But within that period of six years, when was the moment I became an *apikorus?*

My memories themselves are filled with contradictions.

I remember one particular week with Gitty and the children on a rare family vacation, when we took two rooms at the Chalet Hotel in the Catskills. It was a sprawling property, its structures decrepit, the basketball and tennis courts filled with tall grass sticking up from between concrete slabs that had, over the years, as if slipping and sliding, shifted out of place, sinking into the ground in one corner, rising several inches in another. Decades before, the place had served as a vacation resort to a more discriminating clientele, but now it was advertised as a summer getaway for Hasidic families, who didn't need basketball and tennis courts and were happy just to have gourmet kosher food and a ritual bath and a small synagogue.

It must have been the lack of routine that got me thinking. At home, going to shul was like brushing my teeth or putting on my shoes. It was what I did, without giving it much thought. But away from home, I felt a sudden need for purpose. I had no routine for going to a little bungalow shul, worshiping with strangers, and using unfamiliar prayer books, and it suddenly all felt so strange: *I am no longer a believer. Why am I doing this?* I remember holding a prayer book and mumbling the words of prayer, and thinking: *This is pointless. There is no one listening.*

Afterward, in the communal dining room, I sat with Gitty and the children and looked at all the other families, each assigned their own table, a modified version of what they must've looked like in their own dining rooms, boys on one side, girls on the other, some parents sitting side by side while others sat at opposite ends. They came from all over—New York, New Jersey, Montreal, families of five, ten, fifteen, men in tall, stiff shtreimels, women wearing their best wigs and elegant Shabbos dresses, children in matching outfits. As waiters in crisp black vests brought trays of sautéed liver and egg salad and chulent, I looked around and wondered: Am I the only nonbeliever here? At home, I couldn't imagine it otherwise, but here, among strangers, it made me wonder.

And yet, I remember the night of Shavuos that same year, when it was customary to stay up all night studying Torah. I sat for five hours with my friend Motty over the laws of betrothal, the various ways in which a man might "acquire" a wife, rising from our Talmuds only as the sun's first rays came through the tall synagogue windows. I remember on that Shavuos morning feeling as if nothing mattered but the wonderful pleasure of spending hours immersed in the scholarly wrangling of ancient precepts. Was I not a believer *then*, even as I sat and studied on the night we celebrated the giving of the Torah?

I remember only the haze of months, then years, passing as I desperately wished for my faith to return, even as I realized that, like a broken porcelain dish, the pieces might be glued back together and the dish might hold for a while but soon enough it would break again, along that very same crack.

Losing your faith is not like realizing that you got an arithmetic problem wrong. It is more like discovering your entire mathematical system is flawed, that every calculation you've ever made was incorrect. Your bank balance is off, your life savings might be gone, your business could be in the red when you've imagined it to be flourishing. Except you seem to be the only one who realizes it, and how is that possible? Is everyone crazy? Could you really be the only sane one? And if the entire world goes by a flawed system, doesn't it, in some odd way, make the wrong way right? Or at least, there is consistency; they're in sync, zigzagging together, while you walk the straight line all alone. And yet, you know, you *know* that you are right and they are wrong, and that you can demonstrate it if given the chance, but they won't give you the chance. You cannot speak of it because if you do, you will be like the lunatic who prophesies end-of-times doom and gloom, or like the one heralding some New Age brand of salvation and redemption. Passersby can barely be bothered to snigger.

++

The inner turmoil left me dizzy with grief over my lost faith. I wanted it back. I wanted the feelings of ecstasy I'd had from reciting Nishmas Kol Chai or singing Yedid Nefesh. I wanted to feel the words of Torah as, in the words of the Talmud, *black fire on white*. I wanted to study the Hasidic texts I had once found so much joy in, experience again the euphoria of singing "God, the Master of All Creation" with thousands of other Hasidim, and feel the near-tangible presence of the sublime.

But it was all gone.

The comforts of prayer, too, were no longer available. For some years, I tried to hold on to them, even as I wasn't sure there was value to it, clinging particularly to the meditative experience of reciting Psalms. Yet as the years passed, I began to see in those words only the mounting frustration of attempting to retrieve something I had lost, even while knowing it was futile. Chezky had tempted me with the rational, and I had succumbed to its allure. The universe, as if in response, said: *You want rational? Well, here's rational.* And it removed from me all those irrational but vital comforts.

Worst of all was the realization that I had to build myself a new value system. When everything you've ever known is suddenly up for question, what are the values you retain and what do you discard? What is the meaning of right and wrong when there is no guidance from a divine being? And most of all, if we are all but accidents of matter and energy, with no greater purpose beyond our immediate natural needs, what, then, was the point of it all?

PART III

Chapter Sixteen

In the dining room of our new home, two men, employed by the moving company, were reassembling the breakfront. One of them, tall and broad-shouldered, was concentrating on the work, a power drill in his hand and a handful of screws in his mouth, pointy sides in. The second man, short and stocky, looked around, vaguely distracted. Then his gaze fell on the two kids around me.

"Hey, there, little guy," the man said to Akiva, who was now almost three and clasped my hand, vaguely frightened of these strangers in our strange new home.

In my other arm, I held one-year-old Hershy, who was born in November 2001. With five children, we'd long outgrown the two-bedroom apartment on Bush Lane, and were now moving to a new place one block away, on Reagan Road. Finally, we could afford to buy a home of our own, two floors, four bedrooms, two and a half baths, and our very own front lawn, with a newly planted Japanese maple and a pair of white rosebushes.

The boys and I watched the movers go about their work. A few minutes later, the girls stomped in, home from school, and dropped their schoolbags in the hallway.

"*All* these kids yours?" the short one asked, his eyes opening wide.

"Yep." I tried to look proud.

"Some brood," the taller one said. The screws were no longer in his mouth, and now he, too, looked up from his work. "You rich or somethin'?"

"No. But each and every child is a blessing," I said. That was the line, when outsiders asked.

The men nodded and pursed their lips with what appeared to be tentative admiration.

It was true, each child was a blessing. Yet I couldn't tell these men that if I'd have had my way, things would be different.

Gitty and I had talked about birth control. Or rather, I brought it up, and Gitty always had the same three words in response. "It is forbidden." Her resolute tone declared the discussion over.

I hadn't known about birth control until years after our marriage. Once, back when we were expecting Tziri, I heard an acquaintance say that, on average, Borough Park Hasidim had fewer children than other Hasidim. Eight instead of twelve, the man said. I was baffled, but too embarrassed to ask: how do they do it? I knew only the barest facts. Sex brought pregnancy, which brought babies, and that was that. None of it, as far as I knew, was optional. Not even the sex, which, according to Jewish law, a husband was to provide weekly—it was all in the marriage contract.

Eventually, I learned about birth control the way I learned about much of modern life: through the Internet. I also learned that its use was not permitted. Or permitted only under special circumstances. Or permitted only by certain rabbis, and our rabbi was not one of them.

After three children, I thought it would be wise to take a break, but Gitty wouldn't consider any form of birth control without rabbinic permission. Since our rabbi wouldn't permit it, any rabbi who would was, ipso facto, not a good enough rabbi.

After our fourth, I tried again to reason with her, but Gitty protested that she would feel naked if she wasn't either pregnant or pushing a baby stroller. "People will look at me funny," she said, and I sympathized. Who wants to be looked at funny?

After our fifth, I finally declared it was time.

"Which of them would you give up?" Gitty asked, and we looked at our children, the four older ones around the kitchen table, and Hershy on her hip.

Which would I give up?

We were a family of seven now, and I could not imagine it any other way. I loved my children for the ways they resembled one another, but even more for the ways in which they were distinct.

Tziri devoured books. *Just like me*, I would say to anyone who listened. Wins every spelling bee. Corrects her teacher's grammar mistakes. Beats me at Scrabble. I was proud when, a year or so earlier, she leaned in as I read the *New York Times* at our kitchen table. I thought she was scanning the advertisements, until she looked up and asked: "Who's Pope John Paul Eye-Eye?" I was proud, though a little concerned. The pope was in the news because of the sex-abuse scandals of Catholic priests, and I began to worry about what else Tziri might be reading over my shoulder.

Freidy, sixteen months younger and eager to stand apart from Tziri, wouldn't touch a book unless it was absolutely necessary—only for schoolwork and prayers. Rosy-cheeked and plump, she was vivacious and quick with an eager laugh. She had more friends than Gitty and I could keep track of. "Oh, hello there, nice of you to visit again," I'd say to whatever friend Freidy brought home on Sunday afternoons, imagining it to be the same as the little girl who came last week, and Freidy would hiss at me desperately, "This is a *different* one!"

Chaya Suri, five, was a shy little girl, with big, dark eyes and chestnut hair. She resented being grouped with the little ones, but families orient themselves in natural ways, and such was her lot: earlier bedtimes, the colorful, cartoon-covered dishes and fat little forks, always being shooed away from Tziri and Freidy's collaborations on arts and crafts projects or impromptu dance performances. Instead, Chaya Suri turned to the little boys behind her, showing early signs of a tomboyish nature. Later, I'd think of her as a Hasidic version of Harper Lee's Scout, skinny and agile and often up in a tree, gazing out at the world from a place in which no one would bother her.

Akiva, three, was always by my side, reaching for my hand, silent, with a smile that could melt stone. A beautiful child, with an angelic face and silky blond hair, he brought squeals of delight from his dozen aunts and his many older female cousins, and often, too, from strangers on the street.

Hershy was just a toddler, but within a few years, he would show his personality, which was one of effortless indifference to convention. He was the kind of kid who would wear one roller skate but couldn't be bothered with the other, and he'd go half-skating, half-limping down the sidewalk.

Which would I give up?

The thought made me fidget, sending my mind into a twist for a minute, but of course, there was a difference between preventing a child that did not exist, and contemplating which of our children I would rather not have. I wanted these five, no more, no less, and not a different set of five. If we had a sixth, I was certain that I would love him or her, as I did the others; yet the sixth did not exist, and so I could imagine life without it.

I tried to explain this to Gitty, but she declared with finality: "I don't want to talk about it," and transferred another load of laundry from the washer to the dryer.

If we could not talk about it, only one option was left. The nuclear option. The Samson option. I felt like a bad husband, a *wrong* husband, lacking some essential masculine quality. Men were supposed to want sex, always, regardless of the consequences—that, at least, was what I had read on the Internet—and perhaps I wasn't so different either, except that I was not prepared to have another child. I was no longer a believer, and in some far recess of my mind, I wondered if I might one day leave this lifestyle behind. I had no such plans—it didn't seem even remotely possible—but I knew that, should that dream become a possibility, having more children was the first thing not to do.

More than anything, though, we simply didn't have the resources. Each child brought new expenses—food and clothes and school tuition and extra bedrooms and Lego sets and colorful pencil cases and, soon enough, there would be bar mitzvahs and weddings, exorbitant expenditures that caused relentless anxiety for every Hasidic man through three decades of middle age and often far beyond. It simply made no sense to let nature take its course, so I presented Gitty with an ultimatum. Without a reliable method of birth control, we would cease our twice-weekly postmidnight amusements.

Whether it was the ultimatum itself, or the realization of how much this truly mattered to me, Gitty finally relented. If I could find a "real" rabbi—not some English-speaking, clean-shaven, university-degree-holding one, but one close enough to our kind—she would accept a dispensation, if it was granted.

I called Chezky, who gave me the name of just such a rabbi. This rabbi had quite a beard, Chezky said, with not a hair trimmed, as far as he could tell. The rabbi spoke Yiddish, too. He had studied at the finest Lithuanian yeshivas in Jerusalem, but never, to anyone's knowledge, had set foot in a university.

"And he's easy," Chezky said. "He rules by law, not ideology."

Easy was good, and so a few nights later, I drove to the Monsey address I'd written on a Post-it note, a small ranch house on Calvert Drive, just across the street from the rabbi's shul. I watched as a trickle of men left after evening prayers, and then made my way up the driveway to the side door. Hanging from the doorknob was a white supermarket plastic bag, in which there seemed to be a pair of women's underwear.

"What is the problem?" the rabbi asked, after he invited me into his basement study and showed me to a metal folding chair opposite his desk. Large photos of Lithuanian sages graced the walls, as if to remind both rabbi and supplicant who the real authority was in the room.

The problem, I told the rabbi, was that I didn't think it sensible to keep having children without a responsible plan on how to provide for them. I had spent years struggling to find a job, and while I was now doing well financially, the stresses of providing for five children was burden enough. I didn't think I had it in me for six, twelve, or seventeen.

The rabbi tapped his fingers impatiently on his desk. *"Parnosse kumt fun himmel,"* he said. God has the financial plan. This was not the concern of mortals.

This was unexpected. Chezky had said this rabbi was easy. This was clearly not easy. I tried to restate the problem, using different words, gesticulating for emphasis, but the rabbi was unmoved. He shrugged and shook his head lightly. "Eh," he said.

There was something in his manner, however, that suggested he could be talked into this. He seemed like an affable fellow, with a broad smile, and I had a vague notion that his curt responses were deliberate, as if to elicit from me the right words. I could not leave without the necessary dispensation, but what were the right words? I racked my brain for the kinds of circumstances for which Jewish law allowed special accommodations. Then it dawned on me: make it a health problem. Health problems could always be counted on for loopholes in the law.

And so I offered a lie.

"The truth is," I told the rabbi, "my wife just can't take any more of it. She feels like she's going out of her mind. It's just too much." I told the rabbi that my wife was suffering from depression and a variety of other ailments, and was emotionally and physically spent. "She just . . ." I paused, and sighed deeply, hoping to look sad and convincing. "She . . . needs a break."

Now it was easy.

"That's a different matter," the rabbi said, and he shook his head with a gravely sympathetic expression. "If your wife is stressed, that isn't good for the marriage and it isn't good for the children. And it isn't good for you, either," he added with a wink and a twinkle in his eye.

He promptly proceeded to explain the options. "Condoms are never permitted. But she can use spermicide gel, contraceptive pills, or an IUD." He gave me the rundown on how they all worked, as if he were a doctor, describing the benefits and drawbacks of each.

"If you use gel," he said, "it must be inserted shortly before the act." The rabbi shook his head from side to side a couple of times, as if considering some thorny legal matter. "The problem with gel is that it can spoil the mood. You understand what I'm saying?" The Great Sage of Jerusalem looked out at me gravely from above the rabbi's head.

I felt gleeful, triumphant—I'd tricked the law onto my side. Just as I was about to leave, though, the rabbi held up his hand.

"This isn't for using indefinitely." He wanted to make sure I understood. "She can use it for a year or two. Then come back, and we'll discuss it further."

A year or two was a start, I thought, although I did wonder about the parameters. "How long must one continue to have children?" I asked as the rabbi escorted me to the door. "What's the upper limit?"

"There is no upper limit," he said. He quoted a passage in the Bible: *In the morning thou shalt sow thy seed, and in the night thou shalt not rest thy hand.* "As long as nature allows. Each child is a blessing."

As I drove home, my good feelings subsided. Yes, I had the rabbi's permission, but I had lied for it, and if I was going to lie, I could've lied years ago. I could've just told Gitty that I had received permission from our own rabbi. Gitty would never have known. In her entire life, she hadn't spoken to a rabbi, not even once—this was a husband's job, exclusively.

I told myself that my lie was not the same as not going to a rabbi at all. This was a smaller lie. Softer and whiter, and I could keep a straight face more easily when I delivered the ruling to Gitty. Although I'd elicited permission under false pretenses, the pretense was that it was for Gitty's sake. Didn't that give it a redemptive quality, maybe?

Yet it was no small comfort to me when I realized that to continue to live in this community and within this marriage, as I negotiated my own needs in accordance with my secret nonbelief, lies would be a necessity. Soon enough, my lies would become routine, the destiny of anyone in my circumstances: I was a heretic among believers.

◆◆

Late one afternoon in the following year, I was sitting on the Monsey Trails bus on my way home from work, hoping for an hour of reading and maybe a short nap. A man named Moshe Wolf, with whom I was vaguely friendly and had seen around Monsey, boarded the bus and headed to the empty seat beside me.

"*Vus machsti epes, vus?*" he asked as he placed his briefcase on the overhead rack. "How you doing, how?"

He was a fervent Satmar Hasid, and he spoke with a linguistic tic common among certain Satmars, repeating the first word at the end of each sentence.

How you doing, how?

What's up, what?

Anything new in the world, anything?

I grimaced inwardly. Moshe Wolf was something of a gabber. There go my reading plans, I thought. And my nap. From my previous interactions with him, I knew he styled himself an amateur sociologist-slash-political pundit. His Yiddish was heavily peppered with big English words: he liked *antithetical* ("aunty-tetical") and *ideologue* ("idyeh-lug"). He had a fondness for politician-intellectuals, like Senators Daniel Patrick Moynihan and Adlai Stevenson. I would often see him at the Getty gas station on Route 59, eating a bowl of chulent while reading the *New York Post*, which would be spread on the hood of his car. He was an odd combination of worldly and pious, and while I sometimes found him entertaining, I wasn't eager to engage him at the moment.

"What are you reading, what?" he asked as he made himself comfortable next to me. He leaned in to read the title at the top of the page. I flipped the front cover for his benefit, and he read it out loud, in his heavily accented English: *One People, Two Worlds: A Reform Rabbi and an Orthodox Rabbi Explore the Issues That Divide Them.*

"What is the meaning of this, what?"

As the bus snaked its way through traffic into the Lincoln Tunnel, I offered a quick overview of the book. As the subtitle explained, it was a debate between two rabbis about the merits of their respective worldviews, the liberal versus the traditional. The book had been recently published and widely written about in Jewish publications.

Moshe Wolf's eyes grew narrow. "I don't understand," he said. "This is interesting for you, this?"

I said that it was.

"But you're reading the other guy, too, but."

The *other guy*, I assumed, was the Reform rabbi, and so I explained to Moshe Wolf that I was curious to hear different views. I was fascinated by varieties of opinion.

I remember his steely look as my words sank in. He was clearly growing unsettled, and I chuckled reflexively, mildly amused. To Moshe Wolf, however, this was no laughing matter.

"This is *kefireh*, this! *Apikorsus!*" His voice was strangely, alarmingly high-pitched. "This is heresy, this! How can you read this, how?" His voice rising, he began gesticulating wildly. "This is a *rabbi*, this? How can he speak to a heretic? Who does he think he is, who!"

"Shh, quiet down, please." We were attracting stares from other passengers, and I was growing uneasy. I had been amused, for a short moment, but now I was annoyed. Yet I could not stop him. My responses, clearly, were only making things worse.

Moshe Wolf's eyeballs now appeared like spitfires of rage. What had started as a low insistent whine erupted into maniacal shrieking: "*KEFIREH! APIKORSUS!* HOW CAN YOU READ THIS, HOW? THIS IS FORBIDDEN, THIS!"

The bus fell silent. Passengers stood up in their seats to have a better look. Moshe Wolf, realizing I wasn't going to engage him further, grew even more enraged, his face bright purple. All of a sudden, he was on top of me, lunging for the book, wrestling me for it, his long arms a pair of clumsy but furious tentacles. I held on to the book, and for a few seconds we had a tug-of-war, like a pair of first-graders. This is stupid and ridiculous and more than a little comical, I thought, but Moshe Wolf clearly thought otherwise. With a sideways shove of my elbow against his chest, I managed to wrest the book from his grip, and then grabbed my briefcase and shoved past him into the aisle. Dozens of eyes watched as I headed toward the back of the bus, and all the while Moshe Wolf kept shouting: *"KEFIREH! APIKORSUS!* HERESY! BLASPHEMY!"

I found a seat in the rear, and for several minutes, I could hear Moshe Wolf carrying on down the aisle. "Who does he think he is, who? Reading a heretical book, he is reading! Right in front of our eyes, he is reading it!" Some of the other men turned to regard me, holding my gaze unself-consciously, a stare-down of the righteous against the wicked.

The bus continued past the New Jersey Meadowlands and up the New Jersey Turnpike, arriving in Monsey. I tried to keep reading in my seat in the back—to demonstrate to myself, if to no one else, that I would not be cowed—but I was shaken by Moshe Wolf's reaction. As the bus began dropping off passengers in Monsey, I realized that I had been staring at the words for almost an entire hour without reading any of them.

At home, over dinner, I told Gitty about the incident, and she listened quietly. When we were done eating, as she reached to clear our plates off the table, she lingered a moment. Her face flushed, as when she felt embarrassed, and then she looked away.

"Maybe he was right," she said as she stacked our empty plates one on top of the other. "Maybe it's best not to read those books."

In the weeks that followed, I wondered about Moshe Wolf, whom I had always taken to be somewhat worldly and, in fact, of above-average intelligence. This incident highlighted something I had often thought: the most vociferous advocates for unthinking adherence to principles, the ones inclined to protest loudest, perhaps even to resort to violence, were not necessarily those with the weakest minds. In fact, it was often those with superior minds who offered the strongest reactions, as if by doing so, they closed their own minds with that force, precisely because they were more attuned to the challenges.

Zeal compensates for fear. A soldier is whipped into a jingoistic frenzy before battle—because how else does one withstand the fear of death? The religious zealot who shouts, beats, and kills is perhaps not the one who is secure with his faith but the one who is so fearful of the challenges, so aware of the fickleness of conviction, that he has no choice but to strengthen it with the drumbeat of mindless fanaticism.

✦✦

If you don't belong in New Square, you just stay out. That's just how it is. Those were the words of Matt the car mechanic, from years earlier. I remembered them now, and they sounded strangely prescient, except that it wasn't just New Square I didn't belong in but all of the Hasidic world.

Several weeks after the incident on the bus, I heard of a Williamsburg man beaten for leading an Internet group in which matters of faith were raised for discussion. One day, the forum closed down, and the rumors passed via e-mail from one group member to another. The man was lured into a Williamsburg office late one night, and beaten by Williamsburg's Vaad Hatznius, the Modesty Committee. Was it true? No one knew for certain. Several days later, someone suggested that the man was beaten not for heresy but for sexual indiscretions. But did the reason matter? I knew that such incidents were not out of the ordinary, and it reinforced what I already knew: I would have to keep my own views secret.

It was hard to keep my anxiety at bay, though, and over the following months, my mind went into a tailspin through a gallery of horrors. I imagined walking down the streets of our village, or stepping into the large shul in the village's center, and people around me staring in silence: *there goes the apikorus.* I imagined a letter in the mail informing me that my children were expelled from school. I imagined Gitty's parents and siblings turning away in my presence, their disgraced son-

and brother-in-law. I imagined a vehicle with tinted windows driving alongside me on the street, a group of men, Vaad Hatznius members, pulling me inside and taking me to an unknown location for interrogations. I imagined Gitty discovering that I was no longer a believer and deciding she could not live with a heretic husband. Estrangement from my children would follow, expulsion from the community, excommunication.

On the Monsey Trails bus to work, I would look around to see who else might be paying attention. Did anyone notice that I no longer prayed with the rest of the men? Was anyone else paying attention to what I was reading? I tried to tell myself that no one really cared, that Moshe Wolf was an exception, a busybody who pried and intruded but that most others were not like that. But I also knew that in our world, people paid attention even without paying attention.

When my brother Mendy married in the summer of 2002, I led him to the wedding canopy in place of our father. As I walked him to the courtyard of a Monsey yeshiva that doubled as a wedding hall, a braided beeswax torch in my right hand, my left arm entwined in his right, I looked around and felt something I hadn't fully grasped until that moment: I was a fraud.

I saw the faces of those around me, watching as I guided my brother toward creating his Faithful Home Among Israel, and saw what I imagined everyone must have seen: a liar, a man pretending to be pious, to be sharing their faith, when in my heart I was an apostate. At the same time, I imagined my fraud to be ineffective, the word *apikorus* branded on my forehead, with those around me, as a dubious courtesy, withholding condemnation until a more opportune moment.

Chapter Seventeen

The deep, dark secret was threatening to burst. I found myself consumed with anger and bitterness, the stresses of a double life channeled into day-to-day irritability and resentment.

The Internet provided a small remedy, a therapeutic outlet through which to express what felt like an unending inner battle over how to negotiate my circumstances. Interacting with others online helped to solidify my identity as a heretic, lending me the confidence to accept the side of myself that I had been suppressing.

Early on, the big draw was chat rooms, where I fell into long debates on matters of religion. Later, when I discovered Usenet newsgroups, I found more of the same, except that now I would encounter not only Jews but also Catholics and Protestants, Muslims and Buddhists. Soon I was in steady correspondence with people whose worlds, utterly strange to me, were also utterly fascinating.

It wasn't long before I discovered my own fellow travelers. We found one another, scattered across various discussion groups, and proceeded to create our own: "Hasidic and Enlightened," "Frum Skeptics." One Hebrew forum for raising challenging questions about faith was called "Stop! We're Thinking Here." All of us were hiding in our homes and offices, seeking forbidden knowledge and forbidden connections. From across the world, Brooklyn to Tel Aviv, Montreal to Antwerp, from all sects and subgroups, we were able to say to one another: I, too, am asking forbidden questions.

And yet, paranoia reigned. We stuck to our handles, never divulging identifying details. You never knew who was a spy, and the fear of exposure permeated all discussions. Lives could end in ruin from one carelessly slipped remark.

"You know anything about this blogs thing?" I asked a coworker one day.

We were discussing a report in the news: Google, the search giant still barely five years old, had purchased a small start-up company that created a tool for something I had never heard of before. Blogs. It sounded like something out of a fantasy novel, vaguely Middle Earth-y. Frodo Baggins might get stuck in one. Or maybe fighting one.

"They're like diaries," my coworker said. He was a fellow programmer, our workstations face-to-face, and he always seemed to know about tech things before I did. "But they're online," he added. "So they're open to the public."

A public diary sounded both strange and intriguing. The journals I had kept through adolescence were filled with embarrassing ruminations, confessions of envy and shame and bursts of self-loathing. I would've been horrified had anyone read them. Yet I would write as if for an audience, crafting careful sentences, adding a literary flourish here, a flash of humor there, as if nothing was truly worth writing if it wasn't worth reading.

It turned out that blogs weren't exactly diaries, at least not the blogs I would come across. It was early 2003, and George W. Bush was preparing the nation for the invasion of Iraq. "Shock and awe" was the catchphrase of the season, and debate raged among bloggers, as among everyone else, about whether the military campaign was righteous, opportunistic, or foolhardy. Instapundit, a popular political blog—which soon inspired the Israpundit and the InstaConfused—epitomized the trend: ordinary folks bypassing corporate media and publishing, the traditional gatekeepers of our cultural discourse, and gaining popular followings.

All at once, there was a whole world of them. Little Green Footballs, Alas a Blog, IMAO. From the left and from the right. In commentary, political cartoons, angry rants, stories, photography, amateur journalism. Most intriguing to me was an emerging Jewish corner of the "blogosphere." There was the Head Heeb ("knocking down 4000 years of icons"); An Unsealed Room ("a window on life in Israel"); Protocols (three "elders," "endeavoring for total domination of the blogosphere").

They argued and they kibitzed, and they argued some more. They had readers who commented, and they commented on one another, and together created a kind of community.

I knew I could be one of them. I could tell stories. I had opinions. All I needed was a theme. And readers.

Ever since I was young, I had secretly dreamed of being a writer. As a child, I filled notebooks with fragments of stories, disjointed scenes involving an ordinary Hasidic boy who wanted to be extraordinary. One day, I hoped, I would stitch it all together into a great work of literature, and it would be sold in all Hasidic bookstores across Brooklyn.

At fourteen, I tried to set down the outlines of my autobiography—I imagined I'd fill it in over the years. Throughout my years in yeshiva, instead of Talmud commentaries, the traditional obsession of an aspiring young rabbinical student, I wrote pages and pages of philosophical musings in florid rabbinic Hebrew. I would scribble them on loose-leaf sheets, then stick them between the pages of whatever Talmud volume I was studying. I would fill so many of them that, years later, they would come slipping from between the pages each time I took one of those volumes off the shelf, scattering across the gleaming hardwood parquet of our living-room floor.

In the early years of my marriage, I wrote Yiddish essays. They were on religious themes, mostly, and for a long time, I showed them to no one, until one day I sent an essay, in longhand on several loose-leaf sheets, to a local Yiddish publication, *Maalos*. I was proud of the piece. I had woven together several disparate elements—a tale of an old Hasidic master, several Bible verses, a teaching from a favorite work on Hasidism—and framed them with a personal situation: I was having trouble with my toddler daughter. In particular, I was frustrated that my daughter preferred her playthings to bouncing on my lap. *God, too,* I wrote, *wishes we'd come to Him. But we humans prefer our silly playthings.*

When at first I heard nothing from the publication, I figured they didn't much care for it. Three months later, paging through the latest issue of *Maalos*, I discovered a small notice at the bottom of one of the pages. *To so-and-so who sent the essay about his daughter: We've misplaced your essay along with your contact info. Please call us.*

When I called, a woman asked if I could resend the piece. "It was so beautiful!" she said, and offered fifty dollars for it. "Is that acceptable?"

I had not expected to be paid. I could scarcely believe it was accepted. Payment arrived several weeks later: two third-party checks, along with seven dollars in cash. The essay was published a month later with one minor revision: they switched the gender of my child. I felt chastised. I should've known that to write so expressively about loving my female child violated some unspoken matter of propriety.

Within a year after purchasing my first computer, I became consumed with computer technology, and I soon forgot the pleasures of writing. I thought myself a computer expert, and placed an ad in a local bulletin announcing that I was available to teach private computer lessons. A Hasidic man in Monsey hired me to teach him how to use Microsoft Windows and Word and Excel. We sat in his basement office for several hours, and I demonstrated how to use dropdown menus, how to copy and paste, how to use print and save commands. His eyes were glazed over most of the time, but he paid me handsomely, and insisted that I come back for more. After three days with him, the man's wife, a matronly Hasidic woman, came down to the basement.

"You are Shulem Deen?" she asked.

I said that I was. She stood at the edge of the room, maintaining a proper distance. I could hear the ruckus of a large family upstairs. It was dinnertime, and the man had told me earlier that he had a dozen children.

"I'm the publisher of *Maalos*," the woman said. "That piece you wrote several years ago—it was so beautiful! Could you write more for us?"

But I could no longer write for *Maalos*. I was no longer sure about the things I believed, could no longer write with conviction about loving God, about Torah study and prayer. I could no longer quote Hasidic texts with any real reverence. Doubtful of all that I'd been taught, I would have nothing to say to readers who expected morality fables and homilies on biblical and rabbinic texts.

A blog would allow me to get back to writing, but I wasn't sure what I could write about. Clearly, I would not be offering religious messages. For a moment, I thought I might write about politics, or maybe the

Mideast conflict. I could rant, like dozens of other American Jewish and Israeli bloggers, about the world's unfair attitude toward the Jewish state. But now I felt conflicted about that, too. When I had first encountered the Internet, I had been a staunch supporter of the State of Israel. I still loved the land and its people, and yet, I had begun to feel uneasy. Decades of Palestinian suffering and the occupation of their lands could no longer be ignored, justified in the name of security. I couldn't possibly offer my opinions, if they were always changing, still unformed.

Yet blogs were clearly an opportunity. Blogger was handing them out for free. The least I could do was take one.

I created a Blogger account, and named my blog "My Blog." In the sidebar, I wrote: "Shulem Deen's Blog." I placed my personal e-mail address next to it. And then promptly forgot all about it.

One Sunday in April, the news spread through New Square about disturbances in Williamsburg. Tension had been mounting for weeks. An *eruv*, the practice of stringing wires from one pole to another to create an enclosed space, utilizing a loophole in the Sabbath laws to turn a public domain into a private one, had been erected around the neighborhood by some of Williamsburg's Hasidim. In Jewish communities all over the world, from Jerusalem to Montreal to New Square, eruvs were common practice. This allowed people to carry items out of their homes on the Sabbath, on which it would otherwise be forbidden. Young couples could bring food home from their parents, mothers could take their babies out in their strollers. The wheelchair-bound could be transported to the synagogue.

The Satmar Hasidim objected. Their rebbe had ruled that an eruv in New York City was forbidden. That week, around noon on Saturday, hundreds of Satmar men, cloaked in their white-and-black striped prayer shawls, marched through Williamsburg crying, "Shabbos! Shabbos!" Bedford and Lee Avenues were lined with thousands of New York police, but that didn't stop some of the Satmar men from spitting and hurling insults at those who violated their rebbe's ruling. Fisticuffs broke out here and there, and, according to the *New York Times*, five men were arrested.

This incident came after several months of sporadic violence toward those who relied on the eruv, and now I could no longer contain myself. Outraged, I turned to my blog. I had no readers, as far as I knew, but my intestines felt like a cauldron of rage, and I needed an outlet.

Someone needs to show the Satmars that their terrorism won't work in the land of the free and the home of the brave. America was for Hasidim, too; and so the eruv proponents, too, had a right to practice their religion as they chose, without fear of harassment by the Satmars.

A few hours later, I forgot about the Satmars. Now I was thinking about how else I might make use of the blog. I checked my visitor logs to see if anyone had read my rant, but other than my own visits, the logs remained empty.

Trying to think of something insightful to share, I wrote in my next post. *Nothing so far.*

Later that day, I wrote about a book I was reading. Soon after, I had a disappointing meeting with a prospective employer. I was supposed to be hired for a new job, with a significant salary increase. I had been all but assured of it, but the prospect fell through. They were not hiring, they decided at the last minute, and I went to sleep that night terribly upset. The next morning, I blogged about how disappointed I was over not getting that job. So disappointed, that I was staying home from work to recover.

Called in sick to work today, I announced to the world. I hoped that my boss wasn't reading. I checked my visitor logs—still empty. My boss clearly wasn't reading, and neither was anyone else.

That afternoon, I thought back to the eruv disturbance. I thought about the ways our Hasidic society kept people in line. We could control not only the masses but even the leaders. The eruv was not a rebellious project by a fringe group; it was supported by prominent Hasidic rabbis. As far as anyone knew, they were God-fearing men. Except, in that narrow grid, between Lee and Bedford, from Broadway to Heyward, there was only one way to fear God. The Satmar way. And the Satmars were willing to use violence to ensure that everyone knew it.

But these attitudes were not limited to Satmar. The same rabbis who were in favor of the eruv were themselves part of the structure that demanded conformity on everything else. In Skver, violence was used to enforce communal norms. In Vizhnitz and in Ger and in Belz and among so many other sects, there were always rumors of similar incidents. It was how our world worked. We kept people in line by whatever means possible.

What kind of world was this? And who could possibly save us?

George W. Bush, that's who. That was the thought I had on that Monday afternoon in April 2003. George W. Bush, I wrote, should've sent troops to New York's Hasidic neighborhoods. If Americans were so insistent on spreading freedom, there were places closer to home that needed it. Before we went off to bring democracy to Afghans and Iraqis, maybe Williamsburg and New Square could be liberated first.

As military campaigns go, mine was perhaps weakly conceived. A battalion of U.S. Marines marching through Williamsburg or New Square wasn't likely to impress the rabbis. There were no statues to topple, no insurgents with IEDs or RPGs, and no nation-building to embark on. But I was fed up, and I wanted the world to know that in our dark corner of the world, right in the middle of New York, there was in fact very little freedom. I wanted to shout it to the world, and I didn't care who heard me.

Actually, on second thought, I did care. A moment after I clicked "Publish," I reread my post. It was four paragraphs long and very clearly expressed criticism of my own community, my own people. My name and e-mail address were right there in the open.

This isn't good, I thought. *Someone isn't going to like this, and I'm going to get in trouble. I should take my name off, maybe.* Anonymity! That was it. And why not? This was the Internet. I drummed my fingers on my desk and tried to think quickly. I needed a name, any name. "Hasidic Rebel." That's it! I can always change it later.

Then the readers came. First in the dozens, then hundreds, and soon thousands. My visitor logs grew and grew, the numbers rising, doubling and tripling by the day. Across the Internet, I found other bloggers who linked to me, excitedly, with a discovery they seemed to think astonishing: "Look at this! A Hasid writing in secret about his insular world."

Apparently, people wanted to read about my world, and it appeared that I had a compelling enough voice to bring them back for more.

It was magical. Every day, another link would pop up somewhere. The Yada Yada Yada Blog and the Head Heeb and Allison in An Unsealed Room and the elders over at Protocols, all of them were linking to the "Hasidic Rebel."

"Fascinating stuff." "A unique perspective." "A rebel with a cause."

It gave me the encouragement to keep writing, about the parts of my life that I loved and the parts that frustrated me to no end. I wrote about my wife and about my kids. I wrote about the rebbe. I wrote about what it meant to live as a Hasid, within and around New York City, both as part of a broader culture and also, tenaciously, grittily, distinct from it.

The anonymity allowed me to be critical, but I tried to write honestly. There were things about my world that I still loved, and I wrote about them along with our extremist practices and the narrowness of our worldview, the frustrations with which I was now consumed day and night. I wrote about the stresses of trying to embrace modernity and aspects of outside culture while living in a world so steeped in tradition. I wrote about hiding videotapes after secret runs to Blockbuster, about sneaking my daughters into the library, about the wonders of a rebbe's tisch, and about Hasidic hitchhikers who didn't approve of the music I played in my car.

Readers could not get enough. And yet, I could not tell my readers everything.

I could not express outright heresy. My persona was still one of a believer, despite my critical views. Questions of faith, I believed, required a more solitary struggle, a search within, not one aired for public entertainment and submitted to the rapid-fire bursts of Internet comments. *I believe in God and the Torah*, I wrote in one post, even as I knew it was not true, not really. Even under anonymity, I could not yet say otherwise. To declare myself a heretic was a step so terrifying and so bold that I could not say it out loud, even to myself. *Apikorus*. Heretic. It was such an awful, awful word. Shameful and wicked. And I still desperately hoped, deep inside me, that I was not one.

Chapter Eighteen

At first, I told Gitty nothing about the blog. I wanted to tell her, and I knew that I would eventually, but the right moment felt elusive. We had just barely recovered from a difficult episode: only several weeks earlier, I had purchased a television set.

It was a shock to Gitty, the day she discovered it. It was a Sunday, and I had gone to Costco, where I'd noticed the tall pile of cartons on four pallets, 32-inch models, $39.99. I had wanted to get one for a long time but had feared Gitty's reaction. Now I couldn't resist. I placed a carton in my cart, and picked up a package of rabbit-ear antennas a few aisles down. I covered it all in a large black trash bag in the back of my car and brought it home. I laid the television set on the dining-room floor, still wrapped in the bag, and shut the door.

An hour later, Gitty walked into the dining room. Ten seconds later she emerged, her face frozen. For three days, she kept silent. She cooked meals, fed the kids, did laundry, but she would not say a word to me.

On the third day, I snapped. "Stop acting like a child," I said.

She broke her silence with a scream: "A TELEVISION . . . *IN MY HOME!*"

It burst from her like a force of nature. A shriek that even she could not have anticipated. For a moment, her face contorted into something grotesque, and then she turned away, toward the kitchen sink, a dish towel in her hand. Behind the sink was a window, and she stood there, her controlled posture from behind looking almost peaceful, as if she was gazing out at the birds, at the sky. From the tiny tremors of her body and her shoulders, though, I could tell that she was sobbing. A moment later, she ran from the kitchen, hiding her face in her arm, and locked herself in our bedroom.

The violence of Gitty's reaction shook me. Over the years, she had begun to accept that I had changed. We had just passed a decade of marriage. For our tenth anniversary, we spent a rare night out, dining at a kosher Italian restaurant in Monsey. We had learned a lot about each other, how to stay out of the other's way when things were tense and draw closer when the mood was light. There was little passion between us, but there was real feeling. And sometimes, even love.

Still, conflicts constantly arose. Barely a week passed when our differences would not stand in contrast, and each time, I felt resentment all over again toward those who had brought us together.

"This isn't how I married you," she would say, sometimes in anger but also on occasion tenderly, her eyes pleading. "It's not fair," she would say, and a single tear would trickle down the curve of her nose.

And yet, we'd made it work so far. I imagined that, as with the radio and books and movies and the Internet, the TV would be just another boundary to cross, not easily but inevitably.

I had misjudged. Television was a taboo so entrenched that to violate it was nearly inconceivable. Television was the symbol of all the outside culture we were meant to avoid. The Internet might have become the real culprit for corrupting minds, but the television had been, for decades, *de tumeneh keili*. The profane vessel. So abhorrent that many would not even utter its name.

I was almost prepared to return the TV to Costco, but a few days after Gitty's outburst, we talked it over. She was still angry but also forgiving. "If you want to keep it," she said, "I won't stop you. But I will *never* watch anything with you. And don't you dare let the children see it."

She said it as if she knew what was coming—that once she gave in, I would not be content to transgress alone but would try to get her to join me, and then I'd try to reel in the kids. This had happened before. When I first began to watch movies, renting DVDs from Blockbuster and playing them on my laptop computer in the darkness of our dining room, she refused to join me. For months, I would ask, plead, tease, promise to choose something with no objectionable content, no nudity or violence or profanity, until finally she relented, even as she swore that we would never let our children join us, ever.

The old computer cabinet in our dining room had been sitting empty for a while. I had purchased it seven years earlier, with double doors and a lock to hide the computer on Shabbos. Now it would serve as a home for the television set. I would keep it locked at all times, and the children would never know.

I soon began to spend an hour or two each night in our dining room, alone with the TV. Mostly I watched the news, and occasionally one of the late-night talk shows, but really, I was fascinated by all of it, in the same way that I had once been fascinated by the radio. I was riveted by soap operas and public-access programming and late-night infomercials. "Order now, for only $99, and get the full set of Frank Sinatra videos on VHS!" What a deal!

As Gitty grew accustomed to the TV's presence, I grew bolder.

"Want to watch something with me?" I asked her one night.

She shook her head coolly, refusing even to entertain the notion.

But eventually, she gave in. One night, as I sat alone in the dining room, she opened the door. "Can I join you?" Her expression was bashful. From then on, each night after the children went to bed, we would lock the doors and windows, draw the curtains, and sit together in the corner of our dining room in front of the small television set, the volume on near-mute to avoid raising suspicion with the Greenbergs through the wall.

We would watch whatever was on: *Friends, Charlie Rose, Eyewitness News, Big Brother.* There were no guilty pleasures—we were guilty for all of it: *Masterpiece Theatre* and *Jerry Springer, Nightline* and *American Idol.* Everything, all of it, was part of America's great crescendo of profanity.

It was during one of those nights in front of the TV that I ended up telling Gitty about the blog. I had implemented a new feature that day: Each time a reader posted a comment, I received an alert on my cell phone. As we sat in front of the TV, watching a rerun of *Everybody Loves Raymond,* my phone buzzed, harshly interrupting the grainy images on the screen. I ignored it, and Gitty kept her eyes fixed on the TV. Frank was haranguing Marie, who was haranguing Ray, who was already being harangued by Debra. All the while, Brad Garrett was musing about "life's imponderables." Then my phone buzzed again, and then again soon after. Gitty finally turned her head just slightly and raised an inquiring eyebrow. I shook my head to brush her off, and then my phone buzzed twice more in rapid succession.

"What is *all the buzzing?*" Gitty blurted.

"Nothing. Just alerts."

"Alerts?"

"Comments. From . . . this website."

"What website?"

I turned off the TV and told her all about it. I told her how I'd always wanted to write, and now I was writing, and I had readers, too, lots of them. I was the Hasidic Rebel.

She let out a grunt, as if to say, *Well, how unsurprising.*

"What do you write about?" she asked.

"Just . . . about my life."

"Do you write about me?"

"Sometimes."

I could see in her eyes that she was intrigued.

"You're welcome to read it," I told her.

The next day, when I came home from work, she sat down and put her hands flat on the table. "I read your site," she said.

I looked for disapproval in her eyes, awaiting her outrage.

"I kinda like it," she said.

"You do?"

"Yeah. I mean, if it makes you feel better, maybe it'll do you good. You know, like therapy."

"You seem less tense these days," a friend said to me one day. I said nothing, although I knew it was true. The ability to speak my mind gave me a peace I had been lacking for years. A small community had sprung up around the blog, and it gave me a sense that there was a world somewhere in which my thoughts were appreciated. Reader comments on my posts often went into the hundreds.

I didn't know these commenters in real life, but their names were soon as recognizable as my real-life friends: Ani Yesheinu, JK from KJ, Susan in Queens. Some commenters earned followers of their own. One man went by Isaac, and soon there was an "Isaac's Fan." They came from across the Jewish spectrum, from Hasidic to Yeshivish to the Modern Orthodox to the Reform. There were regulars who were non-Jews. Susan in Queens was Catholic. Evy was Mormon. PadrePaz was a Protestant minister somewhere in the South.

One day, I received an e-mail from a reporter for New York's *Village Voice*. He wanted to write a story about my blog. Would I agree to an interview?

Several weeks later, at a kosher café near Manhattan's diamond district, one block from my workplace, we met for lunch. A small tape recorder lay on the table, next to my beaver-fur hat. The writer looked younger than I'd imagined, in his twenties, with hipster eyeglasses and a polite but slightly detached manner. "Can we be friends?" I wanted to ask him. "Can you tell me about *your* life?"

He was a journalist, though, and I knew he did not want my friendship but my story. He asked broad questions, and I offered long-winded philosophical ruminations, which he listened to patiently, smiling and nodding encouragingly. I imagined that every word I said was important to him, not realizing that out of a ninety-minute interview, he would quote me for a total of about ninety seconds.

The article, titled "The Sharer of Secrets," appeared in the *Village Voice* a month later, accompanied by an image of a Hasidic man in profile, with a bloated torso and a long, tangled beard. The top of the Hasid's hat was sliced horizontally across, its upper half raised like the spout of an old-fashioned teapot, a cloud of yellow-and-blue six-pointed stars, the Hasid's secret ruminations, rising from within.

I disliked the image and disliked the article even more. In my blog, I had taken pains to write simply as I experienced my world, subjectively and judgmentally, but also honestly. I had written not with malice but my own truth. The *Voice*, however, had *its* truth, which was clearly different from mine. To them, I was not merely a curiosity, a Hasid offering a glimpse of his world, but a *sensational* curiosity, a Hasid dishing dirt on his own people.

"Have you heard of this website, 'Hasidic Rebel'?" my friend Zurich asked me in shul a few days after the *Voice* article appeared. He spoke in a low voice, as if sharing a secret.

"I've heard of it," I said.

Zurich didn't have a computer or Internet access, but he'd heard the news: a renegade Hasid, an Internet website, an article in some newspaper. He couldn't understand it. "Why would someone do something like that?"

"Do something like what?"

"Write about us that way. Make the non-Jews hate us."

"Why would it make the non-Jews hate us?"

"Well, he's telling the whole world how bad we are. And so he's confirming what all the non-Jews already think."

I quickly changed the subject. Zurich had no idea that I might have something to do with the website, but there were others who had their suspicions.

"Just so you know," Yossi Breuer said to me one day, "Some people are saying you're the Hasidic Rebel."

Instinctively, I opened my mouth to deny it, but Yossi held up his hand.

"I have no opinion. Just thought you'd want to know." We were in the basement of the shul, near the mikveh, and as soon as he said it, he turned and walked past the large bins of towels, thick with the smell of industrial bleach, and headed up the stairs.

Chezky, too, called me with a warning. He was one of the very few I had told about the blog, and when he heard talk of it in the coffee room of the Vizhnitz shul in Monsey one morning, he grew alarmed. "They were discussing the Hasidic Rebel. They were talking about hiring private detectives, scheming to draw you out. They're going to send you e-mails pretending they're women. They say you won't be able to resist. You've gotta be careful."

On the Internet, too, I encountered hostile reactions. On Tapuz, a Yiddish forum, one irate commenter going by the name of Muzar found his own creative voice in his condemnation:

I have come across the blog of Hasidic Rebel: a loathsome swine,
a disgusting poisonous snake, a revolting outcast, the shit-covered

*asshole of a sick dog. A gruesome death upon him. . . . May the
cholera descend upon his limbs, may he be ensnared within
·the devil's clutches, may he be buried alive, his mendacious tongue
skinned, his mad eyes gouged; may he hang, strangle, and choke.
May we live to see it speedily and with joy.*

The violent imagery shook me, even as it did not entirely surprise me. I
also found it perversely amusing. *May we live to see it speedily and with
joy.* The same phrase we used for the coming of the Messiah. The thing
we've been waiting for forever, and will likely go on waiting for forever.

I did not know who Muzar was, but I recognized him, the maniacal
language echoing so much of what I'd heard from rabbis and teachers. I also recognized in him aspects of my younger self—the swagger,
the lazy resort to overstatement. I knew that we were not as quick to
punish offenders as we were to issue threats; and to declare minor sins
capital offenses, only to have passions cool the next morning.

At the same time, I remembered the slashed car tires and broken
windows of Amrom Pollack, when he chose to perform his son's bris
outside our village, denying the rebbe the honors.

I remembered the tales of Mendel Vechter, the rumors of how he'd
been stripped naked, beaten, his beard forcibly shaved by his former
Satmar comrades for having absconded to their arch-nemeses, the
Lubavitchers.

I remembered the story of Itzik Felder, a former Skverer Hasid
who left to follow the rebbe of Rachmastrivka. When he came back to
New Square one evening for a family wedding, he was slapped in the
face and punched in the gut and instructed to never again defile our
streets with his presence.

I remembered my own incident with Moshe Wolf on the bus. I remembered the eruv disturbances in Williamsburg that had driven me
to begin writing the blog in the first place.

*We must determine the identity of Hasidic Rebel, find out where he lives,
and hold a not-so-peaceful demonstration,* wrote another commenter on
the same Yiddish forum.

"What will we do," Gitty asked one evening, "if people find out it's
you? What if something happens?"

I did not believe we'd be harmed, I told her, even as I secretly worried about it.

"What if the children are expelled from school?" she asked.

This was more likely. School expulsions were the primary method for maintaining ideological conformity among parents.

"Maybe we can move to Monsey. Find a more relaxed environment."

But Monsey wasn't an option for Gitty. "Whom will the children marry?"

This was the Great Anxiety of our world: *shidduchim*, the system of arranged marriages. Good marriages were available only for those with perfect, unblemished families. Those who would not conform, though, who stood out in ways colorful or unconventional, suffered the heartache of having their children consigned to the scrap heap of the matchmaker's notebook.

I reminded Gitty that our eldest was barely nine years old, but she only looked at me glumly.

"It is *never* too early to worry about *shidduchim*."

Chapter Nineteen

Summer evenings, when New Square felt suffocating, after the children were in bed, and Gitty would join other women on lawn chairs outside our home for another evening of chatter, and the men gathered at the synagogue for prayers and several hours of study, I would drive my Honda Odyssey down the Palisades Parkway and over the George Washington Bridge, seeking an escape with no particular destination. Often I would end up in Greenwich Village, strolling the leafy streets, gazing at its nineteenth-century row houses and NYU campus buildings, observing the vibrant nightlife around MacDougal and Thompson and Bleecker, and imagine a different life.

I was aware that here, too, there must be regrets, dreams of youth shattered by the realities of modern living. Here, too, I was sure, there were unhappy lives, stalled careers, loves lost and loveless connections maintained for all the wrong reasons. Here, too, I knew, there was the need to conform, with social codes just as arbitrary and stifling. Yet I would return, again and again, drawn to the mystique of freedom, only an hour from home but so many worlds apart.

One evening, I thought I might visit a bar. Bars, I had come to learn, were a celebrated institution of Western culture, where humans went to meet other humans, at least those without synagogues and mikvehs and coffee rooms. But how did it work? Did one buy a drink, and then simply strike up a conversation with a stranger? Was there a protocol to it? Or did one simply sip one's drink in silence, and then leave? I wondered what kinds of drinks I might order, whether there were rules and conventions that I should first learn. In our world, alcohol was consumed with few rituals, cheap whiskeys and vodkas straight up in one-ounce "schnapps cups," at kiddush on Shabbos morning or at a *vach nacht* for a baby boy. In movies, I had seen James Bond order his martinis, "shaken, not stirred" and seen people drink beer out of tall glasses, thick layers of foam at the top, but I did not know what martinis or beers tasted like or how to choose one.

I passed several bars along Bleecker Street and peered inside. Some had TV screens showing sports games, others had crowds huddling over the bar counter, chatting with the bartenders. Others seemed subdued, couples sitting at small tables, chatting over flickering candles in small glass cups.

I would pick one at random, I decided, and I stepped inside a crowded bar near Bleecker and Seventh. The noise was disorienting, loud conversation and laughter and shouts across the room. Did all these people know one another? I wondered. The seats at the bar were taken, and the standing areas were crowded as well. I wondered whether I looked out of place. I had left my hat and long coat in my car, but still I wore my yarmulke and sported a full beard, with my sidelocks twisted up in knots over my ears.

I would order a drink I had seen in the movies. "Gin and tonic," I'd say to the bartender, as if I'd been drinking it all my life. I had never had gin, or tonic, but it sounded like something one might order in a bar. Yet what if this, too, was wrong? What if "gin and tonic" was not a drink but an inside joke of some sort, an allusion I had missed? What if it was like moonshine, something sold in another place and another time, and I'd appear foolish for asking for it?

My eyes fell on a series of framed photographs on the wall. They were of smiling men, although something was odd about it all. They appeared to be striking sexually suggestive poses. Some of the men in the photographs wore pants with large circles cut open to reveal their buttocks, flashing their backsides to the camera. Some of the men were grabbing one another's crotches or tucking their hands inside one another's pants.

Then it hit me. This must be a gay bar. Did straight people go to gay bars? Did my being here suggest that I was gay? Would I be approached for gay sex? Before I could give it much thought, I fled, out the door and into the street and back to my car, back to my home in New Square, where I knew the rules, and where pants generally covered butts completely, at least in public, and where a schnapps cup of Old Williamsburg whiskey could be had without worrying about looking foolish.

Still, I could not stay away from New York City for long, and soon returned, spending evening after evening searching for entry into this world. Some nights, I would head to Dizzy's Club Coca-Cola, on the fifth floor of the new Time Warner Center, where, behind the band, through floor-to-ceiling windows, I could take in the backdrop of Columbus Circle and Central Park, which gave me the feeling that the jazz club itself was in the park, its stage lights iridescent against the moonlight. Sometimes I would go for a movie at Loew's at Sixty-Eighth, or to Barnes and Noble at Sixty-Sixth and Broadway, to browse its shelves until the store's midnight closing time, then head around the corner to Starbucks, where I would sit with my laptop and soak in the pleasure of simply being in Manhattan. I knew that there were other Hasidim who spent time in the city, tucking their *payess* up behind their ears, donning less conspicuous headgear, trading in their wide-brimmed hats and long coats for Ascot caps and short leather jackets. But I didn't know them and didn't know where I might find them, and so I wandered the streets of Manhattan alone.

One day, I received an e-mail from a stranger named KeaLoha. She was a photographer, she said, with an idea for a new project. She wanted to photograph Hasidim. Would I help? she asked. Could I tell her more about my world and what it was like?

I could help, maybe, I said. More important, I craved a meeting with an outsider. I wanted to speak to somebody, anybody, from the world outside my own. After blogging for six months, my regular stream of posts had slowed to a trickle. The attention my blog received had been gratifying, if a little overwhelming, but it also turned what was originally a casual outlet for off-the-cuff musings into an energy-sapping frenzy of thinking up ideas for new posts, and the growing need to write with more consideration for maintaining reader interest. The initial burst of satisfaction soon dissipated, and what I wanted now was a real-world engagement with the outside world, not merely a virtual one.

KeaLoha and I arranged to meet at the Barnes and Noble café at Sixty-Sixth and Broadway. It was a Sunday afternoon, and the place was crowded when I stepped off the escalator on the fourth floor. I hadn't thought to ask how I'd recognize her, until I saw someone waving. She was a young black woman, who looked to be in her thirties, and I wondered if it struck anyone as odd: a black woman and a Hasidic man having coffee.

I'd been interviewed several times by then. Aside from the *Village Voice* reporter, there had been Pearl, a twenty-four-year-old Columbia journalism student, who was writing about renegade Hasidim for her master's thesis. There was Isabella, a producer for a German-language program on a Swiss radio station. I clung to these encounters as potential anchors for life outside the Hasidic world, although I had to remind myself that these people sought not friendship but my story. Still, these engagements offered a glimpse into the lives of ordinary people.

KeaLoha and I had meant to talk about her photography project, but we quickly switched to talking about our personal lives. She had recently returned from several years of living in West Africa, and she eagerly shared her experiences. When I described my life to her, KeaLoha appeared stunned.

"You met your future wife for only *seven minutes?*" KeaLoha shook her head in disbelief. "And you've never had sex with anyone else? Ever?" She fired off the questions one after the other, sometimes circling back and asking the same ones over and over again. "Do you love her? Are you attracted to her?"

The questions put me off for a moment. The answers were no, to each one, and made me fidget in my seat. I wanted to tell KeaLoha the truth. That if I'd had a choice, I would not have married Gitty. But it felt unkind to say it, even cruel, and I didn't want to be cruel, and I didn't want KeaLoha to think me cruel. *Why, then, did you marry her?* I imagined her asking in outrage. *How could you? The poor woman.* I was ashamed of my own feelings, afraid even now to be misunderstood.

KeaLoha did not judge me, though, nor did she misunderstand. She shook her head and let out a long sigh.

"Can't you get divorced?"

I remember seeing sadness in her eyes, which were unusually large, the whites visible around her irises. Not pretty but striking nonetheless. I looked at her long locks of curly brown hair and the soft brown skin of her cheeks and forehead. And again those eyes. Something about them repelled and mesmerized me at the same time. In her voice was something both gentle and insistent.

"Lots of people get divorced," she said. "You can live the life you want. You have that right."

It was all so simple to her. I didn't know how to explain that it was nearly impossible. How divorce came with a dreadful stigma, that the effects on my children would be so terrible that it felt too cruel even to consider.

I looked around at the others in the café. There had been a young couple ahead of me at the counter a few minutes earlier, and now they were sitting a few feet away, leaning over the table, nuzzling noses and nibbling at each other's lips. I wondered what that felt like, to have the burning desire to be so physically close to someone, to have no restraints about being so in public. Then I thought back to Gitty and to KeaLoha's insistent questions.

"We do have good sex," I said.

"You have nothing to compare it with," she said with a scoff. After a moment, she asked, "Would you ever have sex with someone else? Would you cheat? Would you have an affair?"

In later years, I would learn of the stereotypes of Hasidic men as patrons of sex workers of all kinds. Strippers, prostitutes, dominatrices, even male escorts. At the time, however, the thought would've shocked me. I could not imagine any of my friends being of that sort.

We spoke for almost three hours. For KeaLoha, this was a project; but to me, the experience had a lasting effect. For days, my thoughts were preoccupied with how different KeaLoha's life was from my own. More than anything, though, I couldn't get one comment out of my mind: *Lots of people get divorced. You can live the life you want. You have that right.*

My sister's husband, Gedalya, had seen me change, had watched me go from devout young Talmud student, oblivious to the ways of the world, to what I had become. He was a Bobover Hasid, several years older than I. Gedalya and I didn't see each other much, but on those occasions that I dropped by my sister's Borough Park home, we would end up talking for hours.

He was shocked, however, when I told him that I was no longer a believer. "You believe in *nothing at all?*" He thought it was perhaps understandable to reject the Hasidic lifestyle, or belief in the rebbe, but he could not fathom how I could reject the Torah as God's word. It was even harder for him to accept that I no longer believed in the power of prayer. When I told him that I no longer believed in any conventional notion of God, or of a divinely imposed order to our universe, he stared at me wide-eyed. "What are you, *nuts?*"

After several hours, he finally accepted that my beliefs had changed and that he wouldn't be able to talk me out of them. But now he had a different question.

"So why are you still here? Why are you still living the lifestyle?"

"Because it's complicated. I'm married. I've got kids. What am I supposed to do, drop it all?" He knew as well as I that it wasn't so simple. "But who knows? Maybe one day."

"It'll never happen," he snapped, scorn shooting from his eyes like darts. "You'll never leave."

"Why do you say that?"

"You, my friend, don't have the guts."

Those who leave simply cannot resist temptation. This mantra was repeated so frequently that I felt the accusation acutely, whenever the prospect of leaving crossed my mind, even if only as a fantasy. What was it that I sought in encounters with outsiders, in my meetings with KeaLoha and Pearl and Isabella? What was it that I really wanted?

It wasn't clear to me at the time; but later, I would realize that I wanted no more than a world in which I was not lying and hiding. I wanted the freedom to simply be who I was, without fear or shame. When caught in a world where your very essence feels shameful, life turns into a feverish obsession with suppressing your true identity in favor of a socially accepted one. I knew that something, soon, would have to give.

Chapter Twenty

If during the week, I found ways to relieve the tension of living a double life, on Shabbos I had few such options. Worst of all were Shabbos morning services. For three hours each Saturday morning, every adult male member of the community, and a good portion of its male children, packed into the village's synagogue, and I had no choice but to take part.

"Tatti, can I come to shul with you?" Akiva would ask. And I would sigh, and say, "Not this week, *shayfele*." I couldn't imagine a three-year-old enjoying what I, at thirty, now found excruciatingly humdrum.

Women and girls did not attend shul except for special occasions, but for any male above bar mitzvah age, to stay home was unheard of. Gitty would be furious if I stayed home. The children would ask uncomfortable questions. Neighbors might catch a glimpse of me through the window, or one of our children's friends would come to visit and spot me and report me to her parents.

And so I attended each week, even as I despised the monotonous grind of bowing and swaying and mumbling and chanting. In the summer, with two thousand bodies packed into one hall, the heat was oppressive. The layers of clothing—small woolen *tallis katan* worn over one's shirt, the long black caftan on top of it, all of it covered with an enormous wool prayer shawl, with its heavy silver brocade adornment as a headpiece—made it even worse.

One Saturday morning, I discovered that the yeshiva building across the plaza was unlocked. The building was cleared of its usual bustle, and I wandered the corridors, peering into empty lecture rooms in which, all week long, students gathered to study the laws of betrothal and divorce, property damages and court-ordered floggings, sacrificial lambs and burning red heifers. At the end of the corridor were the doors to the cavernous study hall, now completely empty. It was the perfect place for a heretic to pass the time while everyone else prayed.

The first few weeks, I brought along a book, but soon I realized I was not alone. In an alcove of the study hall, or in some of the farther lecture rooms, I began to find other men passing the time, sometimes in twos and threes. Each was there for his own reason—some simply disliked the crowds in shul, others just didn't care for prayer—and within several months, we came to form a group that gathered each Saturday morning. While the rest of the village men spent three hours praying, reading from the Torah, and engaging in the tedious call-and-response between prayer leader and congregation, I, along with Yitzy Ruttner, Hershy Brizel, the three Dunner brothers, and several others, would gather to discuss the important topics of the day—general news, Hasidic politics, community gossip—identical to the discussions one heard in the ritual bath, in the shul's coffee room, or the yeshiva dining room.

There was one difference: this was one place in which I could speak my mind. We were all deviants in one way or another, of various ages, but mostly twentysomethings. Most of these men were unmarried and drifting toward the fringes. Some of them watched movies, listened to secular music, and occasionally sneaked out of the village to play blackjack at Atlantic City casinos. They were an intelligent group, and while few of them had given issues of faith much thought before, they were not bothered by my views. The fact that I considered the parting of the Red Sea a fanciful myth, that I was fairly certain that our prayers reached no heavenly ears, that I saw our worldview as backward and fanatical—it was all fine with them.

One week, we had a newcomer: Leiby Einstein. Nineteen years old, he had a boyish smile and dark chocolate-brown sidelocks framing his mildly acne-ridden face.

Leiby was not a stranger to me. His father had been the yeshiva dean in my time, and his older brother Menashe had been my classmate and best friend. Leiby and I weren't formally introduced, but I noticed from across the table that I'd caught his attention in some way.

He kept looking toward me, throwing me uneasy glances, nervously raising his right hand to twirl the base of his sidelock, sometimes wrapping the lock of hair tightly around his index finger and releasing it into a perfectly coiled spring. He said little. Every few moments, he would bite his lower lip, as if uninterested in the conversation but expecting something more momentous to happen. Finally, during a lull, when Yitzy and one of the Dunner brothers left to fetch coffee from the enormous urn in the coffee room near the dean's office, Leiby came around to my side of the table.

"I've been wanting to talk to you," he said.

We stepped away a few paces from the group. He was interested in computers and computer programming, he said. He'd heard that I worked as a programmer. Could we chat about it?

"Sure," I said. "We can talk computers."

He looked at me as if unsure where to go with that. Over in the corner, the group laughed raucously over a comment someone had made. Leiby looked back nervously, and then turned back to me.

"There are other things." He raised his hand to pat his sidelock, and chuckled. "I don't know what you believe. Maybe you'll disagree with me." Looking away, as if speaking to some invisible presence off to the side, he said, "Yitzy told me you might be a person I can talk to. I don't believe in any of this anymore."

"Don't believe in what?"

He looked at me directly now and shook his head. "None of it. God. The Torah. This whole lifestyle. There's no truth to the things we're taught. We just accept it, without thinking. But none of it is based on truth." His eyes searched mine for a sign of understanding, his fingers never leaving his right sidelock. When I asked how he had come to all this, he told me that he'd found his way onto the Internet several months earlier—he'd managed to get himself a laptop and discovered an old phone jack in his bedroom, to which he was able to hook up a dial-up modem—and had begun to research how we knew the things we knew.

"I don't know your beliefs," Leiby said again, almost apologetically. "But it's pretty clear, the rabbis have been making shit up!" His voice now had an edge to it, betraying an inner rage that had until now been suppressed. "For thousands of years, they've been making shit up! And we just believe it!"

The next week, and the week after, Leiby joined our group, and each time, he would call me away to share his thoughts. He needed someone to talk to, someone who wouldn't judge him. I was nearly thirty. I had a job in Manhattan. I could read English books. I was the elder man of wisdom.

Finally, one week he told me, "I want to leave. This place has nothing for me." His father had only recently stopped beating him, he said, when he realized that Leiby, at nineteen, could easily overpower his paunchy five-foot frame. Now, his father only abused him verbally, calling him a "bum" and a "small-brained *am hu'uretz*," illiterate in matters of Jewish learning. Leiby had no interest in sticking around for more of his abuse. He already had plans to leave and was just waiting for the right moment. He was going to join the army, he said.

As we chatted, Leiby and I moved toward the front of the study hall. The windows faced the shul across the plaza, and through them we could see hundreds of swaying worshipers, the late-morning sun glistening off the silver brocade adornments of their prayer shawls.

"Why the army?" I asked.

"Where else could I go? I want to learn about the outside world. Goyish culture. I want to see what it's about." The army, he thought, would give him the structure he needed for a soft landing—feed him, house him, and give him access to a social life he would otherwise struggle to find. I was impressed with how much thought he'd given to this.

Services were soon over, and through the windows we watched as a trickle of men left the shul. Moments later, the trickle turned into a sea of white prayer shawls and black shtreimels.

"I might have another suggestion. Let's get out of here, we'll talk on the way." I grabbed my prayer shawl, still lying folded on a nearby table, flung it over my shoulders, and we headed out, joining the masses of men and boys heading home. We walked along Washington Avenue, alongside the bright blue posters taped onto lampposts and mailboxes designating it the "Men's Side." Leiby looked at me eagerly as we walked. "What's your suggestion?"

"Have you looked into going to college?"

He looked at me as if I'd suggested something at once brilliant and baffling. "I—I don't—" he stammered, but then looked as if something had just clicked in his mind: "You think I can get in?"

Like most boys in New Square, Leiby had little secular education. He had taught himself to read English but could barely speak it or write it. I told Leiby what I knew about college, which wasn't much. My own secular studies had been better than his, and I'd taught myself a lot over the years, but my education still contained vast gaps. Still, in a village where grown men turned with grudging admiration to anyone who could read an English-language newspaper on his own, I was the expert on all things worldly.

"The army is a fine idea, if that's what you want. But know your options. In the outside world, most kids your age are headed to college. Look into it."

Several weeks later, Leiby told me of his decision. He had discovered an organization in Manhattan called Footsteps, which offered educational assistance to ex-Hasidim. Through it, he found tutoring help for English and math and assistance with applying to college. He spoke excitedly about his plans, of GEDs and college admissions and FAFSAs. He still had many hurdles but was determined. Through Craigslist, he found a place to live in Brooklyn, a three-roommate share in Brighton Beach, and was planning, as soon as he passed his GED exam, to enroll in Kingsborough, a two-year community college.

"I'll probably major in some liberal arts field," he said, and when I nodded approvingly, he said. "You know what a major is, right?"

"Of course," I said. I was only vaguely familiar with the term and wasn't sure what liberal arts were, but it sounded as though he was on the right track.

I remember parting from Leiby that day, lost in my thoughts, a powerful pang of envy hitting me. Leiby's desire to join the army had struck me as fancifully adolescent, but college was a different matter. I had encouraged him, partly driven by my own wistfulness for the opportunity. Now that his plans were taking shape, I couldn't help thinking about myself.

A short while later, Gitty and I sat down to our Shabbos lunch with our children. As I watched my daughters bring out dishes of hummus, sour pickles, egg salad, and chopped liver and lay them across our dining-room table, I thought of the chaos that would ensue, were I, too, to split from the community. I imagined the friends who would no longer acknowledge me on the street, the shuls in which I would no longer be welcome; imagined my family broken apart, my children traumatized by the knowledge of a father ostracized from the only world they knew. I imagined my mother's tears, the pleadings of my siblings to reconsider, to spare them the shame. Not only would I become a pariah, but my children would also be forever stigmatized, the offspring of a heretic, their reputations blemished by the sins of their father and unfit for marriage with the devout. Most likely, my children would be forced to sever all contact with me, the only way in which to redeem themselves.

We took our seats around our dining-room table: Gitty and I at either end; the girls—Tziri, Freidy, and Chaya Suri—on one side; the boys—Akiva and Hershy—on the other. Together we sang the opening verses of the kiddush before the blessing over wine, the boys' voices loud and eager, the girls, less enthusiastic, mouthing the words lazily, tapping their fingers lightly on the white tablecloth. Gitty swayed along silently.

> And the children of Israel shall observe the Sabbath . . .
> The sign of an everlasting covenant. . . .
> For in six days, the Lord created heaven and earth,
> and on the seventh day, He rested, and was refreshed.

I cut open the golden-brown challahs and passed around slices. Gitty disappeared into the kitchen and returned with platters of gefilte fish, jellied p'tcha, and a large bowl of steaming chulent. I remember watching as my family went about their ordinary Sabbath lunch, watching as if I were not part of them, as if through the glimmering sheen of a thick pane of glass between us.

A single sour pickle remained on a dish in the middle of the table, and Chaya Suri reached for it, while Tziri and Freidy, forever mothering her, gave her disapproving looks.

"There are plenty more pickles in the fridge," I remember Gitty saying, with the calm grace that seemed to envelop her on the Sabbath.

I remember how, facing the girls from across the table, Akiva held up the edge of one of his ritual fringes and brushed it lightly into Hershy's ear. Hershy, startled, slapped his ear with the back of his hand, as if to drive away an insect. I remember the girls laughing, now forgetting their quarrel over the pickles, and Gitty, suppressing a chuckle herself, scolding Akiva, who smirked, red-faced. Hershy forked a piece of gefilte fish into a small dish of beet horseradish, and then, noticing the girls' laughter as he brought his fork to his mouth, barely missed his nose.

Through it all, I could think only: How could I possibly leave all this?

We finished eating, then sang the hymns for the Sabbath meal, the children following along in their *bentchers*, the small hymn-readers passed around as mementos at family weddings.

> *Blessed is God above, who has granted us rest,*
> *Redemption for our souls from sorrow and despair.*
> *He will give respite to Zion, the rejected city,*
> *How long must a soul grieve in distress.*

I looked at my children around the table and knew that I could never leave. Leiby would go on to live a free life, but I would remain, in our suburban American shtetl, its men consumed with the study of ritual law, its women scurrying aside on the streets so as not to tempt them, its children content without art and science, *Star Wars*, and video games.

The call to appear before the bezdin came several days after Leiby's departure. Word traveled fast, and for days the village was abuzz with the news that Leiby Einstein had left his parents' home to "live with goyim and go to college." Leiby would tell me later that before he left, he visited a barbershop outside the village, where his long dark side-curls were swept off the barbershop floor and into the trash can. After his haircut, he visited a nearby shopping mall, where he bought a pair of jeans, several T-shirts, and a pair of sneakers. He moved out of his parents' home without so much as a glance at his wide-brimmed hat and long coat hanging in his bedroom closet along with his black pants and white shirts.

"Word has it that it's all your fault," my friend Yitzy Ruttner told me on the phone.

Leiby and I had been seen together on several occasions, and it was rumored that I'd talked him into his decision. Even prior to this, people had begun to say that I was no longer a Hasid, that I scorned our traditions, that I was an *apikorus*, a nonbeliever. My act had begun to disintegrate. Until Leiby left, however, the idea that there lived a heretic among them seemed too strange to New Square's residents. "There are no real heretics nowadays," people were accustomed to saying. Now, it appeared, they had changed their minds.

On the day that the call came from the bezdin, I had a conversation with Leiby's brother-in-law, Yossi Pal. I had been driving down Bush Lane in my Honda Odyssey, a block from my home, when Yossi, walking home from the kollel with his blue-and-gold velvet prayer-shawl pouch under his arm, walked toward me. Our eyes met as I drove. His eyebrows went up in a flash of recognition, and he waved for me to stop.

"Can I talk to you?" he asked, as I rolled down my window. I pulled my car over to the curb and motioned for him to get in. He settled into the passenger seat. When I looked at him expectantly, he paused, collecting his thoughts, and said, haltingly, "You . . . are, uh, friends with Leiby, right?"

I nodded, and he looked at me as if trying to discern whether this conversation was really worthwhile.

"Maybe," he said, "there is something you can do?" His interlocked fingers rested on the velvet bag in his lap. His voice was soft, almost pleading, now. The family was in a crisis, he told me. Leiby had rejected their pleas to stay. Couldn't I explain to him that his plan was nothing but foolishness?

I watched as boys nearby rode their bicycles, swerving wildly to avoid girls jumping rope or swaying with hula hoops. It was at this very

corner that I'd had my last conversation with Leiby. I had urged him
to rethink the one part of his plan that I found troubling: severing ties
with his family. Why was it necessary? I'd asked, and Leiby responded
that it was what he needed to do. His family, he said, would only be a
hindrance to his goals, always after him to return to observance. His
father had been abusive to him all his life. His mother had experienced
several emotional breakdowns, and he did not think she was a healthy
presence in his life. He was the youngest of seven siblings, and close
to none of them. Leiby was determined to do it his way, and I realized
that there was something to his resolve that went beyond reason. He
needed to be free, perhaps, before he could return to them.

Now I sat with my arm leaning on the open window, while Yossi
waited for my response. I knew I had to hide my own views, my secret
pride in Leiby's courage to forge his own path, but I, too, had felt unsettled by Leiby's decision, and here, perhaps, was an opportunity to
mend the rift between Leiby and his family before it became irreparable.

"There isn't much I can do," I told Yossi. "But the family might still
have options."

Yossi looked at me eagerly, while I thought of how best to make
my point. I knew I had to weigh my words carefully, to seek a balance
between my conflicting sympathies.

"Meet him halfway," I said. "Focus on the important things, instead
of trying to control him completely."

Yossi's eyes narrowed with suspicion. "What are you suggesting?"

"Attending college is not a sin. He'll be no different from thousands
of Modern Orthodox Jews. Show him some support for his needs, and
in return, ask him to come home for Shabbos."

Yossi looked at me as if I had suggested something truly awful.
Leiby's family wanted him back, within this community and within
the lifestyle in which they had raised him. Compromise hadn't occurred to them.

"Would you rather he leave and be completely cut off from it all?" I
asked. "He's an adult. He has a plan for his life. Neither you nor I nor
anyone else can stop him."

Yossi looked startled by all this. These were ideas he'd never considered. We spoke for a long time, and by the end of it, Yossi appeared

to understand. Going to college was bad, but things could be worse. Then he looked at me as if it had just dawned on him. "Do you think he's *already*"—he hesitated, as if afraid to mouth the actual word, then gathered his strength—"eating trayf? Not keeping Shabbos?"

"I don't know," I said. "But he certainly will soon, if his family doesn't care to understand his needs." Yossi nodded slowly. Then he said that he thought Leiby and his family might come to some understanding. He would speak to Leiby's father and explain it to him.

Later that day came the call to appear before the bezdin. By midnight, I was officially expelled from the community. As I walked home after the appearance before the bezdin, the words of Matt the car mechanic rang again in my ears: *If you don't belong in New Square, you just stay out. That's just how it is.*

I thought about how I was going to tell Gitty, and then I thought about Leiby, and wondered about my part in his decision. Had I guided him irresponsibly? I had applauded his desire to determine the course of his own life, offered a listening ear and a sounding board for his plans. But Leiby was nineteen, an adult. The army would've taken him, if he'd followed through, sent him out into the world to make decisions about life and death, and to place his own life in jeopardy.

In our world, however, adulthood did not exist, not really. Everyone was influenced by *someone*, who was in turn influenced by someone else. Both good and bad behavior were guided not from within but by the books and authority figures who declared one thing forbidden and another thing virtuous. Self-determination was an unrecognized concept. To the bezdin, it was clear: Leiby's escape was my fault, and mine alone.

Later, I would learn that Leiby's father had come to them in the very hours following my conversation with Yossi, and demanded that I be held accountable. Yossi had repeated to him our conversation, told him how I had defiantly declared my support for Leiby's goals. It was clear to them all that I was the story's main villain. During my conversation with Yossi, I had hoped to encourage understanding between Leiby and his family. In that regard, it was now clear: I had failed.

Chapter Twenty-One

I wasn't overly upset by the bezdin's verdict. For several months, I had been trying to convince Gitty that if I was to continue living an Orthodox lifestyle, then, at the very least, we would have to leave New Square. Gitty had resisted, though, wanting to remain near her parents and her twelve siblings. This was the only community she'd ever known, and she wouldn't know how to live elsewhere, how to engage with neighbors who didn't understand people from our world—people who, she was sure, would mock her provincial manner, her flawed English, her outmoded fashions.

Now, however, we had no choice. The bezdin had ordered me out. Unless we decided to end our marriage, Gitty would have to move with me.

Over the next few weeks, as Gitty and I packed our family's belongings, sold our house in New Square, and closed on a new home in Monsey, I thought back on another time when I had suffered the shame of expulsion.

When I was thirteen, when I first came to know the Skverers, the Skverers thought they might do better without me.

At the Skverer yeshiva in Williamsburg, I had earned myself the distinction of uncooperative student. According to the official yeshiva schedule, we were to arrive each Sunday morning at seven, stay in our third-floor dorm rooms throughout the week, and return home on Friday afternoon for the Sabbath.

I, however, had established my own routine.

On Sunday morning, instead of waking at six and rushing through the cold December and January mornings to catch the bus to Williamsburg, I would stay in bed until ten, then stroll off to the Munkatch shul on Forty-Seventh and Fourteenth, where the ritual bath was open late and prayer groups assembled every twenty minutes. "You have to get to yeshiva!" my mother would cry, but I had few anxieties about it. Most Sundays, by the time I returned home, ate a leisurely breakfast, and determined that it was time to start the day, it would be long past noon. No point in going to yeshiva *now*, I would think, and then I'd spend the day lazing around at home.

On Mondays, I would repeat the routine.

On Tuesdays, I would show up at the yeshiva around lunchtime.

The Skverer teachers, unlike the cheder rebbes at Krasna, were warm and gentle, scholarly and pious, lax with discipline. "I am very afraid I will have to suspend you," my morning instructor would say to me, and I would nod, sympathetically. He had to do what he had to do. In the end, he wouldn't bother. "Can you make an effort?" he would ask, and I would say that I would, knowing that I wouldn't. I studied well, when I was around, but by lunchtime on Thursday, I would decide I'd had enough yeshiva for the week. My tefillin pouch under my arm, I would make my way down Bedford Avenue, to the entrance ramp to the Brooklyn-Queens Expressway, and hitchhike a ride back to Borough Park.

"I don't want to use the word *expulsion*," Reb Chezkel, the dean, said to my mother over the phone. Unbeknownst to either of them, I was listening in from another extension. "He is a very fine boy. But if his week lasts from Tuesday afternoon to Thursday morning, there isn't much sense in keeping him here."

"What do you suggest we do with him?" my mother asked. She sounded surprisingly calm, as if arranging a delivery of groceries.

"Maybe a yeshiva out of town," Reb Chezkel said. There were many options. London. Zurich. Montreal. Jerusalem. My heart leaped. I would travel, make new friends. I was all in favor. He could use the word expulsion, too, if he liked.

My father was ill at that time, in the hospital with a strange condition. For years, following the practices of obscure Jewish mystics, he had lived a life of asceticism and taxed his body severely. The practices were known as *sigufim*. Self-punishment and bodily deprivation. Mystics of old rolled their naked bodies in snow-blanketed fields, hammered holes through ice-covered rivers to immerse in frigid waters. They spent their days in fasting and prayer. My father did not roll his body in snow or break holes through ice, but he slept little and fasted frequently. When he ate, it was with such regimented discipline that it was barely enough to sustain him. Breakfast would be a toasted rice cake and a couple of spoonfuls of plain yogurt. Lunch, a bowl of steamed vegetables; supper, a thin slice of specially prepared rice bread that my mother would bake for him. Sometimes, he also had a tablespoon of peanut butter.

Finally, in the summer of 1987, a month after my bar mitzvah, he collapsed, and was hospitalized. He was six-foot-two, weighing in at ninety pounds. His body had worn away, unnourished. According to my mother, he was suffering from a rare form of anorexia nervosa. He was not only physically ill but psychologically ill.

"He's gone crazy," my mother would say, and I would get angry at her. I had always thought of my father not only as brilliant but saintly. A man who truly lived for otherworldly aspirations. I could see no other way to explain his behavior.

"He has become intolerable," she would tell us, knowing certain things about him that we children did not. Soon she was dropping hints of divorce.

When I argued that she was being unfair to him, she would grow exasperated. "*Shayfele*, your father is a brilliant and unusual man. But he is very, very sick." She explained that sometimes, those who practiced extreme behaviors for what seemed like religious reasons were really afflicted with psychological conditions. My father, she claimed, was suffering from a mental illness that drove him to treat his body cruelly. Religion and spiritual practices provided the cloak, but underneath was a terrible malaise that was destroying him.

My father would scoff when I'd ask him about it. "Nonsense. Mommy means well, but she reads things in books or hears things from doctors and thinks they must always be true."

I didn't know which of them was correct, and I was upset with it all. I loved my father, but I wanted him to start eating and to get better and to stop being crazy and go back to being just saintly. I loved my mother, but I wanted her to stop berating my father and to stop threatening to break up our family. I knew they cared deeply for each other, but if they couldn't take responsibility for their own lives, they would have no authority to instruct me on mine. When adults misbehave, I reasoned, they forfeit the right to tell children what to do.

"When the two of you shape up your acts," I told my mother, "I'll shape up mine."

The yeshiva in Montreal was not the panacea that my parents had hoped for, nor was it the fulfillment of my own dreams for travel and adventure.

"*Nu! Nu!* Wake up! Wake up for the service of the Creator!" Reb Hillel, the *mashgiach*, would shout as he walked through the dorms at six o'clock each morning. I could see his scowling face even without opening my eyes. These rabbis were not Skverers but Satmars. They shouted, they slapped, they pinched, they thwacked. There was no way to hitchhike home on Thursday afternoons. There was serious studying and serious punishment. The doors to the study hall would be locked at the beginning of each session, and anyone who didn't make it in time was punished—either fined or, with repeat offenders, slapped. The yeshiva was headed by the Ruv, a rotund and austere man, the scion of great rabbinic dynasties, whose presence in the study hall was so thick that when he was around, the already-high decibel level in the study hall would reach an eardrum-pounding pitch.

In June, the yeshiva moved to the Laurentian Mountains. Our summer campus was a converted resort on the edge of a small lake with a private beach, once used for swimming but now forbidden to us students. Behind several bungalows that had been converted to lecture rooms, past the gravel road that led to the main road, past a large clearing on a hilltop, a path led into the woods. After a five-minute walk, the path forked sharply to the left, where, past tangles of brushwood and scattered thornbushes, stood a tremendous boulder, twenty feet high, abutting a wide creek on the other side. Around the far side of the boulder were a series of ridges, where I could climb to the top for a magnificent view of cascading waterfalls a hundred yards upriver.

On that boulder, during our one-hour lunch break at midday or during the dinner break in early evening, my friend Avrum Yida and I would spend the time in brooding conversation. Avrum Yida was from Williamsburg, the Satmar stronghold in Brooklyn, and he, too, came from a family with troubles. His father, he told me, was a drug addict, and his parents, after years of domestic strife, had recently divorced. We found commonality in our respective miseries.

In July, my mother called to say that my father was in the hospital again and that he wanted to see me. He'd been out of the hospital for a couple of months but apparently had not been entirely cured. My mother didn't elaborate. She said only that she'd already made flight arrangements and spoken to the Ruv. One of the rabbis would give me a ride to the airport.

After the flight from Montreal to New York, after lugging my suitcase up to our second-floor apartment in Borough Park, I opened the door to find my mother standing in the hallway, waiting. She gave me a silent hug, then looked at me sadly, her gaze steady.

"He's gone," she said.

My father was dead.

The adults hadn't shaped up their act. My father hadn't gotten himself better, and my mother hadn't been much help, either. Before she had time to follow through on her threats of divorce, my father had died, leaving our family in a state of turmoil.

After the seven days of mourning, I returned to the yeshiva, more apathetic than ever.

"My plan," I said to my friend Avrum Yida, "is to end up a shaygetz." A shaygetz drove a sports car or a motorcycle. He cavorted with shiksas. He wore jeans and leather jackets. He didn't bother keeping Shabbos or kosher. He was, in short, no different from a goy. The shaygetz declared God and His laws irrelevant. The shaygetz was unprincipled—there was no principle in sin. For spite, for temptation, for mindless apathy, for sheer wickedness—the shaygetz defied God, the rabbis, his parents, and all that was good and righteous and noble. I had no clear formula for becoming a shaygetz, but I was determined, in the meantime, to show my general intentions.

Reb Mordche would attempt to put a stop to it.

Reb Mordche delivered his lectures each afternoon, for an hour and a half, in one of the tiny converted bungalows, where we sat cramped against one another on wooden benches around a three-sided arrangement of tables. He sat on the fourth side, facing us. My place was the first to his left, within easy reach.

One day, all of us were restless from the heat, the broken air conditioner a teasing reminder of the comforts we lacked, and Reb Mordche struggled to hold our attention. To my left sat Chaim Nuchem Ausch. Reaching silently from behind, I flicked my middle finger against his left ear. Chaim Nuchem flinched, then looked angrily toward the boy on his left: "Why you flicking me?"

The boy to Chaim Nuchem's left protested, declaring his innocence, and Reb Mordche threw me a stern glance.

A plastic straw lay on the table in front of me, alongside an empty soda can. I reached for it and held it between my index and middle finger, pretending to twiddle it absentmindedly, while at the same time, I put a small piece of paper in my mouth and let it soak in my saliva for a few minutes. A few minutes later, I shot a prodigious spitball across the room, watching with delight as it whizzed past Pinny Greenfeld's nose and landed on Yossi Hershkowitz's forehead with an audible *sprrt*. I remember the laughter, and how it stopped abruptly just as I saw, from the corner of my eye, Reb Mordche's arm jerk up from where it rested on the table, his open palm headed directly to the right side of my face.

There were no thoughts in my head at that moment, only reflexes, and my right arm went up to block his strike. My arm struck his forcefully. I remember the stunned look on Reb Mordche's face, his arm still partially raised in front of him. I was aware that the room had gone frightfully silent. I had committed the greatest offense possible for a yeshiva student: striking an instructor.

My punishment would be severe. If I was lucky, I would be slapped senseless. More likely, Reb Mordche would summon Reb Hillel, and together they would beat me as no student had been beaten before.

There was only one thing to do: escape.

I sprang backward up onto the bench. With one arm in the air for balance, I jumped toward the door, pushing it with my free arm midair.

The last thing I heard, as the flimsy screen door banged shut behind me, was: "All of you! Go get him!"

I was fast, and I knew where I was headed. By the time my classmates had bounded out of the lecture room and determined the direction I'd gone, I was already halfway up the trail to the woods. By the time I heard their shouts—"Which way? Where'd he go?"—I was halfway up the boulder abutting the creek, hidden behind a dense thicket, climbing to the top and settling into the familiar ridge.

The minutes passed, and the sounds of my classmates receded. From my perch, I watched the rushing cascades of the falls and the pools of white foam in the water below. I wondered what I was going to do now. Certain punishment awaited me back at the camp, but where else could I go? I was hundreds of miles from home. My transportation had always been arranged by the yeshiva, chartered buses that brought all the New York students back and forth over the various term breaks. I had no money for a bus or an airplane ticket.

I wondered what it was that had led me to all this trouble. I wondered why I found myself, over and over again, on the wrong side of adult expectations. Overcome with self-pity, I thought of jumping off the edge and sinking into the rushing torrents. But the water didn't look very deep, and I wasn't likely to drown easily. I considered taking off through the woods to the railroad tracks that passed not far from our camp, and walking until I reached some destination or collapsed from exhaustion. I needed to get away, far from the yeshiva and its tedious grind of Talmud studies, far from the rabbis and teachers, with their beatings and their insistent scoldings and their buffoonish piety, far from the friends who sided with a teacher and pursued me into the woods.

I checked my watch. There were fifteen minutes until afternoon prayers, and I realized with a start that it was my turn to lead prayers. If I wasn't there, a new offense would be piled on to all my existing ones. I listened carefully to the stillness of the forest and to the sounds of rushing water. Here and there, a bird called and another responded. The sounds of my friends had quieted down, but who knew if they were lurking somewhere, behind a tree or a rock?

Then again, what if they were?

It was unfair that life presented only bad options. It appeared that whatever I did, I was bound for trouble. I would head back and face whatever punishment awaited me. Adults were often unpredictable—maybe they'd spare me this time.

Stepping tentatively out of the woods, I looked around and saw no one. The afternoon sun beat down on the trampled grass around the cluster of buildings, the two-story dormitory, the study hall and dining room, the small cottages serving as residences for faculty members, who brought their wives and children with them for the duration of the summer. From above the study hall doorway, set within the transom, a massive air-conditioning unit hummed loudly, a steady drip of condensation falling on all who passed beneath it.

I pushed the door open slowly. My classmates were all in their places. I looked for Reb Mordche and noticed that he wasn't in the room. Neither were the other instructors, or even the Ruv, who ordinarily sat up on a platform at the end of the hall, eagle-eyed over his domain. Here and there, students began to close their texts, reaching for their hats, offering concluding remarks to their partners as they headed to the sink in the rear to wash before prayer.

The clock on the wall read two minutes to four. No one looked my way. Slowly, I angled my way through the maze of tables and chairs to the front of the hall, and took my spot at the prayer leader's podium. I turned and saw my friends at the other end of the room noticing me and whispering.

I watched the clock. The moment it struck four, a side door opened and the Ruv walked in, followed by the rest of the faculty. I could not read their expressions. The Ruv looked around at the students, then made his way toward his lectern, opposite the one for the prayer leader, where I now stood. I watched him, my heart pounding wildly, trying to discern his intentions, but he appeared not to notice me. Perhaps he's saving my punishment for later, I thought. Or, I dared hope, maybe Reb Mordche decided to keep quiet about the incident.

The Ruv was now at his lectern, opening his prayer book. Clearly, my punishment was not at hand. I looked at him, anticipating his signal, ready to launch the opening verse: *Ashrei. . . . Fortunate are those who dwell in Your houses.*

All of a sudden, the Ruv turned to face me, then raised his arm and pointed a pudgy index finger toward the door: *"AROIS FIN DU!"*

I froze. The hall fell silent, and I could feel the stares of fifty pairs of eyes on me.

"GET OUT OF HERE!" the Ruv shouted, louder this time. "I won't tolerate gangsters in my yeshiva! You are now expelled!"

For a moment, I was struck by the word *gangster*, thrown into his furious Yiddish. Was I a gangster? The word was meant to shame me, I knew, but instead I felt proud. A gangster was worse than a shaygetz, and so I had achieved something.

I turned and made my way through the hushed study hall. The students stepped aside to let me pass, through to the rear, past the last tables, where my classmates, the youngest group of students, stood watching me. I nodded to a few of them as I passed, offering a hint of a smirk, and opened the main doors and headed up to my dorm room.

A hour later, I finished packing my things into my suitcase, but not before Reb Hillel appeared suddenly and delivered a slap to my face so forceful that the world went black for a long moment and I thought I was going to faint. When I finally looked up, Reb Hillel stood there in silence, contempt all over his face, and then turned on his heels and left the room.

That night, I slept at the home of a kind rabbi in Montreal, who offered to let me stay until I could get a bus back to New York. As I dragged my suitcase into the small guest room on Durocher Avenue, I felt a sort of melancholic emptiness. I had been expelled twice now—first by the Skverers, and now by the Satmars. After I had been branded an outcast, my plans to become a shaygetz no longer seemed so hot.

Duly chastised, I began to rethink my strategy. I was a Hasidic boy, and I realized that I could be nothing else. I had been shown up for my hubris, and what I wanted most now was acceptance. I wanted back at the yeshiva.

The next day, I called Reb Mordche and offered an apology that was as sincere as it was desperate. Then I called the Ruv and promised to change my ways. A week later, I was allowed to return to the campus in the Laurentians. I hunkered down and set my mind to studying the laws of the Sabbath, when and how one may or may not remove olive oil from a lamp to season a salad—nearly a whole chapter on that subject alone. I was determined to change. I would take my duties seriously and prove that I had what it took to achieve both scholarship and a pious disposition. I would make these rabbis proud. I would be just like them.

I had veered off the path, nearly lost my way, but had gotten right back onto it. After a year in Montreal, the Skverers took me back, and I spent two years at their yeshiva in Williamsburg, and then three more at their flagship institution, the Great Yeshiva in New Square. I had become not a shaygetz but a serious student and later a respectable young man.

Until now, at the age of thirty, when I had veered off the path once again. The reasons were different this time; yet in so many ways, they felt the same, as if I were a child again, a teenager, naturally inclined to rebel against authority. Except that this time, my sins were far greater. And this time, I had no intention of pleading my way back.

Chapter Twenty-Two

A month after the bezdin ordered me out, Gitty and I and the children moved to Monsey, a nearby hamlet with a Hasidic population several times greater than that of New Square. In Monsey, there were not only Skverers but also Vizhnitzers, Belzers, Satmars, and Lubavitchers, all living cheek-by-jowl with old-school Litvaks.

The area we moved to, a hilly road studded with one-story ranch houses and modest colonials, looked like any other suburban neighborhood in Rockland County: backyard swimming pools shaded by dogwoods and Japanese maples, manicured hedgerows along property edges, front lawns so green they seemed almost painted. Behind the halcyon facade of two-car garages and well-maintained landscaping, however, were attitudes not much different from those of New Square. The men wore the same broad fur hats, the women wore the same wigs covered with hats and kerchiefs, and many showed the same suspicion and intolerance for those who were different, for those whose fur hats just weren't furry enough, or just the right height or weight or hardened sheen.

Walking home from the little shul at the corner one Friday night, I got into a discussion with a neighbor about the challenges of science to religious faith.

"If science contradicts the Torah, it is false," the man said resolutely.

The man's son, a chubby, redheaded little boy, pulled on his arm. "Come already," the boy whined. I could see Chaya Suri looking for me through our dining-room window, her hands cupping the sides of her face, better to see into the dark. But the topic at hand burned inside me, and I couldn't let it go.

"You can't say that," I said to the man. "The study of science is every-where in your life. It's in the car you drive. In the medicine you take when you're ill. It is in the production of your food, in the manufacture of your clothes. You rely on science when you fly in an airplane, or when you visit your doctor. Science has put a man on the moon, for goodness sake!"

The man remained unimpressed. "I see you're an *oifgeklerter*," he said. "Only an *oifgeklerter* believes in scientists the way you do."

An *oifgeklerter*. An enlightened one. Not a heretic but in many ways just as bad. The heretic declares his godlessness openly, and so the righteous can choose to avoid him. But enlightened ones are deceptive, wrapping their heresy in a veneer of plainspoken inquiry.

I was reminded of an old Hasidic teaching, on the verse in Psalms: *God peers down from heaven to ask: Where is the enlightened one who seeks God?*

Said Reb Noach of Lechevitch: "*Where is the enlightened one who seeks God?* The answer, of course, is that he is nowhere." The Psalmist had asked a rhetorical question because enlightened ones do not seek God. They seek only to destroy the faith of those who do.

"They *merely question*," one of my teachers once said of the Maskilim, the enlightened Jews and the reformers who studied science and philosophy and attempted, during the eighteenth and nineteenth centuries, to create a new Jew for the modern era. "In their questions, however, lie their malevolent intentions. They seek to destroy faith, not to uphold it."

The transition to life in Monsey brought our family new challenges. In New Square, I had felt alienated from those around us; now Gitty and the children did, too.

I had hoped that the children would make new friends. The Mandelbaums, across the road, had three girls; the Illowitzes, next door, had four; the Richters, a couple of houses down, had seven. During the first weeks in our new home, Tziri, Freidy, and Chaya Suri would regularly head over to the Mandelbaum house, a split-level cottage almost identical to ours. After several weeks, I noticed that they went less frequently. Soon they stopped going altogether.

"Those girls are different," Gitty said when I asked about it. They spoke English instead of Yiddish. They wore more fashionable outfits. My daughters were shy, uncomfortable around girls so unlike them. In

New Square, they'd been surrounded by family and friends, cousins, classmates, children raised as much in one another's homes as their own, and they'd never felt the sting of outsiderness.

Gitty, too, missed her parents and her dozen siblings, and scores of nieces, nephews, and cousins. She tried befriending the neighbors but, like our daughters, found it hard to blend in. It wasn't long before she gave up trying, and kept busy with housework, scanning the advertisements in the Community Connections, or selling old baby outfits on eBay.

"Can I ask you something?" Gitty asked one evening just as I walked in from work. In her hand was an envelope, and she was reading what appeared to be a credit-card statement.

"Can it wait?"

Gitty slapped the statement on the kitchen counter. "What's *this*?" she asked, and jabbed her finger at one of the lines on the page: *D'Agostino's*.

I remembered the purchase: I had been in Manhattan late one evening, and I'd stopped at a supermarket to buy a quick dinner of roasted salmon and a side of potatoes from its hot-food bar.

"Was it nonkosher food?" Gitty asked.

I told Gitty that I would not give her an accounting for a ten-dollar purchase that could've been for anything.

She turned furious, convinced of my guilt. "Why?" she cried. "Why must you do this?"

I didn't know why. Salmon and potatoes from D'Agostino's weren't any better than salmon and potatoes from a kosher place, but I no longer kept kosher when there were no neighbors or family members to hide from. I simply no longer felt the need. Manhattan didn't have nearly as many kosher options for a quick dinner, and it seemed silly to go to such effort when it felt so pointless.

"Would you rather I lied?" I asked.

"No," she snapped, her teeth clenched in anger. "I don't want you eating trayf, period!"

During our Shabbos meals, I sometimes prodded my children to think about the weekly Bible portion in new ways.

"Do you think it right," I asked my daughters one week, "that an Israelite soldier may abduct a woman from an enemy nation and force her to be his wife?"

Tziri appeared pensive and said nothing, while Freidy looked up at me, surprised, and shook her head.

"*M' fregt nish kein kashes oif de Toireh,*" she said, and went back to her plate of chulent and noodle kugel. At eleven years old, it was as clear as it could possibly be: *one does not question the Torah.*

Freidy needed nothing more, but Tziri looked as though she was still processing the thought.

Gitty, from the far end of the table, glowered at me. Over the years, she had made it clear: she could imagine no greater betrayal than infecting our children's minds with heresy. I tried to be careful, to keep my real thoughts well concealed, but sometimes it was hard to resist a nudge.

Late on Friday nights, after the Sabbath meal was over and the children were tucked into their beds and Gitty, too, said she was tired and went to bed, I would sit on the living-room sofa and read. When I sensed that the house was entirely still, I would open the creaky door to my study, located right off the living room. I would close the door as quietly as I could and leave the light off so as not to alert the neighbors. In the dark, I would jiggle the mouse, and the computer would come alive, its light casting a soft glow on the mess of papers, the printer, my bookcase filled with forbidden literature. Checking my e-mail and browsing the Internet, I would listen carefully for sounds coming from the house. I would press the keys gently, one at a time, pecking with my index finger instead of touch-typing, anxious not to let the familiar sounds of keyboard typing penetrate the Sabbath silence of our home.

But all the care I took was no match for Gitty's intuition. I never understood how, but each Friday night, minutes after I would sit down at my desk, the door would creak open, and Gitty would be standing in the doorway in her nightgown. The glow from the screen would partially illuminate her face and cast a shadow of her profile against the wall. In the dim light, I could see her face ashen, her eyes pleading.

"How *can* you?" A cry of anguish, perhaps even a genuine desire to understand: How could I be so dismissive of God's law?

By the glow of my computer screen I would explain, yet again, that I was no longer a believer. The rules were meaningless to me, my private desecrations were my way of carving out a personal space of freedom from a world in which my nearly every move was scrutinized. I was sorry she had to see it, I'd hoped not to wake her, but I wouldn't accept restrictions during private moments.

Gitty would grow offended and angry. "You think you're so much smarter than everyone?"

In my anger, I would say, yes, that was exactly what I thought. And then we would fight, and then make up, in an endlessly exhausting cycle. Afterward, we would lie in bed for hours and sigh about where to go from here and how to make it work, and always, we would end with the question: What about the children?

I would feel tenderness for her in those moments, despite all that was tearing us apart. But the next week, the same thing would happen, until eventually I grew bolder and would turn on the light in my study and tap the keys without fear. Gitty would still come down, but it was no longer in the dark, and she would sit on the floor near the door and glare at me and my desecration of the Sabbath.

"Why do you have to be so different?" she would cry. "Why can't you be like everyone else?" She would come up with the answer on her own: "It's all those books, and movies, and newspapers, and the Internet.

"The rabbis were right," she would say again and again. "It's all that garbage that's changed you."

The tension in our home only grew worse. Gitty would continue to scold me for my transgressions, and eventually, in the interest of keeping the peace, I would begin to hide from her, using cash for nonkosher purchases, hiding receipts and creating alibis. At Starbucks, I would carefully calculate my purchases. A five-dollar purchase could be for a latte, which was kosher. A ten-dollar purchase would give away the turkey-and-Swiss-cheese sandwich that I'd bought with it, and so I'd rush to find an ATM.

I needed to stop hiding. I needed to stop lying. But was there a way to do it without shattering everything?

I would grow frustrated with Gitty's unwillingness to bend. When I suggested one day that instead of always requiring me to drive her places, she might learn to drive on her own, she exploded: "Why should *I* change for *you?*"

Most Hasidic women did not drive cars, but still, some did. I did not care so much if Gitty drove, but it annoyed me that she wouldn't even consider it. As a family, we kept everything in strict accordance with Jewish law. I was careful to keep up appearances for the public, now even more than before. Unlike in New Square, where I'd had my small circle of deviants on Saturday mornings, here I had no choice but to sit through three hours of prayer and Torah reading, to listen to the other men speak without being able to offer my own real thoughts. Much of it felt taxing and stressful; yet I kept doing it because Gitty wanted it for our family. Was it so much to ask that we relax on minor matters of Hasidic custom?

"Let's take a vacation," I suggested to Gitty one day. I thought it would be good for us to get away. "How about Europe?" Gitty had relatives in London. I wanted to visit Vienna and Prague and Kraków.

Gitty, however, had little interest in traveling. Newness disoriented her. She didn't care for foreign cities and the stresses of unfamiliar foods and other people's beds. Through our decade and a half of marriage, we'd taken only one vacation out of state, a week in Florida to visit an aunt and uncle near Boca Raton.

I persisted, though, and Gitty finally relented. "Maybe just a few days. Somewhere close."

We made arrangements for the children to stay with relatives, and Gitty and I took a three-day trip to Niagara Falls. After we saw the falls, rode the *Maid of the Mist*, and purchased armloads of souvenirs, I wondered if we might get away from the high-rise hotels and the masses of tourists in Bermuda shorts and cheap sunglasses.

"Look!" I pointed to several brochures I found in the hotel lobby. "Vineyards! Wine tours!" Gitty agreed to go for a wine tour, but in the parking lot afterward, we quarreled bitterly.

"You drank trayf wine!" she cried. During the tour, I had ignored her dark glances, and had drunk from the small cups offered for tasting—Chardonnays, Cabernets, Malbecs.

After an hour of arguing, screaming, and crying, we made up, agreed to put it behind us, and drove to our next destination. In the nearby town of Niagara-on-the-Lake, the annual ShawFest was taking place, a celebration of "the witty and provocative spirit of Bernard Shaw," and I persuaded Gitty to attend a play with me. The play was *Hotel Peccadillo*, based on a French play by Georges Feydeau. It was, in the words of one reviewer, "a romp about the respectable middle-class behaving less than respectably." Neither Gitty nor I had ever been to a play before, romp or non-romp. The reviews were good, and we had only one night left. I bought tickets without investigating further.

When the play was over, Gitty stalked out of the theater ahead of me. No, she said when I finally caught up to her. She did not enjoy the play—could not, in fact, make out the story line, but understood enough to know that it was dirty and disgusting and vulgar and goyish and if I asked her to join me in one more of my stupid and crazy and goyish interests, she would never see me or speak to me again, and then I'd be free to go off on my own and watch all those stupid plays and have sex with the actors, too, if I wanted.

In an effort to reason me out of my pleas for compromise, Gitty would remind me that she had moved to Monsey for my sake, how unhappy she was to be so far from everything she knew, how unhappy the children were. I knew that she was right; yet I would look at her during those times and feel nothing for her. Old resentments would rise, and I would wonder: Why were we still together? The answer was, for the children, of course. But if they, too, were unhappy, what was the point?

"I don't think this is working," I said to Gitty one day.

Gitty thought that maybe we could still save things. "Maybe we can move someplace else," she said.

"Move again? To where?"

Gitty looked down, silent. There weren't many options.

"Would you live among the Modern Orthodox? The Upper West

Side? Teaneck? Flatbush?" The Modern Orthodox allowed the study of secular subjects, they watched movies, boys and girls went on dates. Our children would have more opportunities, and I would perhaps feel a greater sense of freedom.

Gitty shook her head. "The children need a Yiddish-speaking environment." After a few moments of silence, she said, "But maybe we can relax certain things."

"Like what?" I asked. "You won't even get a driver's license!"

"I don't know." I could see her hazel irises glistening. "What will I tell my parents?" she asked in a near whisper, her voice catching halfway through.

On a breezy night in November, Gitty and I looked out in silence from behind a low fence at the edge of the Hudson River. The river's gentle waves broke against the stone wall as the wind blew gently in our faces. A mile or so upriver was the Tappan Zee Bridge, its lights cutting brilliantly through the darkness of the sky and the river. The shops behind us, along the Piermont Pier, were closed, and aside from a lone dog walker up the road in the distance, there was no one in sight.

It was a night of scheduled intimacy. Earlier that evening, I'd picked up Gitty on Viola Road at the women's mikveh, the ritual bath that she attended once a month, and when we came home, I suggested we do something. "Want to go for a movie?" I asked.

She said that she was not in the mood and did not like movies all that much, anyway.

"How about a drive down to Piermont?" I asked, after we sat in silence for a while longer.

Piermont was a hillside village ten miles away, right on the Hudson River, known for its trendy art galleries and restaurants and a handful of celebrity residents. At this hour, the waterfront would be empty, and I thought it would be a pleasant place to spend the evening.

"What are we going to do there?"

Was there irritability in her tone? I wasn't sure. Then again, she seemed irritable almost every time we spoke now. I considered giving up. I could go into my study and watch a movie on my own, and we could just go to bed alone. Yet through the years, physical intimacy had remained important to both of us, and I felt it my duty to keep that aspect of our life from going stale.

"I don't know," I said. "We'll take a stroll. Look at the stars. Gaze at the lights."

"Fine," she said.

Now we stood watching the lights passing in the distance over the bridge, like colored dots against the black backdrop of a low-resolution video game. She was dressed in a warm coat, but she'd forgotten her scarf. She got a tissue out of her pocket to wipe her nose, and I realized that my mustache felt moist on my upper lip. I reached my hand behind her arm, then moved to take her hand. Her hands were in her pockets, and I put my hand inside. Her fingers reached for mine, interlocking, although I could feel hesitancy in her movements. She would never have allowed it in public within our own neighborhood.

I remember thinking that it would make a nice photograph, the two of us against the night sky, the lights of the bridge glistening against their reflection in the water.

"Isn't this nice?" I asked.

Her shoulders were hunched, her eyes darting around. She noticed that I was looking at her, and she smiled stiffly. After a minute, she said, "I'm cold." Then, looking away, "I want to go back."

It was chilly, not freezing, but cold for November. Still, she'd said it irritably, almost as if the weather was my fault. Frustration, annoyance, a touch of anger finally burst inside me.

"For once, can we want the same thing?"

Gitty scowled, and I regretted saying it, but it was too late.

"You want different things," she said, repeating what she'd said a thousand times already. "Weird and crazy things. Goyish things. All those things you read in books or see in the movies. I have no interest in any of it."

She unclasped her hand from mine, and we lapsed into silence. When she looked at me, I could see the wetness on her cheeks.

"Maybe you're right," she said softly. "Maybe we just can't make it work."

PART IV

Chapter Twenty-Three

On a Tuesday afternoon in December, during Chanukah of 2007, Gitty and I climbed two rickety flights of wooden stairs to the meeting room of a local rabbinical court. The room doubled as the women's section for a neighborhood shul, and through the slats of the latticework along the far wall, we could see down to the sanctuary, where several dozen men sat over their Talmuds, swinging their thumbs and stroking their beards. Nearby, in a room the size of a large closet, a scribe, feather quill in hand and inkwell at his side, wrote twelve lines of Hebrew script onto a square of parchment. A short while later, the rabbis, the scribe, the witnesses, and several curious busybodies assembled.

"Thou art hereby divorced from me. . . ." The words stuck in my throat as I held the square of parchment in my hand. Gitty stood with her palms together, open and upward, tears running down her cheeks, her body trembling. I could barely see anything but could only hear, as if from inside my head, the silence in the room. I could imagine the rabbis' thoughts, *Nu, finish already.* But I couldn't get the words out. It was fifteen years, almost to the day, from when we'd first met, and now, after I said these last few words and dropped the parchment into Gitty's palms, our bonds would be severed. I swallowed hard, and forced my mind into numbness. "And thou art hereby permitted to all other men."

"A beautiful divorce," one of the rabbis said afterward. "Such lack of acrimony, such genuine tenderness." Gitty and I smiled through our tears and rode home in our car together.

◆◆

Before we split, Gitty and I had agreed that the children were the most important thing. Evenings, as the children slept, we would talk late into the night, sweetly, sadly, of civility, of continued friendship, of co-operative parenting. For the children's sake, we said, we'll make this the most amicable split in the history of amicable splits.

Gitty and the children moved back to New Square, while I took an apartment in Monsey, a ten-minute drive away. The children came to my place twice a week for dinner and homework, and visited every other week for Shabbos, rotating three at a time. I bought a bunk bed from IKEA, along with several air mattresses and lots of pillows and blankets in bright, gender-neutral colors, and set it all up in the extra bedroom, which doubled as my office. It wasn't very roomy, but the kids didn't mind. It felt like camping, they said. I stocked up on books, toys, board games. Gitty and I spoke on the phone nearly every day, and with her guidance, I learned to prepare basic meals.

When the children came on Shabbos, I kept up appearances, wearing my shtreimel and *bekishe* for their sake. I took the boys to shul, and we ate the Shabbos meals and sang the Shabbos songs. I tested the boys on their Bible and Talmud studies, and warned my daughters that playing Monopoly was forbidden according to some opinions, as it was a simulation of weekday business practices. I maintained a strictly kosher kitchen, with two sinks and two sets of dishes for meat and dairy. I even disallowed watching movies—Gitty had become more strict about it, and I made it clear that, wherever the children were concerned, we would go by her rules.

On Saturday afternoons, the children and I took walks down an old country road a mile from our home. At the end of the road was a pond shaded with elms and weeping willows, where we would watch the geese swim and catch glimpses of deer in the nearby woods. Once we spotted two turtles resting on a tire that stood upright in the shallow end, its bottom half buried in rocks and dirt. The turtles faced each other, their necks outstretched, as if in a stare-down. For a long time, we stood and watched, waiting for them to move, until dusk fell and the turtles were barely perceptible bumps on the tire's dark silhouette.

I was thirty-three. After fifteen years of marriage, and five children, I did not feel very young. Still, I told myself, it was not too late to begin a new life as a citizen of the world, a life guided by my own values, no longer driven by the fear of social ostracism.

My job kept me occupied during the day, but in the evening, I could catch up on the education I had missed. I would make new friends and learn about the world. The future seemed bright. I wanted to be a writer and an academic. I would get my GED, my bachelor's degree, my master's, my doctorate. I dreamed of leafy New England college campuses and ivy-covered stone walls and a tenure-track professorship. I wanted to be a scholar of Near Eastern studies or of comparative religion. Or a professor of psychology. Or creative writing. There were suddenly so many options. For now, I would start the process. Within a decade, our youngest would be nearing adulthood; with an empty nest, I'd have the second half of my life to pursue my dreams. I would create possibilities not only for myself but also for my children. I would teach them that they, too, could pursue their aspirations, to be writers or academics or scientists or car mechanics or circus performers. "I want to be a mom," Freidy would say, and I would tell her that was a fine thing to be, if she chose it herself.

None of it was going to be easy, but we would make it work. I would continue to support Gitty and the children, and we would find a reasonable way to share custody. Soon enough, Gitty would find someone to marry. She had many good qualities, and I was sure that there was a man somewhere who would make her happy.

A week after Gitty and I moved to our new apartments, I drove to the Rockland Community College campus, nestled in a forested nook at the tip of Monsey. Down a corridor from the gleaming lobby of the main building, I found a room with brochures and course catalogs and application forms of all kinds. I took one of everything, and spent the better part of a long night reading registration policies, tuition details, and course descriptions.

I wanted to study it all: art history and ornithology and cartooning and calculus I through III and automotive technology and restaurant management. But I could take only night classes, and I was further restricted by my lack of a high school diploma. After two semesters, I would get my GED; but for now, I had to stick with a limited list of classes. I chose English 101 and elementary algebra from the list of requirements, and added one class in psychology and another in general philosophy.

During my first algebra class, after I found a seat in the last row, a woman sat down beside me. She had chin-length, soft blond hair and the clearest skin I'd ever seen on an adult human. Her features were exquisite, almost doll-like. She wore a white jacket and tight jeans and short white boots with furry cuffs. She struck me as vaguely Eastern European. I imagined a Russian accent.

I knew that at some point, I would want to begin dating. But now, sitting next to this woman, I did not think I wanted to date her, or be friends with her, or even speak with her—I only had the visceral awareness that next to me was such an extraordinary presence that I wondered how I was to concentrate on the algebra lessons. As the professor spoke of polynomials and rational numbers and factorization, I could think only of the woman beside me, her knees nearly touching mine, the pen in her slender fingers moving steadily, filling her notebook with gracefully looping numerals.

Were my feelings normal? Did other men's minds, too, freeze into a near-comatose state in such situations? I wondered what would happen if I tried speaking to her. Would she respond? Or would she cast me a withering glance?

By the end of the first class, I had worked up enough courage to look her way. When our eyes met, she smiled lightly. During the next class, one week later, she leaned over and asked if I'd caught something the professor said. I pointed to my notes, and she copied from them eagerly. Emboldened, I turned to her during the five-minute break. I do not remember what I said, but I remember being astonished that she not only spoke to me but that she was shy and soft-spoken and entirely, though still exquisitely, human. Her name was Aliona, she said. She was twenty-six, lived two towns over, and was in her second year in college.

I wondered if we might become friends.

I thought I knew all about the outside world by now. I had watched hundreds of movies, read dozens of books, devoured thousands of newspaper and magazine articles. I imagined that the language and the cultural nuances and the behavioral peculiarities of non-Hasidim would come to me like a second skin, once I shed my old one.

I would learn soon enough: A world presented on film or on the page was not reality. One does not become a homicide detective from reading crime novels, or a trial lawyer from watching courtroom dramas. All the movies in the world could not adequately prepare me for living in this new world. Even without my yarmulke, with my *payess* shorn off and my wide-brimmed hat and long coat abandoned, I could not shake the feeling that I still carried the aura of a Hasid, emitting vibrations of alienness to all around me.

My attempts to strike up conversation with my classmates felt awkward and strained; it seemed as if their sentences carried a subtext I could not decipher. "Hey, man," a classmate said to me one day in greeting, and I wondered about the meaning behind the idiom. "Man" struck me as a strange form of address. Could one say, "Hey, woman"? What about, "Hey, person"? The dictionary did not say.

Another man peppered his speech with "yo," "dude," and "bro." Even though I knew these words, it felt odd hearing them in real life, and I wondered whether there was some crucial element to living as a non-Hasid that would prove forever elusive. I had been told over the years that my English speech carried a slight Yiddish accent, and I now found myself self-conscious each time I spoke. My name, too, was a source of discomfort: "Shulem," with its Hebrew and Yiddish distinctiveness, felt wholly incongruent with the ethnically neutral persona I now sought for myself.

When shopping for clothes, I found that I could make little sense of contemporary fashions. After I bought a new sweater and wore it to work one day, an acquaintance from the office next door stepped into the elevator with me, looked me up and down, and said, "Preppy sweater." I looked at him for clues to a deeper meaning, but he looked away, hummed a tune to himself, and stepped off the elevator. I was left to wonder: Was preppy good? Was preppy bad? I turned to the Internet, but the answers were elusive. Preppy. Urban. Sporty. Business casual. So many terms, but how did one know what was what? What style suitable for whom, and for what occasion?

One day, I came across the term "dad jeans." Dad jeans, I came to understand, were bad, so I immediately ran to my closet and held up the single pair of light-blue washed-out denim I'd purchased only a few weeks earlier. Dad jeans!

One day, Aliona told me that she hoped to graduate with an English degree. She wanted to be a schoolteacher, she said. English majors liked English, I thought, which meant they liked words and sentences and strange language constructions.

"Do you know the longest grammatically correct sentence containing only a single word?" I asked.

She gave me a puzzled look.

"Buffalo buffalo Buffalo buffalo buffalo buffalo Buffalo buffalo."

She offered a half smile but looked no less puzzled. "What?"

I had seen that fact on Wikipedia earlier that day. The word "buffalo," the article said, with its various definitions—as a regular noun (the animal), a proper noun (the city), and a verb ("to annoy")—made this construction possible. I found myself reading this information with such delight that I immediately filed it away, hoping for an opportunity to share it.

"It means—" I began to explain, then noticed her blank expression. Perhaps offering random bits of information collected from Internet encyclopedias was not a good way to make conversation.

"Sorry," I said, with an embarrassed chuckle. "I guess not everyone's a word nerd."

She laughed. "A word nerd. I like that."

Her laugh encouraged me. Also encouraging was that each Wednesday evening, as soon as I arrived, she would look up and nod: "Hello, Shulem." Her voice was like silk, soft and smooth and precious in its sparseness. Occasionally, she would look at me with a kind of expectant expression. Yet I could not think of much to say, and my meager attempts at conversation fizzled into nothingness.

Months passed, and I found myself with a kind of loneliness I had not anticipated. For nearly fifteen years, my wife and children had been right beside me. I'd had scores of friends, hundreds of acquaintances, and a community of thousands. Suddenly unmoored, I began to worry: How was I going to replace it all?

A small handful of old friends still called occasionally, but there was a chill to our interactions. "So, are you happy now?" they would ask, their tones flat, rhetorical. I would say that yes, I was happy, or happier than before, or what did it mean to be happy, really? Or I would turn the question back at them—"Are *you* happy?"—and they would grow annoyed. "You're the one who made this big change." Those conversations were awkward and stilted. We were careful to skirt sensitive issues, questions of faith, the details of non-Hasidic life, whether I *really* no longer kept the Sabbath, or if it was all just theoretical, as my brother Avrumi had once asked. Invariably, my friends would say, "You'll be back, Shulem. You'll be back." They would offer their best wishes, hopes that I find myself soon, find peace of mind, find whatever it was I was looking for, so that I might, the sooner the better, stop all this nonsense for the good of everyone involved.

"We should hang out sometime," I said to Aliona after class one day. "Maybe get coffee or something." I placed my books into my bag, then flung the bag over my shoulder and slipped out between our seats. I had hoped for a casual effect, as if the thought had just occurred to me, as if I hadn't prepared those words in my head, rehearsed them with different cadences and tones to get the effect just right.

Aliona looked up. "Yeah, we should."

Did she say it brightly? Did she seem eager? Was she just being polite?

"We'll figure something out," I said as I took off, not knowing what else to say. Later, I agonized over it: How will she react when she learns about my past? What if we have nothing to talk about? Scenarios of rejection—catastrophe!—played out in my head, which soon became not only possibilities but certainties, as if they had already occurred, instead of the imaginations of my frenetically anxious mind.

Soon there was only one class left. I was dismayed at my own failure to turn Aliona into a friend. I could not bear to attend our last class, so I skipped it and pushed Aliona out of my mind.

A fellow blogger, a Hasidic man in Brooklyn, with whom I'd been in touch over the years, called me one day. He'd become acquainted online with a Hasidic woman who had confided in him.

"She wants to leave," he said. "But she wants to speak to someone who's already done it. Someone who is not a fuckup."

Was that me—*not a fuckup?*

I told him to give her my number, and a few days later, the woman called. She sounded out of breath.

"I'm sorry, I'm—" I heard her panting, then silence.

Moments later, she was back.

"Sorry, I'm on my way to the library. I thought I saw a Hasidic man following me, so I started running." She sounded distracted, and I heard a groan. "Ooh—sorry, I almost fell into a ditch here. I think he's gone now. Gosh, it's so dark!" Then she laughed. "You must think I'm nuts. I'm not nuts, I promise!"

Her name was Malky, she said, and she lived in Kiryas Joel, the Satmar village in Orange County, thirty minutes north of Monsey. Could we meet? she asked.

We arranged to meet a few days later, at an Applebee's near enough to Kiryas Joel for her to walk. No proper Hasid would step into a non-kosher eating establishment, so as long as she wasn't seen entering, she'd be safe meeting a strange male.

I arrived several minutes late. A middle-aged man sat alone in a booth, eating dinner. A few tables down, a teenage couple leaned into each other, side by side, a half-eaten plate of dessert between them. The server at the door raised an eyebrow. "One?"

"I'm supposed to meet someone." I wasn't sure how to describe her. "Have you seen . . . a woman in a . . . ?" I raised my hands to indicate a covered head. Before I could finish the question, the waitress pointed to a corner booth at the far end of the restaurant. Peeking from behind the high-backed bench was a head covered with a floral lavender kerchief, facing away from the entrance.

I walked over slowly. A Hasidic woman sat bundled in her winter coat, upright and stiff, her hands folded in front of her. On the table was an untouched glass of water. The woman looked up at me, her expression blank.

"Malky?" I said.

Her jaw hung slightly down as she stared. I sat down, and she kept looking at me, her eyes wide.

Finally, she spoke. "You look like a regular shaygetz!"

We eased into conversation. She was twenty-three, she said, married with two little daughters. She described how she had been raised in a typical Satmar family, with nearly a dozen siblings and scores of cousins, and had once been happily ensconced in her world. Then she discovered the Internet and began interacting with others online, and the world opened before her. The library was now her place of refuge. Every evening, she would ask her husband to babysit their two daughters, saying that she was going to visit her sister or her mother. Then she would walk for thirty minutes down dark, wooded back roads to the library in the nearby village of Monroe. Her inner life had completely changed. She was determined to make her way out but had no plan and still saw too many obstacles.

In the days and weeks that followed, Malky and I spoke on the phone several times, and then began to meet up regularly. The pretense was that I, already out, was giving her a line to grab, a sounding board for her own plans. In reality, Malky meant as much to me as I did to her. She was all that was saving me from what was beginning to feel like soul-crushing solitude.

And yet, however disorienting my transition, I knew that I had chosen the right path. On Saturday mornings, those weeks when the children were with Gitty, I would drive to nearby Harriman State Park and hike miles of crisscrossing trails. As morning passed into afternoon, I would think of what my children were doing—at noon, they would be in shul, finishing prayers; at two, home with Gitty, or perhaps at their grandparents' or with cousins, having their chulent and kishke and onion kugel and singing the Sabbath songs out of worn *bentchers*.

I would think of those songs now, and the Sabbath atmosphere, and feel pangs of nostalgia that were both painful and pleasing. Stepping carefully across streams, climbing cliffs, up one mountain and down another, I would sing the songs I had sung so many years during Sabbath afternoon meals: "This Day Is Most Esteemed of All Days," "A Sabbath Day for God," "When I Keep the Sabbath, God Will Keep Me." My favorite trail went up the Popolopen Torne, where, at the peak, twinned with Bear Mountain several miles away, I would have a 360-degree view for miles. On a clear day, I could see Hoboken and sometimes even New York City. Near a tall cairn, a makeshift memorial for members of the U.S. Armed Forces, I would stick my hiking poles into the soft ground, take off my sweaty backpack, and get out my turkey-and-cheese sandwich.

It was Shabbos afternoon, and I was desecrating it by hiking and eating trayf. I would reflect on the fact that such simple pleasures were so meaningful. It felt exhilarating to be able to do what had for so many years been forbidden for fear of not heavenly but human judgment.

Chapter Twenty-Four

"Do you think you'll get married again?" Malky asked me one day. "Do you want to have more children?"

We were in the middle of a hike up Bear Mountain, headed to the Perkins Memorial Tower at the peak. Malky had told me that she wanted to join me on my hikes but could not get away on Saturdays, so I switched my hiking day to Sunday.

"Not sure about marriage. But children, yes."

"Really?" She looked at me, her ponytail wig bobbing behind her.

"I want to raise children without having to hide my true beliefs."

"I see."

"I'll be honest, though. Part of me feels it would be wrong. Something about it does make me uncomfortable."

She looked at me quizzically, but I wasn't sure how to explain. We fell silent as we scrambled up the face of a jagged crag, stepping carefully onto sharp outcroppings of rock to maintain our footing. Up on top, after we caught our breath and felt the breeze of the open skies on our sweaty necks, Malky took off her backpack and withdrew her water bottle, while I sat down on a large rock nearby.

"Why does it make you uncomfortable?" She tilted her head and fixed me with a look, her brow creased, as if staring at an object she couldn't quite make out.

"Maybe this is absurd," I said. "But . . . it just feels disloyal. Like the kids I have now aren't good enough. Like I cherish them less because of the world they're in and need other kids to replace them."

She edged beside me onto the rock, and we sat silent, both of us lost in our thoughts. It had been an unusually mild March day. The sun above a cloudless sky had warmed us for most of the afternoon. Now, however, the sun was quickly moving to the west, and a gust of wind reminded us that dusk and an evening chill were approaching.

We stood up and gathered our packs, but Malky's movements were slow, dreamy, as if she was still processing something.

"I think I understand," she said finally, as she reached to fasten the chest-strap of her backpack. "For me, there's only one option, though. If I leave, it's not without my daughters."

The thought of taking my own children with me had not occurred to me. Later, there would be those who would tell me that I had no right to leave because—among other things—I had no right to expose my children to a worldview and a lifestyle to which they were not accustomed. Others would tell me that I had been cruel to leave without fighting to take them, to change their lives along with mine. But at the time, it seemed as if living with Gitty was truly best for the children. She loved them, too, and wanted what was best for them. I was not at all convinced that the path I had taken, this transition, was necessarily the path to happiness for all.

One day, Malky called me, nearly hysterical. "Shulem, my father wants to kidnap my girls!"

She'd been at her parents' home a few days earlier, she said, for the haircutting ceremony of one of her three-year-old nephews. While standing in her parents' kitchen, immersed in the babble and cheer of the assembled women and girls, she noticed her husband and her father speaking earnestly in the dining room nearby, and she leaned in to listen from behind a door.

"They were talking about taking my daughters away! Shulem, I am so frightened!"

Several days earlier, she told me that whispers were spreading about her in the community. She had stopped wearing the special stockings of beige fabric with the seams sewn up the calf. Her husband noticed that she was no longer shaving her head. She'd taken to wearing pajamas to bed instead of a nightgown. She considered these minor transgressions, but her husband, to whom she had once, in an unguarded moment, expressed a fantasy about leaving the community, reported her to her father.

"He can't possibly be serious," I said. A kidnapping sounded far-fetched. "There are laws in this country!"

"You don't know him, Shulem." Her father was an *askan*, a *klaktier*. An activist and a political liaison. He delivered votes to elected officials. He advised rebbes. He stood at the head of important institutions. He wasn't accustomed to being defied. "Besides," Malky said, "you know this place isn't exactly law-and-order central."

The next time I saw her, I realized immediately that something had changed. She had taken a bus to Monsey to run some errands, and had only a few minutes for a quick chat before she returned. I picked her up from behind a local shopping center, where she stood waiting behind an enormous Dumpster.

After looking around carefully, she got into my car. I leaned in for a hug, and for a moment she hesitated, then leaned in and pulled back quickly. "I can't hug you anymore, Shulem."

She'd spoken to a divorce attorney, and he advised her to avoid any appearance of impropriety.

"Here?" I looked around the empty lot.

She shook her head. "I can't risk it." I could see her eyes glistening. "Shulem, what am I going to do?"

She needed to pull back, she said. We could speak on the phone occasionally, but that would be it.

She wants to meet someone who is not a fuckup. My friend's words played over and over in my head as the months passed. It was the common stereotype of those who left: fuckups. Troubled youths. Men and women from broken homes, bad marriages, victims of abuse—physical, sexual, emotional. Only those afflicted with a psychological ailment would choose to abandon the loving embrace of the Hasidim. And sometimes I wondered: Could they be right?

On the outside, I functioned well enough, went to work each day, continued my studies. But I began to feel a small part of myself crumble. I did not regret my choice; yet I was growing uneasy. Malky was gone.

I had failed to strike up a lasting friendship with Aliona. On Friday nights, when the children did not come, I would ache for a friend to call, but there was no one. Sometimes I would go to a movie theater, but the movie would end, and I would have nowhere to go but back to my Monsey apartment, alone. I took to driving into Manhattan to wander the streets of Greenwich Village, looking for something but I did not know what.

Once, at two in the morning, I strolled past a middle-aged man leaning with a cane against a wall at the corner of University Place and Washington Square Park. He pointed at me with his index finger: "You. You're beautiful." I looked behind me, but there was no one else. He pointed more emphatically: "You." He shouted an offer for a sexual service, assuring me of our mutual pleasure, then chortled as I hurried away. And yet, I could not help but take small pleasure in our interaction. I had been noticed.

Another evening, I saw a man and a woman smoking outside a door on West Houston Street, near Sixth Avenue. For some reason, I slowed as I passed.

"Looking for the meeting?" the man asked. "Second floor." He pointed at the door, then crushed the cigarette under his shoe. It was around midnight, the streets filled with the clamor of Greenwich Village nightlife, women in tight skirts tottering on high heels, men at their sides, hailing cabs, jittery with the night's promise.

"Come on," the man called. "Don't be shy." He held the door, and I followed him up a narrow staircase. Upstairs, a sign said, "Midnite Meeting." In a large room, several rows of chairs were laid out on three sides, facing a small platform. Piles of brochures were spread out on a table near the door, and from their titles I realized what I had already assumed: This was an Alcoholics Anonymous meeting. Men and women of various ages, looking respectable and earnest, took their seats. A man got up on the platform, and began to speak about how alcohol had destroyed his life and how the "itty, bitty, shitty committee" had interfered so many times when he tried to sober up. He spoke of persevering against the odds, of falling and picking himself up, repeatedly. Others shared, telling stories about lives of ruin and failed promise and picking up the shards of what was left of them, after their families, jobs, and life aspirations had left them. Each one announced his or her length of sobriety. Seven years. Three months. Five days.

I returned to that meeting several times, on lonely Friday nights when I had nothing better to do, nowhere to be, no one to meet. I was not an alcoholic, but I felt a kinship with these people, each in his or her own way suffering from a combination of bad choices and unfortunate circumstances. They had been fuckups, and yet, they were not. They were there, determined to go on.

I found a therapist, a birdlike woman in her sixties. I wanted her to tell me that there was something wrong with me, but she wouldn't. "You made difficult choices, and they led to real consequences. You'd be a fuckup if you *didn't* feel a little bit lost."

I thought about Footsteps, the organization in Manhattan that offered assistance to people who had left the ultra-Orthodox world. Leiby, whose departure from New Square three years earlier had prompted the bezdin to expel me, had sought its assistance. Leiby had moved on and was pursuing a degree in chemical engineering at Cornell University, but the organization was still around.

In the first weeks after I'd left, I had looked up its website and read its program calendar: education night. GED tutoring. Résumé writing. Assistance with college applications. I didn't need those things; I had a job, had enrolled in college without much difficulty, and my English skills were fine. I called the number to inquire about any other services they offered, but there was little they could do for me, and so I thanked the staff for their wonderful work and put the organization out of mind.

Now, however, I realized that I needed the people. If I didn't need the services, maybe I could mentor others, tutor some of the younger members in English or math. I could offer assistance, and perhaps that alone would help me in return.

It was the second night of Passover when I arrived at the downtown location. The tables were laid out with boxes of matzah next to piles of pita bread, gefilte fish and sushi platters, pasta salads, potato kugels, and apple compote. A table off to the side with a "kosher" sign had been set up for those who still maintained degrees of religious observance.

As a potluck dinner, though, the food was mainly provided by members, and most of it did not appear to be kosher. Most startling to me were the products that were clearly *chometz*, made of leavened dough—bread, pastries, pasta. *He who eats chometz [during Passover] shall be excised from his people*, the Bible said. So severe was the sin that, before the holiday, Jewish communities large and small burned all *chometz* in backyard trash cans or enormous communal Dumpsters. During the eight-day holiday, Hasidim even refrained from eating anything prepared outside their own homes. But here sat a group of men and women exercising the freedom to choose for themselves.

A man who looked to be in his twenties and was wearing a gray AC-DC T-shirt sat down next to me.

"AC-DC fan?" I asked.

"Huh?" He looked at me blankly as he forked a slice of gefilte fish onto a plate.

"AC-DC. Your T-shirt." I pointed at the logo, with its three-dimensional lightning bolt slashing through Gothic lettering.

The man looked confused, and then looked at his shirt. "Oh. Yeah. AC-DC. They're, like, a band, right?"

I thought he was joking, until he told me he was a former Belzer Hasid, only vaguely aware of popular music groups. "I just liked the shirt," he said, laughing. "Someone told me later it's the name of a band, but I know nothing about them." If I'd seen him on the street, I'd have taken him for a fashionable academic type. He was tall and thin with a shaved head and smart-looking glasses. He worked as a truck driver, he said, and was studying for his GED. He hoped to get into college eventually.

"Good for you, man," I said.

He shrugged. "It's rough, you know. I'm twenty-four. I have a daughter. And I feel like I'm in the first grade."

Another man, whose name was once Burich but who now went by Brad, told me of his frustrating attempts to make new friends in the outside world. He'd only recently joined this group but had been out for two years. The entire first year, he didn't know how to speak to people.

"Then I bought a book." He grinned, with a twinkle in his eye. "*101 Ways to Make Small Talk*. It helped me make friends, start conversations on the subway or at Starbucks or in a bookstore. Now I make new friends wherever I go."

The themes I heard that evening were all too familiar. Some people appeared broken by their pasts, when their lives as individuals had been subservient to the welfare of family, community, sect, people. Almost everyone spoke of feeling suffocated, compelled to act and behave in ways that were not true to themselves, until finally they could take it no longer, and risked ostracism and alienation in return for a chance to live more authentic lives. Many were still adjusting, struggling with linguistic limitations, learning basic concepts about the outside world: how to buy clothes, what to do on a date, where to buy a Halloween costume. One former Chabad woman mentioned that she had taken to listening to hundreds of rock bands in order to become familiar with secular music. An ex-Satmar man sitting nearby perked up his ears. "Vat it means a rock band?" he asked. It was the first time he'd heard the term.

Later that evening, I met some who had been out for years and were now indistinguishable from other New Yorkers. Many were college students, pursuing degrees in psychology, medicine, art, engineering. There were aspiring filmmakers and writers and actors. Several already held advanced degrees, with a disproportionate number of attorneys, especially among the men—years spent honing analytical skills on Talmud study had apparently led to lifelong appreciation for the nuances of legal texts.

During the months and years to follow, I would meet many "Footsteppers" for whom this group had become a surrogate family. Founded in 2003 by a former Chabad woman, Footsteps was officially a service organization but had also built the framework for a fledgling community. There were holiday dinners and summer camping trips and weekly discussion groups, where members could drop in to speak to others who had been through similar experiences. Some of the meetings were facilitated by hired social workers, and others were free-form conversations. The peer support, I learned, was valuable even to those who felt as though they'd "made it," who already held degrees and jobs and had lovers and closets full of secular clothes and years of secular experiences. Many members had been disowned by their families, and now they attended one another's college graduations, celebrated birthdays and holidays together, and, in later years, served as best men and bridesmaids at one another's weddings. Soon there would be childbirths, too, and the sparks of a second generation would glow from the cracks of so many broken hearts.

♦♦

One day, during a conference with a prospective client, my employer looked around the table, and made introductions: Eileen. Amber. Jeff. Lisa. Shulem.

"The *new* Shulem!" my boss said with a laugh. "There once was an old Shulem. Now there's a new Shulem."

My coworkers laughed nervously, while the clients smiled, throwing glances at me, clearly bemused by my boss, a small man in a red bowtie with a big laugh and a stunning lack of social graces.

Several days later, as the children ate their dinner around my small kitchen table, I wondered: Was I new to them, too? They had seen me change over the years. They had seen my beard grow shorter. They had seen my clothes grow increasingly casual, after I traded in my long coat for a short sport jacket, my large velvet yarmulke for a small suede one.

"Where are your *payess?*" Chaya Suri asked one day, as if she'd suddenly noticed. They had once been long and dense; unrolled, they had come down almost to my waist. For years, I would twist them into a coiled knot and tuck them behind my ears, until I began to snip them, a few millimeters each time. After a year or so, they were completely gone.

I tugged on some hairs at my temple. "They're here. I just keep them short now." She looked more closely at the spot, doubtful, and ran off.

"Family hug," I would announce as the children prepared to leave, after they were bundled into their coats and hats and mittens, and the six of us would gather near the door and squeeze together in a tight circle. "Kiss, kiss, kiss, kiss, kiss," we would all go, puckering lips against cheeks and foreheads.

The children appeared to be doing OK, but as the months wore on, things grew tense with Gitty.

"Why do you have to wear jeans when you pick them up?" she snapped at me one day over the phone.

"I stay in my car," I said. "No one can see my pants."

"You got out of your car once," she shot back.

It was true. *Once*. I had come to pick up Hershy and Akiva for the weekend. The girls had a special event that weekend, and the two boys, aged six and eight, had come alone. They came out of the apartment carrying their sleepover bag between them, each holding one end. I watched as they struggled to carry it, and then laid it down near the car. I wanted to help them but was wearing jeans. Through the mirrors, I watched as they opened the back door of my Honda Pilot, and together they lifted the bag into the rear, and then looked up at the door, now high above their heads. I stepped out of the car, closed the rear door, and in a flash, I was back in the driver's seat.

It had taken no more than ten seconds, but as the boys got into the car, a little boy on a bicycle called to Hershy in a loud whisper: "Who is this goy?"

I did not want my children to be embarrassed by me. Still, I wondered: What were the limits for accommodating a child's anxieties about a nonconforming parent? Were children so lacking in resilience that they could not overcome the trauma of a parent wearing the wrong kind of pants?

The liberal-minded side of me believed that it served children well to be exposed to different worldviews. But perhaps these were special circumstances. I had assured Gitty that I would maintain strict observance of Jewish law in the children's presence. Hasidic custom was of a lesser priority, although I promised to be sensitive to their lifestyle and to avoid exposing them to practices that might unsettle them.

More challenges arose. During the intermediate days of Passover, the children and I took a trip to Six Flags in New Jersey. After hours of riding the bumper cars and roller coasters and pirate ships, we took out the lunches I'd packed, matzah and cheese and yogurts and other specially prepared "kosher for Passover" foods. The matzah I brought for the children was the traditional kind—round, handmade loaves—

but I soon realized that I'd brought along too few, only seven or eight of them. The children ate them quickly, and Akiva turned to me and asked: "Do you have more matzah?"

I had thrown in a box of square, machine-made matzah before we left—fully kosher according to Orthodox law but frowned upon by Hasidim. Still, they were kosher, and even Gitty had allowed these in the past from time to time. They were better-tasting, and they cost a lot less.

"Have some of this," I said to Akiva quietly, and handed him a square matzah from the box beside me.

Hershy noticed. "Can I have one, too?"

I handed him one, even as I wondered if this wasn't going to cause trouble. For a moment, I considered telling them to keep quiet about it, not to tell their mother.

The next day, Gitty called, livid. "How could you feed them machine matzahs!"

I tried to calm her. "It was all I had. And I gave it only to the little ones."

She screamed. "You're feeding my children trayf!"

I reminded her that there was no such thing as trayf matzah and that not only was it a minor transgression but that she herself had permitted it on occasion. My responses only infuriated her, and it wasn't long before the arguments snowballed.

"You let them watch television!" Gitty yelled at me one day.

There was a TV in my bedroom, and the day before, Akiva had wandered in and asked, "Why do you need a computer in your room?" I told him it was not a computer. "What is it, then?" he asked, and I wouldn't say, because I knew the word "television" would unsettle him. "Turn it on," he said, and I thought there could be no harm if I did so for a quick minute. He then watched, mesmerized, as a man and woman on the screen delivered the evening news. Hershy, hearing the commotion, popped into the bedroom, followed by Chaya Suri. "OK, that's enough," I said, and the three of them moaned in unison. "Just one minute longer!" Akiva pleaded, as I herded them into the kitchen for dinner, where Tziri and Freidy were setting the table.

I promised Gitty that I would never allow it again, that it was a momentary lapse in judgment, and that she was right: I should have been more careful, but they had watched for no longer than a minute.

"I can no longer trust you," she said simply. And with that, she ended the conversation.

Several weeks later, the children got into the car and Freidy handed me a note, in Gitty's familiar script. *I am sorry*, it read. *I can no longer be in contact with you.*

All messages were to be passed through a third party. She listed the name of one of her relatives.

I called her immediately. "What's going on?" I asked.

"I can no longer speak to you," she said.

I asked if I'd upset her in some way, if there was something I could do to make it better.

She remained silent.

"We've been doing so well!" I had been grateful for her willingness to keep in touch. If I was not there to see my children each night when they came home from school, to have dinners with them and do homework and take them shopping and work on school assignments, I could at least get regular updates from her. How would I be a parent to them now?

Gitty would not explain more, and when I pleaded for us to have a reasonable conversation, she said flatly, "I can't speak to you. This is final. Please don't call again."

I had a strange feeling of loss, a kind I hadn't felt all these months. Gitty and I had had our difficult times, but we had also grown close over the years. We hadn't fought bitterly the way other divorced couples did. We cared for each other, and we both wanted what was best for the children.

I called the relative she'd indicated in her note. The man's name was Shragi Green, a real estate developer in New Square with a reputation for shrewdness, although I also knew him to be barely literate. We had been friends in the past; on occasion, he would ask me to edit some of his business correspondence, which often reminded me of scam e-mails from Nigeria, written in substandard English with a thinly veiled duplicitous quality.

"Do you know anything about this?" I asked.

I could hear him breathing through the phone, like a long series of deep sighs, as if he had been bracing for the call but hadn't prepared himself fully. Finally, Shragi said, "The rabbis have advised her on this. You've made your choice. Now she's made hers."

I began to protest. The rabbis had no business interfering. This was a private family matter. Shragi interrupted me, his tone steely. "There's nothing you can do," he said. "You've tried to influence her and the children in the past, but those days are over. She is now getting guidance from the right people."

I tried to object, but he raised his voice to speak over me.

"I know it's hard to accept. You're angry now—that's normal." His voice softened. "Don't worry, it'll get easier. You'll get used to it."

Chapter Twenty-Five

Within weeks of Gitty's note, Tziri, as if in solidarity with her mother, stopped speaking to me. She would come along with the others, eat her dinner, and then curl up on the sofa with a book until it was time to go home. I would ask about school, about her friends, about what she was reading, and she would ignore me. Something or someone had gotten to her, and I could not budge her out of her resolve. Now thirteen and ferociously bright, she showed the stubbornness of an ox and the indifference of an alley cat.

Weeks, then months, passed. Tziri remained silent. Gitty refused to take my calls. I ached for news of report cards, parent-teacher meetings, doctors' visits. I had to plead with the children for information. I knew only what they told me, and they weren't offering much.

One day, Chaya Suri mentioned a car accident involving Hershy.

"What car accident?"

"The one where the car ran over his foot."

When did that happen? Where? How come I hadn't heard?

They didn't remember the details. Some guy in a car, right in front of the apartment. Two weeks ago, maybe three. An ambulance came. Was he taken to the hospital? Freidy said no, and Chaya Suri said yes. Was anything broken? Were X-rays taken? What did the doctor say?

"Does it look like anything's wrong with him?" Freidy snapped, looking up from a bag of chips. Hershy was on the kitchen floor several feet away, Game Boy in hand, oblivious. Clearly, he hadn't been badly hurt, but I was furious that no one had bothered to call me.

The suddenness with which I was consigned to irrelevance left me stunned. For fourteen years, I had imagined myself integral to my children's lives. All at once, it appeared that I was not.

When I called Shragi to inquire about the children, he would not give me much.

"They're being well taken care of. There's no need for you to worry." Then he turned the call into a conversation about my wicked ways. "The Gates of Repentance are never closed. Return, and all of this can be fixed." Gitty and I could remarry. All would be as before. "'There is no greater mitzvah than taking back an abandoned wife,'" he would remind me, quoting the Talmud.

In the interest of amicability, Gitty and I hadn't bothered with legal agreements from the secular courts. They seemed unnecessary. We knew very few divorced couples and imagined that family courts were only for those divorces one heard about in the news, between couples who bore such relentless grudges toward each other that they turned their acrimony into sport while their children were left irreparably scarred. Trusting in the goodwill of all involved, I had imagined we'd work it all out between ourselves. Even when Gitty refused to speak to me, when I knew that she was being advised by those with less than noble intentions, I still hoped we could find a way back to the open hearts we'd had just months earlier.

The surprising thing about the final unraveling was that it was precisely the thing I had feared; yet when it came, I was neither prepared for it nor could I have imagined the psychic devastation I would experience in its wake.

Gitty brought our matter in front of a family court judge, where her attorney explained the many ways in which I was unfit to be a father to my children. Shragi sat behind Gitty's attorney, whispering into his ear.

"Mr. Deen has changed his beliefs," the attorney told the court, and laid out the many ways in which my new ways were damaging to the children's well-being:

My clothes were the wrong kind.

My haircut was offensive.

My yarmulke was too small.

I had a television and the Internet in my home.

"And," the attorney concluded, "he has become an atheist."

And so they wanted me out of the children's lives.

"Is your client an atheist?" the judge asked my attorney.

"No, he is not," my attorney said, without missing a beat, and the judge looked relieved. I was stunned that my personal beliefs were relevant to the case, but my attorney clearly knew that they were.

When I asked for the court's permission to take my children on a daytime trip during the intermediate days of the Sukkos holiday, as I had done every year for the past decade, Gitty could no longer contain herself.

"He'll take them to atheist places!" she cried, and Shragi nodded vigorously behind her. I could only surmise that she meant a natural history museum or public library.

At first, I wasn't very concerned. A family court judge could not rule on the basis of religion, I imagined. But when the judge ordered overnight and weekend visitation rescinded and reduced visits from twice weekly to once a week, I grew alarmed.

"It's only temporary," my attorney explained. Until it went to trial and a permanent arrangement was decided.

"How long until the trial?" I asked my attorney.

"Hopefully, within the year."

In the meantime, there would be no more weekend visits, no more long meals and lazy Shabbos afternoons during which we would sing songs and tell jokes and stroll to the pond and watch the geese and the turtles, or, on rainy days, play Scrabble or broken telephone and sit around resolving arguments about who stole whose toys and who was hogging the Calvin and Hobbes comics.

I would still have two hours with the children each Sunday evening. It wasn't a lot of time, not when there were five of them—and I did the math: after subtracting the ten minutes' driving time each way, I was left with exactly twenty minutes per child. But we could have dinner together and play a game or two, and maybe have some time for homework. Within a year, I would get our old arrangement back, I was certain. We would be a family again.

I could not make any sense of Gitty's sudden change. The answer I came up with eventually was that something had snapped. The seeds of her resentment were not religious but personal. "You're living the good life while I'm stuck here," she had said bitterly, several weeks before cutting off contact. "You're out having fun, partying with your goyish friends, living without restrictions. You probably have a million girl-friends by now."

It was an odd accusation, not only because it was so far from real-ity but also because it betrayed what I had long suspected: a glimmer of envy. As if underneath it all, those who begrudge the godless their godlessness do so not because the godless are sinners but because sinners have more fun—and how dare they?

The months dragged on, with complaint after complaint filed in court on minor matters of Hasidic custom. I had fed the children machine matzah. I was wearing jeans. They were traumatized by the television in my home. I could not be trusted to abide by the laws of kosher food. My very appearance was having a negative influence on them.

I thought that these issues would be declared irrelevant by the judge and that a secular court could not be swayed by such concerns, but my attorney assured me that it was not so. *Everything* was relevant in fam-ily court, especially in a county like ours, where judges were beholden to powerful constituencies with very special interests.

The complaints were formally filed by Gitty, but I knew that, aside from Shragi, other community "experts" were involved. I heard through friends that thousands of dollars were being raised to pay for the legal costs necessary to keep me away. I knew how these things worked. I had seen the flyers over the years, on lampposts and synagogue doors in New Square and Williamsburg and Monsey, calling on people to "save the children from a parent gone astray." Common tropes were used to stir hearts—most often, the image of a young Hasidic boy, scis-sors Photoshopped menacingly over his sidecurls.

My brother Mendy came by one day, and told me something Shragi had said to him when he ran into him in shul one morning. "We may not have a legal case," Shragi said. "But we can beat him down emotion-ally and financially. He'll have to give up eventually."

I remember laughing when I heard it. It sounded ludicrous. I was unaware that even with a strong case, custody battles could cost tens of thousands of dollars. I was unaware that, when held in Rockland County, custody battles in our community required rabbis, community leaders, and Orthodox family therapists on your side. I was unaware that family courts were also part of the local political machinery and that elections were never far from a judge's mind. I was unaware that my relatively meager resources were no match for a powerfully resourceful community with an ideological stake in the future of my children. Most of all, I was naive about the power of religious extremists to control even the minds of children.

I did not lose in court. Instead, I lost my children's hearts, and with them, very nearly, my sanity.

Soon after the court proceedings began, the children changed markedly. They grew withdrawn in my presence, eating dinner in silence and showing no interest in their favorite games and books. They began to speak to one another in hushed tones, their manner subdued, looking at one another awkwardly and at me barely at all. They began to inspect the labels on food products and picked at their dinners reluctantly. When I asked what was wrong, they looked at the clock, anxious to leave.

"Has anyone been saying bad things about me?"

Akiva shook his head vigorously, while Chaya Suri's lids turned red around her large glassy eyes. Only Hershy looked me in the eye, and said, "Mommy says you want to turn us into goyim."

I turned to several rabbis for help, but few were sympathetic. "Don't you agree that your children are better off without you?" one rabbi asked, eyeing my too-small yarmulke and my shaved beard.

When I turned to the local, Hasidic-run mental health clinic for assistance with getting the children counseling, I learned that I was too late. Gitty had already come by, I was informed. The clinic had assigned one of its staff psychologists, a young Orthodox woman, to issue a letter to the court with its advisement. The letter, I would later learn, urged the court to forbid me to bring my children into my home.

It also urged that my visits be reduced to once a month, and that they be supervised by a member of the Hasidic community.

"Shouldn't you have met with me first?" I asked the young psychologist, when she finally agreed to see me. Her supervisor, a Hasid whose stomach bulged over his trousers, passed by in the hallway. She glanced at him through the half-open door and looked back at me. She appeared lost, both contrite and defensive.

"You're right," she said, her voice faint. "I didn't think of it." Her supervisor passed by again and looked through the open door. The woman rose from her chair. "I hope things work out," she said.

"My children will never reject me," I had said to my brother Mendy when he told me what Shragi had said. My children adored me, but I soon realized that it was more complicated than that. When a child is taught that a parent is wicked, the child's love for the parent does not subside immediately. What the child feels instead is shame. Shame over her own feelings of affection for someone she has been told is a bad person. Shame over her biological association with that bad person. Embarrassment over what people would say, were they to observe or think about her association with this bad person. It is only natural that the child then wants nothing but to withdraw from the source of all that shame.

Tziri stopped coming, and Freidy followed suit soon after. It was April 2009; Tziri had turned fourteen the previous September, and Freidy turned thirteen in January. I didn't want to fight my own children, but their change was so sudden and so inexplicable that I felt socked in the gut just when I needed clarity of mind. I knew that it could not be the children alone. A parent for fourteen years, I was accustomed to my children's pendulous moods, but this—complete and determined withdrawal from one day to the next—was something else. It had all the hallmarks of bearded, sidecurled puppeteers.

And so I brought the matter into court, and the judge, blessedly, ordered them back.

My two eldest daughters were delivered to my door the next day by Shragi. They brought along their own books to read, no longer trusting the amusements I might offer. The moment they entered, they set themselves down on the edge of my charcoal gray sofa and kept their eyes in their books or stared at the walls.

"How about a game of Cranium?"

Tziri turned a page in her novel. Freidy crossed and recrossed her legs.

"Hey, you want to make mac and cheese? Freidy, you *love* mac and cheese."

For two hours straight, they refused to eat, speak, play, or even meet my gaze. Every few moments, I would catch Freidy glancing at me, but whenever I looked at her, she averted her eyes quickly. She sat slouched in a corner of the sofa. I got the sense that she wanted for us to speak but was being held back by some invisible force. Tziri, suffering no such doubt, sat stiffly the entire time, her back like a rod, her arm never touching the side rest, poised to leave. Only occasionally would she look up from her book toward Freidy, and in their glances I could see some pact remembered, their resolve reinforced.

I blamed the family court judge most of all. Spiteful ex-spouses and religious minds can be expected to have lapses of reason, but the judge had no such excuse. With a single careless thought, under the guise of "temporary," he had declared me a "visitor" rather than a father, and the children's attitudes had changed immediately, as if the courts had confirmed Gitty's accusations. Now it was my job to convince them otherwise.

"Try to speak to them," my therapist advised. "Ask them if they have any concerns they want to talk about." I pulled over a chair and placed it opposite the coffee table, and looked at my silent daughters and cleared my throat.

"Is there anything you want to talk about?"

My words reverberated against the apartment walls, while my daughters pretended that no one had spoken.

"You know this can't go on forever, right?"

I crossed my arms and stared at them. I told a joke or two, hoping to elicit a laugh. I stood on my head. I pulled out a pack of cards and performed a couple of old magic tricks, which they had loved watching when they were younger. But they refused to be entertained. And so I sat with them in silence, until we heard the honk of Shragi's horn.

The three younger ones were now visiting separately from the older girls, although they, too, appeared lost, warming to me during one moment and declaring their unwillingness to visit during the next. Whenever I went to pick them up, only Akiva and Hershy would come out to the car, and I'd make them go back and get Chaya Suri, who would emerge wiping her tears. At my apartment, Hershy got into a new habit. To every remark that I made, his response was, "When can we go home?"

Their visits left me emotionally drained. Later, I would berate myself for taking it to heart as I did and for not thinking more clearly; there were things I could've done, perhaps. But at the time, I felt destroyed. My children loved me, I was sure of it. Yet they were living in a world that could not tolerate difference, and I was beginning to realize that I was powerless to fight it.

"I shouldn't have let those little shits control my emotions," I would tell a friend later, in anger; but at the time, that's exactly what I'd done. After they would leave, I would sit in my empty apartment stewing with anger. I cried so much those days, it felt as if my tear ducts would clog, but I wept still, unceasingly, in anger and in despair and in yearning for my children to return, but all I got in response was the rustling of leaves outside my window and another exorbitant bill from my attorney.

Tziri and Freidy's visits, especially, took an emotional toll that I knew would break me if I let it continue. Shragi called me several times to tell me that the girls were causing Gitty untold grief about their forced visits. They cried. They threw tantrums. They picked fights with the little ones. I believed him and wondered whether it was wise to keep forcing their visits.

During their next visit, while they sat in silence, as always, I turned to them earnestly: "Do you really not want to come anymore?"

For the first time in months, they spoke. "Yes," they said in unison.

I asked and they answered. I told them how much it hurt for me to hear it, but they showed no reaction. For every question that went unanswered, every remark unacknowledged, the brick in my throat grew larger and lodged itself deeper. I could not let my children see me cry, and yet I wanted only to scream.

Instead, I said I was sorry. I said that I would fix it—say the word, and I'm on it. If only they would speak, and tell me what it was they wanted me to do.

Tziri ignored me as before, but Freidy looked up. For a moment, it seemed as if she might say something. Then she rolled her eyes.

In that eye-roll lay the answer, I realized. How conceited of me to think that I could impose a monumental change and then ask *them* how to fix it. My daughters were rebuking me in the only way children know how. This was not about faith or values or lifestyle choices. Children, I would realize, do not have philosophical problems but only emotional ones. What mattered was not what I believed, or the particulars of how I lived, but that, by my own choices, I had placed myself in the camp of those they were taught to shun, and so I had shamed them, shamed our family, shamed all of us. What they wanted was a father who did not represent the wickedness they were taught to abhor, but I could only be the father I was, and that, clearly, was not good enough.

I told them then that I loved them, that I couldn't help it, and that I could not imagine life without them. And that regardless of what happened, I would always be there for them.

Tziri's face remained a mask of contempt. Freidy, who was often quick to tear up, swallowed hard, but when I looked at her, hoping that my eyes would carry my plea, she was busy fingering a spot on her tights, a tiny clump of thread on her knee where a rip had been mended, as if suddenly overcome by the intricacies of navy-blue thread.

"And if you really don't want to come, I won't force you." Moments after the words left my mouth, I regretted them. I thought that by sympathizing with them, by easing up on my demands for their affections, they would feel freer to grant them, but, a split second later, I realized it was unlikely to happen.

We sat in silence for a while longer, until we heard Shragi honking the horn of his minivan. The girls headed to the door in a hurry, but I was ahead of them.

284 : SHULEM DEEN

"Family hug?" I asked.

This was the ritual of only months earlier, when the six of us would wrap our arms around one another giddily. This time, the girls held themselves stiffly, while I wrapped my arms around them anyway, and held them close. I could feel their eagerness to get out from my embrace, to be done. All I wanted was never to let go.

I could not know then that this was the last I would see of Tziri and Freidy for a long time. I could not know then that my many phone calls and letters would go unanswered, my messages unreturned. That for years, I would not know whether they even received my messages, or whether they were intercepted and discarded by those tasked with keeping their minds pure.

I could not know then that four years later, I would hear of Tziri's engagement to a boy she had met for only a few minutes, just as Gitty and I had met twenty years earlier, that I would wait in vain for a phone call or a letter inviting me to her wedding, or that on the night of her wedding, in February 2013, I would sit at my desk in my Brooklyn apartment snacking on a bag of chili corn chips and browsing the Internet, chatting on Facebook, as I did on so many other ordinary nights, trying desperately not to think of the wedding taking place one hour away and the years of my children's lives I had missed.

I could not know all this then, but as I watched my daughters leave that evening, watched through the blinds as they got into Shragi's minivan and swung the door closed, I knew that something had ended.

The next week, Shragi called to say that the girls refused to come.

I had said I wouldn't force them. They were holding me to my word.

In December 2008, nearly nine years after I had been hired, my employer called from his office in Tel Aviv.

"I'm sorry, Shulem. But we are going to have to let you go."

I wasn't surprised. The company had begun outsourcing its programming needs to India. I thought I would quickly find employment elsewhere, but the country was in a full-blown recession, and jobs were becoming scarcer by the day. New York City was crawling with unemployed programmers, many of them with master's degrees in computer science from prestigious universities. Unlike nine years earlier, when computer programmers were practically hired off the street and when I had relied on the Orthodox community's support network to find my job, I was now trying to find a tech position in New York without even a high school diploma to show on my résumé. I could barely get interviews, and when I did, employers quickly determined that I was not qualified.

I drew money from my unemployment insurance and sent it all to Gitty and the kids, while I tried to scrape by on my meager savings. Gitty and I were trying to sell our home in Monsey, but with the downturn of the housing market, it couldn't be appraised for more than three-quarters of what we owed on the mortgage, which was soon foreclosed. My car cost more than I could afford, and I owed my landlord several months in back rent. I had no money left to pay for my college classes and decided to discontinue school until things stabilized. I needed to focus my energy on finding a new job. I had already spent tens of thousands of dollars on legal fees, my reserve funds were quickly depleting, and I was sinking into unmanageable debt.

I had been many things in adulthood—a husband, an entrepreneur, a computer programmer, a blogger—but for fourteen years, fatherhood defined me most. Now, I no longer knew who I was. After months of harrowing court appearances, I felt drained.

I came to a low place, depressed and suicidal and angry at the world and myself. Most of all, at myself. I could not understand how it had all happened. I could not understand how I had lost my children before the fight had even begun. I blamed myself for not having foreseen it, for not being better prepared, for lack of cunning and craftiness to match the qualities so deftly used by the other side.

In June 2009, I spent a week at the Frawley Psychiatric Unit at Good Samaritan Hospital, after my therapist determined that my suicide ideation was more than just a passing notion. I had fallen into a despair from which I could not see myself out. Perhaps I hadn't even known until then how much my children meant to me, but now I could not imagine life without them. For more than a decade, their voices had been the first thing I heard when I woke each morning, the rhythm of my days guided by their needs, even when we were not physically together. The realization that I had lost my role as a father, not by the courts but because my children's minds had been turned against me, sent me tumbling into an emotional sinkhole. I yearned for some way to shut down my mind and was gripped with the increasing conviction that death was the only way to do so.

When I was released from the hospital, my stack of antidepressants in hand, I felt lighter. Grief, I learned, blessedly diminishes over time, and soon the pain would lessen; it was something to work toward and to look forward to. I also forgave myself for some of my failures. I knew that the choices I had made had seemed the best at the time and that if my judgment had failed me at certain points, I could not remain angry with myself forever.

But my resolve had weakened. My fight was gone.

We can beat him down emotionally and financially, Shragi had said. He had succeeded.

We met at a local park, three miles down from New Square. A group of Hasidic kids twirled on a merry-go-round nearby, while Shragi and I sat across from each other at a picnic table.

Shragi shook his head. He wanted to clear up a misconception. "We would never keep children from a father." He was so very surprised, he said, that I'd thought otherwise. "That would be incredibly cruel."

I asked what he had in mind for an agreement.

"What we would like," he said, with a salesman's flourish, "is for you to see the children twice a year."

I stared at him in disbelief, while he offered some vague explanation for why this was really best for the children. I thought I had been prepared to take whatever I got, but I could not accept this.

"You are aware that they don't want to see you, yes?"

When I said nothing, he thought for a bit, and then offered four times a year.

I asked for six.

"Fine," he said. He offered his hand but then pulled it back. "But only the three little ones."

I bit my tongue, and nodded.

"And only until they're thirteen," he said. "Later, it's difficult. Especially for the boys, after bar mitzvah. You understand, of course."

I didn't understand. It didn't matter.

••

The last time I saw my father, he was in the middle of morning prayers. It was spring 1988. He was home from the hospital but still in a weakened condition, so he prayed at home instead of going to shul. I had been home then for Shavuos, the celebration of the giving of the Torah, and was heading back to Montreal that morning. The bus was to leave very soon, and I was running late. My father was wrapped in his prayer shawl and his tefillin, reciting the portion between the Shema and the Shmoneh Esreh.

God, your Lord, is Truth.

I stood near the doorway and watched as he enunciated each word, stressing each syllable, as he always did. *One must pray the way one counts precious gems*, the Talmud says, and I had never seen a more exemplary demonstration of it.

Fortunate is the man who hearkens to Your command, who places Your Torah upon his heart.

I had to say good-bye because the bus would be leaving shortly; but for some reason, I stood and watched my father. He was turned slightly away, the edges of his tallis partly obscuring his face, and I wasn't sure if he saw me.

You have redeemed us from Egypt, God, our Lord. You split the sea, drowned the wicked, led Your beloved across, and let the waters bedeck their foes.

I had to go. In only a few seconds, my father would rise for the Shmoneh Esreh, the silent portion of the prayer, during which his eyes would close and his mind would go elsewhere. I didn't want to interrupt him, but I had to go.

Rock of Israel, rise to the aid of Israel. . . . Our redeemer, the Lord of Hosts is His name, the Holy One of Israel.

"Tatti," I said softly. "I have to go."

He paused, startled. He did not turn his head, but when I came close, I could tell he was giving me his attention. He did not speak or even offer a hug or a handshake, but he smiled and nodded faintly. As I shut the door behind me, I heard the concluding verse go faint as he rose for the Shmoneh Esreh.

Blessed are You, God, deliverer of Israel.

Two months later, when my mother told me that my father was dead, after the first spell of tears and the sinking realization that his death was forever, I could not get one thought out of my head: he never said good-bye. Yet in the weeks and months after my father's death, I didn't think I missed him. I remember making all the right gestures and saying the right things because I knew it was expected of me.

"It is very sad, but God has a plan for all of us," I said to the adults who looked at me, and then at one another, at once charmed and bewildered. "We don't understand God's ways, but we cannot question Him," I would say, not meaning a word of it. "My father's time had come. He must have accomplished all that was destined for him."

The adults nodded and smiled and patted my shoulder and told me how impressed they were, that I was so strong, that I would've made him proud, that I'd be the rock of our family, being the eldest son. They didn't realize I was saying what I knew they wanted to hear. It wasn't difficult.

Perhaps it is hard to truly miss a parent when you're a child—or at least to have the awareness of it, to understand it as such. During childhood, parents are resources. They give and withhold, and you come to tolerate what seem like arbitrary decisions and you can't wait to be out from under their rule. You don't quite understand what it means to love them and to miss them when they're not around, but you might be old enough to understand the language of it and to speak as if you grasp it like an adult. You have feelings about it, but the feelings don't match the words people use, and you wonder if something might be wrong with you because maybe you're not feeling the right things.

And then came the dreams.

A rabbi who was close to our family asked me once, several months after my father's death, "Does your father appear to you in dreams?"

I understood his question in the context of Jewish folklore. There were many tales of deceased loved ones appearing in dreams, bringing precious messages.

Go to the bridge in Kraków, and find the treasure.

My soul wanders in the heavens with no rest. Recite kaddish for me.

Don't let Tzeitel marry the butcher.

So many stories. The dead returning to reveal secrets or provide valuable guidance. Especially the saintly—they were the ones who knew the most. This rabbi wanted to know if my father, too, had appeared to me. Did I know any otherworldly secrets?

"Yes," I told the rabbi. "He comes to me."

"And what has he told you?" the rabbi asked.

I pretended to be too shy to offer the details, and the rabbi did not press for more. He only shook his head and said, "Pssh. Such a holy thing. He comes in the dream, eh?"

My father, however, did not appear to me in dreams. Or at least not in the way the rabbi meant it, as an apparition at my bedside with secrets from another world. Rather, I would dream that my father was alive again. In my dreams, which would recur for years, my father would be in the kitchen of our home, getting a cup of yogurt from the refrigerator, or sitting on our back porch with a glass of tea and speaking to one of his students, or praying at the shul in his usual spot in the last row, carefully enunciating each syllable. I would see him and smile and say, "Oh, you're here! I thought you were dead." And he'd say, "Oh, no. I was just traveling. I'm back now." In my dream, I would feel an unusual sort of happiness, the kind that comes after hearing terrible news and then hearing that no, a mistake was made, that terrible thing did not happen, it was all an unfortunate miscommunication.

Then I would wake and realize it was a dream. There was no mistake. My father really was dead. I would lie in bed for a long time, trying to go back to that place, where my strange and erratic and brilliant and loving father was back, perhaps even scolding me, or just being impatient because he was busy and had to get somewhere and I was getting in his way.

And that's when I knew that I really, truly missed my father.

Chapter Twenty-Six

On a Tuesday in September 2009, I rented a U-Haul truck and packed up my things. I left my long dark coats and beaver-fur hats to gather dust in a friend's basement, along with my small collection of religious texts and audiocassettes of old Talmud lectures. I took my tallis and tefillin and my shtreimel with me, too sentimental to part from them, and moved to an apartment in Bushwick—Brooklyn's newest bastion of hipster faux bohemianism. I moved to be closer to friends, many of whom I had made over the past year, collecting them like seashells, one leading to another and then another, cherishing each one, after having spent my first year out in near solitude.

It was an odd thing, to live suddenly among secular people, Jews and non-Jews, where there were few synagogues and no kosher supermarkets or large families with boys in yarmulkes and sidelocks, girls in long skirts and long-sleeved blouses. Instead, there was a colorful variety of types: young postcollege hipsters and settled yuppies living side by side with Dominicans and West Indians.

I tried to forget the events of the previous year. I met more people. I hosted parties. I smoked pot and tried MDMA, and, once, a spot of cocaine. I learned how to ask women on dates, and fell in and out of love. I took a trip to Spain and Greece, traveling on my own for the first time. For a while, in an attempt to try on a new persona, I went by a new name: Sean. I soon realized that an ex-Hasid with an Irish name does not an Irishman make, and reverted back to Shulem.

Schooling now seemed a luxury I could no longer afford. During my one semester in college, I had paid my own tuition, but now, with my job security gone, all I could focus on were my child-support obligations and my own basic living expenses. Over time, I found sporadic freelance programming work, and soon I would return to writing as

well, publishing articles and essays relating to Hasidic life and the journey away from it.

My mother and my siblings had not rejected me, and I remained
grateful for their acceptance. My brother Mendy and his wife would
invite me to their Monsey home for Shabbos meals, without asking
questions about how I got there, even as they knew that I now drove
on the Sabbath and probably parked my car only a short walk from
their home. My sister, Chani, too, would invite me to spend time at her
home with her family, and insist that I take part when her own daughters celebrated their marriages and the births of their own children.

My brother Avrumi, who had followed me to the Skverers when
we were teenagers, would call frequently, and ask whether and where I
had prayed that morning. When I would remind him that I no longer
prayed, he'd say, good-naturedly, "Eh, I'm sure you do when no one's
looking," and then he'd inform me of all the births, marriages, and
deaths among the people of New Square, where he was still a member
in good standing.

My mother, who had moved to Jerusalem a decade earlier, was pained
by the path I had taken but even more so by the fact that Gitty would
no longer allow the children to see or speak to her. Gitty, I would learn,
sought to punish my mother for not having raised me right, even as my
mother remained as devout as anyone Gitty had ever known.

In January 2010, I started an online journal with some friends. We called
it *Unpious*, a play on the Yiddish phrase *uhn-payess*—"no sidecurls"—
and we published stories and essays related to the fringes of ultra-
Orthodox society. Slowly, a community rose from the many who had
made the journey out, the numbers exploding in recent years—mostly
because of the Internet and the existence of Footsteps, which provided an anchor for hundreds who might otherwise have drifted into
a strange world with few resources. Every few months, there would
be a new crop, finding one another through interconnected networks:
blogs, Facebook groups, or underground gatherings around Brooklyn
and Manhattan.

Within our fledgling community, there were those who would
undertake projects around issues related to both the world we came

from and the community to which we now belonged. Ex-Orthodox activists set up new organizations to advocate for education reform in Hasidic schools, for Orthodox victims of child sexual abuse, for women trapped in forced marriages, for gay and lesbian members of the Orthodox community who loved their communities and traditions but were not accepted for who they were. We would write articles and appear in TV and radio interviews, speaking out about our journeys and our experiences, what we had learned and what we could share with others.

Malky, too, had made it out. We had first met in April 2008, and, finally, nearly two years later, I heard that she had left—and had taken her daughters with her. Her father and her then husband's threats had turned out to be empty. A group of us were gathering for Friday night dinner, and our host had invited Malky to join us and spend the weekend in Brooklyn.

When I walked in and saw her again, for the first time in two years, it was my turn to be stunned. Her hair had grown in and she now sported a short bob. Gone was her tight kerchief and her skirts and long-sleeved blouses, and in their place were slim jeans and a fashionable sleeveless top. "*You* look like a regular shiksa!" I said, as we hugged and laughed.

Soon we were sitting for dinner, a dozen friends, men and women, all of us former Hasidim who'd finally made it out. "Let's drink to this!" someone said.

"Let's do picklebacks!" someone else said. He'd learned it from hipster friends. We were in Williamsburg, America's capital of hipsterdom, and so we were often the beneficiaries of its concoctions. The rest of us had never heard of picklebacks, though, and our friend explained. "A shot of Jack Daniel's chased by a shot of pickle juice."

"Pickle juice?" The strangeness of the outside world still took us by surprise.

"Regular store-bought pickle juice. The stuff that's left in the jar after you eat all the pickles."

We filled shot glasses of whiskey and shot glasses of pickle juice, and held them up. To freedom! To choice! To opportunity! To friendship! We did one round and then another, and the cheer in the room rose. Soon we were singing, banging fists on our host's table in time to Hasidic songs from our youth, from Chabad and Belz and Vizhnitz, about the God we did not believe in and the Torah we did not follow. The songs were still beautiful, and we rose and rested our hands on one another's shoulders and swayed to old favorites, as if we were still in the synagogue or at the rebbe's tisch.

> Ata sakum terachem tziyon.
> Raise up and have mercy upon Zion.
> Ki va mo'ed. Ki va mo'ed. Ki va mo'ed.
> For the time has come. For the time has come. For the time
>   has come.

We'd made our choices and were proud of them and, despite the challenges, lived with few regrets.

The hours passed, and Malky and I found ourselves talking on the sofa. We had so much to catch up on. In a flash, it was six in the morning, and Malky walked me to the door as I prepared to leave. From the kitchen came the smell of chulent, stewing in a Crock-Pot—or what was left of it, after we'd raided the pot hours earlier. In the next room, Malky's daughters, aged three and five, were fast asleep.

At the doorway, Malky pulled me toward her, and put her arms around me. "Shulem," she said. "Now I can hug you again."

And yet, through it all, I could not forget what I had lost.

"Don't you miss your children?" some friends would ask.

I would shrug and say, "It is what it is."

"I suppose you get used to it," they'd say, and I'd say, "Yeah, pretty much." I wouldn't tell them that, no, in fact, you don't get used to it at all, at least not for a very long time. So many memories were sparked by sights and sounds around me—a mother and daughter on a movie screen, a father and son playing catch in the park, parents and children on the subway. These small moments would evoke feelings I did not know were possible, a kind of grief that would, at times, strike me with such force that it would impair my daily function, throwing me for hours, days, into a nearly catatonic depression.

The once-insignificant moments of day-to-day life, snippets of conversation, would suddenly come alive in my memory. I would try to put them out of mind, but the spool of them was relentless. All I could do was close my eyes and let them wash over me, painful as they were.

I would remember weeknight evenings, when I'd get home from work at eight, and Tziri and Freidy would be at the dining-room table doing homework. The little ones would be in bed, and I would head upstairs to kiss them good night. Chaya Suri would hug me close to her small frame and refuse to let go. "Stay," she would plead, and I would lie next to her in silence as she wrapped her arms around me tightly and told me about her day, until finally I'd kiss her good night and pry myself from her grip. Downstairs, Tziri and Freidy would bring their schoolbooks and sit with me at the kitchen table as I ate my dinner, and as we reviewed their studies, they'd pick food from my plate, always complaining that I got better dinners than they did.

I would remember the Friday nights and Saturday mornings in Monsey, when I would take the boys to shul, their company providing a small measure of relief in an otherwise tedious routine. Akiva would sit by my side and move his index finger along the lines in his prayer book, while Hershy ran outside with the other boys. Later, we'd walk home slowly, Akiva always holding my hand, and Hershy running ahead, and we'd gaze at the full moon and occasionally catch the fleeting silhouette of deer passing behind the trees. Then we'd hold hands tightly as we crossed the bridge over the little brook on the path home from the shul.

I would remember Saturday nights in winter, when nightfall came early and the Sabbath ended, and we would order in pizza and French fries and the seven of us would sit around the fireplace, the crackling logs competing with the sound of the wind howling outside. I would remember how, after every snowfall, the children and I would bundle up in our coats and build the largest snowman on the block, the snowballs of its torso so large that the three girls and I would have to lift them together.

People would ask, "Don't you ever feel guilty? For leaving them like that?" And I would wonder about the question, about their assumptions, casting it all into the inglorious tradition of male irresponsibility. And then I would go on, and plan the next Friday night dinner, because what else was there to do?

I would often think of Gitty and the hardships of raising five children alone, and I'd feel badly for her, and then I would feel angry. She was raising five children alone, but she didn't have to, not the way she had chosen. When I heard, in 2012, that she had remarried, to a good man, a pious and kind Hasid, a scribe who made his living writing sacred ritual texts—Torahs, tefillin, mezuzahs—and who took my sons to the synagogue on Shabbos and treated them kindly, I hoped that it would allow Gitty to forgive me for some of the pain I had caused her.

··

In the summertime, as Brooklyn simmered in the heat and Bushwick filled with block parties and backyard barbecues, a group of friends decided to take a break from our frenzied urban lives and participate in the Rainbow Gathering, an annual event of living off the grid for several days with peace, love, and thousands of unshowered bohemians.

We were sixteen men and women in four cars, driving along a dirt road through the Allegheny National Forest in Pennsylvania. Our cars whipped clouds of dust around barefoot, dreadlocked passersby, who all waved, flashed us peace signs, and shouted, "Welcome home!" and "Loving you, brothers and sisters!"

We planned to stay for four days. We packed for a month: massive amounts of food, towels, bottles of soap and shampoo, swimming attire, plasticware, rolls of aluminum foil, beach chairs, a portable shower, and gallons and gallons of bottled water.

A man with long flowing white hair in a colorful unbuttoned shirt sat at the head of the trail to the main campsite. He stared at us unselfconsciously, with his sagging abdomen and his chest of white hair.

"Welcome home, brothers and sisters!" he called in a thick Southern accent, and looked at our bags. We were hauling carry-ons, suitable for airport corridors and train stations, less so for steep hills of eroded soil and bumpy clots of exposed tree roots.

"Haven't y'all heard of backpacks?" the man asked with a laugh. "Which camp y'all headin' to?"

296 : SHULEM DEEN

"The Jewish camp." If we were going to hang with hippies, we preferred the Chosen variety.

After a moment, he said, "Down this trail, across the main meadow. Then take the trail to the right. The Jewish kitchen is called 'Shut Up and Eat It.' Can't miss it."

We found the camp easily. There were Breslovers with flowing tzitzis mingling with former Israeli soldiers, religious and secular Jews together dragging massive bottles of water, half-naked girls working alongside women in long skirts and headscarves.

After we set up our tents, we headed out to the meadow, where drum circles formed throughout the day, and the crowd of several thousand rocked, danced, and twirled. "Welcome home!" people called. "Loving you!"

The atmosphere at Rainbow brought back memories of my first experience at the tisch among the Skverers, the enchanting songs and the warm welcomes from people I did not know, the strange boys my age who shook my hand and made room for me among them on the bleachers, the gruff middle-aged men who offered me plates of roast chicken and potato kugel and bowls of apple compote, insisting that I eat, eat, because there was plenty more.

That tisch had changed my life, and over the following decade, as my attachment to Hasidic teachings deepened and my religious views matured, I had come to see the tisch not merely as a place for song and dance but as a vessel for experiencing what the psychologist Abraham Maslow called "peak experiences"—the transcendent moments of clarity when the whole cosmic mess we call our universe is suddenly beautiful and orderly and one's place within it is stunningly clear. In those moments, our very insignificance is magnified in such a way that all we can do is tremble in awe at the wondrousness of our existence.

In the last years before I left, when I was barely holding on to my faith, I would still sometimes attend the tischen, yearning for the feelings I remembered from my earliest days in New Square. I would head to the synagogue on Saturday evening for the third tisch of the week, traditionally held in the dark in the final moments before the Sabbath passed into weekday. Those final moments, the kabbalists tell us, are times of *ra'ava dera'avin*, a time of expanded consciousness of the divine.

But I had no longer felt it—the experience no longer moved me. The words of "Benei Heikhala Dikhsifin," the haunting poem by Isaac Luria that speaks of the unveiling of cosmic light that comes at that particular time, no longer made the hair on my arm stand stiff. The rebbe's chanting now sounded irritatingly mournful, whiny, like the sobs of a petulant child. The words were still beautiful but carried only a dim reminder of the ecstatic heights they had once triggered within me. I had developed resistance to their effects, and—heretic that I now was—the experience fell flat.

Soon I would lose my faith entirely—not only in Hasidic teachings but in the concept of the divine or the sacred, or even the idea that we, as humans, can intuit anything beyond the empirical. Still, the memories of the tischen lingered, and as I transitioned to the life of a secular New Yorker who didn't observe the Sabbath, didn't keep kosher, didn't attend synagogue or pray or perform any of the religious rituals that had, in my earlier years, been so meaningful, I couldn't help but wonder: Where did secular folks go to experience what I once felt at the tisch?

At one point, I wondered if a rock concert might do it. My mother would eventually tell me of her experiences as a teenager listening to Bob Dylan and the Beatles, of being at Woodstock, and the intensity of those experiences, to which she would later credit her religious awakening. I'd heard from Grateful Dead fans who described their experiences as being similar to what they would later feel at a tisch. But when I sought out such events, they evoked nothing at all.

At Rainbow, however, the energy was palpable, and I wondered if, finally, I had found it.

Hai yana, ho yana, hai ya na, the crowd sang as a small group sat on the ground and banged on their bongo drums. The steady rhythm of percussion instruments of various shapes and sizes attracted a growing crowd, until the group of three or four turned into several dozen. Across an enormous meadow, several thousand people in circles like this one waved their hands and shimmied their hips to the cacophonous symphony of drums, rattles, tambourines, and every other conceivable noisemaking device, conventional or improvised.

Hai yana, ho yana, hai ya na, the crowd kept repeating, and after every repetition, they chanted a line or verse about the elements of nature, the trees, the mountains, the rivers, the sun, the moon, and the sky. A barefoot young woman, olive-skinned with delicate features, wearing a flowing white sleeveless dress, led the chanting:

> *The rivers are our sisters, we must flow with them,*
> *The trees are our brothers, we must grow with them.*

And the crowd swung back to the refrain: *Hai yana, ho yana, hai ya na! Hai yana, ho yana, hai ya na!* It was a mantra both incomprehensible and mesmerizing, and I stared at those around me, each of them smiling at no one in particular, some closing their eyes and shaking their heads to the rhythm, waving their hands in the air, back and forth, back and forth. One man sat on the ground in the circle's center, swaying like a Hasid in prayer. Most others were standing, shifting their feet in a shuffle dance. Suddenly, all I wanted was to join this circle and be part of it, to dance with these people, to feel what they were feeling.

> *We are one with the infinite sun, forever and ever and ever.*
> *Hai yana, ho yana. . . ..*

But I was no longer thirteen, no longer able to embrace such experiences without feeling cynical or detached. Though I wanted to join them, I kept wondering: *"We are one with the infinite sun"? "The rivers are our sisters"?* What do these things even mean? The concepts didn't work for me, even on the level of metaphor. As touching as the sentiments were, I wasn't sure what I would do with them once I got back to Brooklyn, to alternate-side parking, to my cable bill, and to the perpetually unreliable G train. I now lived deeply and fundamentally suspicious of any hint of dogma or ideology, of subjective values presented as Great Truths. While I wanted to care more about the sun and the rivers and the sky, about loving my fellow humans radically, and about finding the sacred within our universe, I found that I was not moved enough to give these issues further thought.

And so I watched those who sang and danced, and when night fell,

I crept back to my tent, where I could still hear the sounds of the drums, the crackling of a nearby campfire, the laughter of the dozen or so people near our tent who called themselves "Goat Camp," a motley group of freight-train riders who picked up every stray dog and cat along their travels and ended up encamped in the woods next to our group of ex-Hasidim.

Soon I was back in Brooklyn, no longer squatting over a ditch in the woods to relieve myself, no longer bathing in the stagnant water of a shallow creek, no longer smelling unwashed bodies in a cramped tent, and, over the days and weeks that followed, I thought often of that weekend. I wondered about that circle of hippies and my odd attraction to them, and I realized, after a time, what it really was: what I longed for was not the tisch of my past but a return to a time and place when ideas moved me even if they didn't make perfect sense, a time when I allowed myself to be fired up with passion for something, anything, because it held a "truth" that had made itself evident during a moment of inspired consciousness.

Sometime later, I accepted the invitation of a friend to attend a non-Orthodox Sabbath service at a synagogue on Manhattan's Upper West Side. I thought I had prayed enough to last me a lifetime, but I had never before experienced a musical service, and when the congregation sang the "Song for David," I found myself unexpectedly moved. When the crowd rose to dance for "Come, My Beloved," I recalled the dancing at the rebbe's tisch, the endless circle snaking around the large shul for hours.

The congregation quieted down for the Amidah, the silent prayer into which each worshiper disappears into his or her private meditations. It had been years since I had recited it, and I found myself tripping over some of the words, surprised at my loss of fluency, however minor.

Atah kidashta. You have sanctified the seventh day for Your Name . . . the end goal of Creation . . . blessed it of all days, and consecrated it of all times, as it is written in Your Torah. Vayechulu. . . .

I imagined a primordial world in which God, Adam, and Eve had only one another for company, and the two solitary humans looked at the sun and the rivers and the trees and the sky, and declared, as the

Talmud tells us they did: *Mah rabu ma'asecha Adonai,* how wondrous are Your works, O Lord.

And for the loss of my faith, for being unable to fully embrace the mythic beauty of those words, for my detachment from all those things that I once held dear, I let the stream of tears fall over the open pages of my prayer book.

Epilogue

Akiva and I sit on a couple of large rocks near a shallow stream, the water cascading over tangles of branches and fallen tree trunks. Akiva has a sandwich that Gitty packed for him and a water bottle. I have a hot dog and a container of sautéed chicken liver from Mechel's Takeout in Monsey.

Hershy was supposed to come, too, but this time he isn't with us.

Six times a year, I come up from Brooklyn to see the boys. Earlier this morning, I took the train from Penn Station to Suffern for my single summertime visit. A friend picked me up and loaned me his car for the afternoon, and before heading to New Square, I stopped at a photo store in Monsey to print photos we'd taken on our previous outing, during the intermediate days of Passover, at Bear Mountain State Park. Outside the store, while I smoked a cigarette and waited for the photos to be printed, Shragi appeared, out of nowhere.

"Amazing to meet you here," he said. "I'd been meaning to call you." He'd meant to but didn't, for unspecified reasons. "I wanted to tell you, just so you'd know, that Hershy doesn't want to come today. I thought you might want to make other plans, but, well, you're here already, so I guess it doesn't matter."

Doesn't *matter*?

"Why doesn't he want to come?" I asked, the message like a blunt knife scraping against my skin, causing a minor bruise, annoying but bearable. It is what I've come to expect.

"I'm not sure," he said, avoiding eye contact. "Does it matter?"

I felt a rising sense of fury. *Does it matter?* It was eight weeks since I'd last seen the boys. Several years since I'd seen Tziri and Freidy— and even Chaya Suri stopped coming soon after I moved to Brooklyn, after she turned thirteen. I wonder often what their lives are like, whether their interests have changed, whether they look different, but I can barely imagine it. My calls and letters continue to go unanswered. The cell phones I bought them must never have been charged, always going straight to voice mail, my messages unreturned. In the beginning, Akiva would call on occasion, but now, even he no longer does. I can sense, with each visit, the growing distance between us. Soon, I am all too aware, the boys, too, will turn thirteen.

I suggested a hike in the woods, to see the waterfalls a mile up the Pine Meadow Trail, off Seven Lakes Drive. Walking along the trail, Akiva eagerly pointed out the blazes of red circles on white rectangles that marked our way, jumping over knobby tree roots, which, because of the erosion of soil, rise inches above the ground. It is one of the most popular trails in the park.

Now, as we eat, I explain the history of the trails, the early hikers who mapped out the hundreds of miles of crisscrossing paths. I answer Akiva's questions about who puts the blazes on the trees, builds bridges over streams, cuts away fallen tree trunks that block the trails. I make him sit still and listen to the sounds of the forest, the chirping of birds, branches swaying in the wind, the rustling *shrrrip shrrrip* of a deer taking off at the sight of us.

He doesn't ask about my life now, and I don't offer much, although I want to. Whenever I do mention something—my apartment in Brooklyn, my new friends, the articles that I write—he goes silent. I know that inside him must be a mountain of turmoil; yet I feel powerless to do anything about it. All I can do is show up and pay attention.

We trek back the mile or so to the parking lot, where a soda vending machine stands. "I want to buy a soda," I say, and he regards the machine with hungry curiosity.

"Can I put the money in?" he asks.

I hand him a dollar bill, but it doesn't take.

"It's spitting it out." He laughs.

I give him another bill, a crisp one. This one takes, and he pushes my hand away when I reach in to make my selection.

"Let me press it," he pleads. A boy for whom a soda vending machine is a novelty.

As we drive home on the Palisades Parkway, he speaks eagerly about school trips and neighborhood news. He notes the speed on the speedometer, 70 mph, and then the 55 mph sign. *"Farchap yeneh car,"* he says, and points to a blue Honda Civic ahead of us. He grins as I switch lanes and press down on the gas, and I wonder if I'm setting a bad example.

The light after the exit ramp is red, and I take the Fotomat envelope lying near the gearshift. "I want to look at these again," I say, and he leans over, stretching his seatbelt to look at them with me. We laugh at the silly poses he and Hershy had struck for the camera, until the light turns green, and I shove the photos into my lap.

"Are you going to look at the rest at the next light?" he asks. The next light is the last before we turn into New Square.

"If it's red," I say.

He points to an empty parking lot at the side of Route 45. "Or maybe you can turn in there." He says it as though he's trying to be helpful, but his concern is obvious. He doesn't want me lingering in front of the house. I tell him I'll pull over near the bus garage, right after the turn, and I sense his relief as he nods.

"Where should I drop you off? At the Brauns' or at home?" The Brauns are cousins who live a block away. Sometimes he asks to be dropped off there, for reasons he won't elaborate on.

"Doesn't matter. Wherever's easiest." After a moment, he says, "Near home, you know, at the corner is fine." As if he doesn't want to trouble me to go all the way.

I sense his unease as we approach, his eyes shifty and alert. A group of women stand at the corner, mothers in turbans and housedresses with baby carriages and young children at their sides, and I see his glance fall on them, anxiety all over his face.

"Better at the house," he says, and I hear a nervous tremor in his voice.

At the house, I lean in to hug him, kiss him on his yarmulke, but he's already grabbed his lunch bag and is fumbling for the car-door latch.

"Here, take the photos," I say, and he grabs the envelope quickly.

"Bye," he says without turning, his eyes scanning warily for passersby.

He closes the car door and steps onto the curb, then turns back briefly, unsmiling. I wave to him, then watch him run up the pathway. The door to the apartment slams shut behind him.

I pull away, stepping lightly on the gas. Just then, I notice a familiar blur passing behind a parked car. It is Hershy on his bike, zooming down Reagan Road with all the energy of an eight-year-old, oblivious to my presence. I think to honk, but before I have the chance, he's already zoomed past. I can see him in the rearview mirror, still going full-speed down the road.

I drive ahead a short distance and make a U-turn. Then, coming back down Reagan Road, I look for the familiar round shape of his head, his *payess* trailing behind, his arms in that outward swagger I'd seen so many times before. He is not outside the house, nor do I see his bike at the door. At the corner, a group of boys of various ages rest on their bikes and huddle in conversation. I scan their faces for Hershy, but he isn't among them. He was here a moment ago, and now he is gone.

Author's Note

Each of us has a story to tell. Rarely, however, are our stories ours alone; typically, we share them with family, friends, colleagues, and so on. And yet, our subjective experiences remain unique. This is true of everyday events, but even truer of contentious moments. When we feel aggrieved, we stew in the passions of our own righteousness, our very experiences often leading us to see only what we want to see. In shaping our narratives, we select facts to our advantage, even if only unconsciously.

Throughout the writing of this book, these thoughts were never far from my mind, hovering like a gray cloud in the middle distance, reminding me that my truth was not the only truth. I am all too aware that some people in this book, either individuals or groups, might offer details and perspectives that I have surely missed. I think particularly of my ex-wife, with whom I shared nearly fifteen years of marriage and who doubtless has a compelling story of her own to tell, perhaps even an altogether different story of our marriage.

Additionally, there are people described in this book who behaved in ways that are, to my mind, less than admirable. And yet, laying blame and casting stones is an ugly business, especially when dealing with people who were once dear to you. However, this story could not be told without a measure of castigation, overt or implied. I have taken pains to describe characters in this book fairly even when I didn't feel entirely inclined to do so. I offer this not to absolve myself of the responsibility to offer an accurate telling of events, or to excuse any errors of fact that have slipped in, but to acknowledge the very real challenges in trying to present a fair and honest portrayal of deeply painful events.

Memoir, of course, is not history, nor is it, strictly speaking autobiography. More than simply a collection of facts, it is a rendering of personal history along with an attempt to find meaning within that history, to weave together narrative threads that might, both to the writer and reader, illuminate aspects of the narrator's life, and by so doing, impart something of value to the reader. That was my sole objective.

A Very Brief Reading List

This book describes a crisis of faith that unfolded over a number of years, a largely internal process of inquiry and examination. I relate here mostly the external, more demonstrably dramatic aspects of that process, and the observable effects upon me and those close to me. My intellectual and philosophical journeys, however, while internally dramatic, do not lend themselves to narrative form in the same way. By necessity, therefore, they have been offered only in collapsed form within the book's main narrative. Furthermore, this book is not intended as an argument against Orthodox Jewish belief and practice broadly, and should in no way be seen as such.

I am aware, however, that some readers might want to further explore some of the faith-related topics presented in this book. I offer the list below as a modest attempt at sharing some of the works that have contributed meaningfully to my own intellectual journey, in the hope that others might find them useful.

This list includes a variety of works, both in favor of and against aspects of religious faith, from popular works to recent classics. Most of them are accessible and illuminating even to non-scholars. They are presented here in the approximate order in which I encountered them, and correspond loosely to the trajectory of my own journey.

The Nineteen Letters of Ben Uziel: Being a Special Presentation of the Principles of Judaism, Rabbi Samson Raphael Hirsch
Permission to Believe: Four Rational Approaches to God's Existence, Lawrence Kelemen
Permission to Receive: Four Rational Approaches to the Torah's Divine Origin, Lawrence Kelemen
Living Up to the Truth, Rabbi Dr. Dovid Gottlieb

Genesis and the Big Bang: The Discovery of Harmony between Modern Science and the Bible, Gerald Schroeder

Lonely Man of Faith, Joseph B. Soloveitchik

Halakhic Man, Joseph B. Soloveitchik

God, Man, and History: A Jewish Interpretation, Eliezer Berkovits

Man Is Not Alone: A Philosophy of Religion, Abraham Joshua Heschel

God in Search of Man: A Philosophy of Judaism, Abraham Joshua Heschel

Beyond Reasonable Doubt, Louis Jacobs

The Dignity of Difference: How to Avoid the Clash of Civilizations, Jonathan Sacks

At the Entrance to the Garden of Eden: A Jew's Search for Hope with Christians and Muslims in the Holy Land, Yossi Klein Halevi

Major Trends in Jewish Mysticism, Gershom Scholem

The View from Nebo: How Archaeology Is Rewriting the Bible and Reshaping the Middle East, Amy Dockser Marcus

God against the Gods: The History of the War between Monotheism and Polytheism, Jonathan Kirsch

The Religion of Israel: From Its Beginnings to the Babylonian Exile, Yehezkel Kaufmann

How to Read the Bible: A Guide to Scripture, Then and Now, James Kugel

Who Wrote the Bible?, Richard Elliott Friedman

The Bible Unearthed: Archaeology's New Vision of Ancient Israel and the Origin of Its Sacred Texts, Israel Finkelstein and Neil Asher Silverman

What Did the Biblical Writers Know and When Did They Know It? What Archaeology Can Tell Us about the Reality of Ancient Israel, William G. Dever

Mere Christianity, C. S. Lewis

Why I Am Not a Christian, Bertrand Russell

The Blind Watchmaker: Why the Evidence of Evolution Reveals a Universe without Design, Richard Dawkins

The God Delusion, Richard Dawkins

Existentialism Is a Humanism, Jean-Paul Sartre

Acknowledgments

Phin Reiss has been a better pal than any man deserves to have—or, at any rate, has paid for more glasses of Johnnie Walker Black than any man deserves to drink. I remain forever grateful for his friendship, his wisdom, and his generosity.

From Netanya to Cape Town to Williamsburg, Jill Schulman has heard it all many times, and still continues to listen. Her insight, humor, and compassion have been invaluable to me. Much love.

I am indebted to Ricki Breuer, Zalmen Labin, Y. M. Schwartz, and Itchie Lichtenstein, without whom this book would not have been possible. Also, those who can be known only by their *noms de guerre*: "Shtreimel," fellow blogger, friend, inspiration. "Mendy Chossid," *baal chesed* extraordinaire. "Hoezentragerin," for giving me the strength when I felt depleted. Thank you, Avi Burstein, Emily Cercone, Meghan Bechtel Lin, Frieda Vizel, Judy Brown, Samuel "Ushy" Katz, and Eve Singer for your many forms of assistance.

I am fortunate to have been a part of Footsteps, a small organization with enormous impact. Thank you, Malkie Schwartz, Lani Santo, Michael Jenkins, Rachel Berger, Betsy Fabricant, Chani Getter, and all other current and former staff and board members. Special thanks to Adina Kadden and Leah Vincent, fellow participants and board members, for their dedication to our community's needs. Many thanks also to Ella Kohn, Anouk Markovits, Alan Lerner, and Monette de Botton for their generosity and support to OTD families.

To my friends in the OTD community: You have given me hope, strength, and love. Together, we have formed the vanguard of a movement. May we continue to grow, to inspire others, and to tell our stories with clarity and strength.

I am enormously thankful to my agent, Rob McQuilkin, for his faith in this project; I could not have hoped for a more tireless and fearsome champion. Thank you, Hella Winston, for the introductions. My deepest gratitude to my editor, Katie Dublinski, for her remarkable patience, insight, and guidance throughout. Thanks also to Fiona McCrae, Erin Kottke, and everyone else at Graywolf; I feel humbled to have been accepted into the "den."

My mother, Bracha Din, has endured much in her life, but her spirit remains one of the strongest, noblest, and most gracious I have known. My siblings, Chani, Avrumi, and Mendy, have shown me nothing but love and acceptance. I know it couldn't have been easy, and I am grateful all the more for it. Much love to you all.

I cannot know what my father would've said about my path in life, had he lived. No doubt, he would've been troubled. No doubt, he would've loved me as fiercely as he always had. He would've called me *shayfele*, even now. His memory is always with me.

A Graywolf Press Reading Group Guide

All Who Go Do Not Return

..

A Memoir

SHULEM DEEN

Questions and Topics for Discussion

1) Shulem Deen is labeled a heretic by his community. Do you feel this was justified, given the governing rules of the Skverers?

2) Do you think Deen's experiences offer insights into fundamentalist religions in general?

3) What most surprised you about the Hasidic community's beliefs, customs, and culture?

4) How do you think Deen's ex-wife's version of the story might differ from his?

5) What does Deen's story tell you about our society's tolerance for extremist communities?

6) Deen's choice to leave the Hasidic community had a significant impact on his relationship with his children. What do you think about the choice he made? Can you imagine making a similar choice?

7) Do you think insular religious communities such as the one Deen describes offer something of value that isn't easily found elsewhere?

8) Do you think that the way that the narrative moves back and forth in time is effective?

9) Deen's various experiences as a student and a teacher are an essential part of his story. Do you think his rigid early education affected his thirst for knowledge as a young adult?

10) How did you feel about Deen's admission of his own questionable actions, such as using corporal punishment as a schoolteacher, or engaging in fraudulent practices to receive government payment?

11) Deen describes a world in which young people are led into arranged marriages, with no education about sex or birth control. Similarly, he describes a world in which boys spend their youth studying Torah and Talmud, and receive very little secular instruction. Do you think our society has an obligation to help prevent young people from the negative consequences of such practices?

Making My Own MFA

Shulem Deen

I don't remember precisely when it began, but at some point, about a decade ago, as a thirty-year-old living among one of the most insular Hasidic sects in the United States, I had this fantasy: I wanted to go away to the Iowa Writers' Workshop and earn an MFA in creative writing.

How exactly did I learn about Iowa, or MFAs, or writing workshops? I can no longer recall. Just a few years earlier, at age twenty-five, I barely knew the difference between a bachelor's degree and a master's, or even what a "major" was. The idea of getting a college degree seemed as remote as meeting the Pope on the Monsey Trails bus. But at some point I learned that the Iowa Writers' Workshop was where people went to become writers. And I wanted to be a writer.

At age thirty-three, I left the Hasidic world. I had learned a lot by then—I knew what a major was, and the difference between a bachelor's and a master's. But I never did get to Iowa, or any other creative writing program. Or even any old bachelor's degree. Life got in the way, and I lost my romantic notions of American higher education. But when an opportunity came to write a book, I knew that it meant committing not only to writing but also to teaching myself how to write.

The Iowa Writers' Workshop had been a dream because the program was legendary—one of the first such programs in the country—but when I began to lay out the first draft of my book, I realized why I really needed it, or something like it; I needed a basic understanding of literary craft, an immersive environment in which I could experiment with form and technique, and an opportunity to spend time with other students as well as with seasoned writers who had already produced bodies of work from whom to learn. But such an environment was not an option at that point—I'd committed to the book and had looming deadlines. I had no choice, I realized, but to create my own MFA writing program.

Read, read, read—this is every seasoned writer's advice to novice writers.

I was poorly read. Secular books are scarce within most Hasidic communities, and formal education—aside from religious studies—is meager. I'd had only spotty exposure to English language books, and I'd never given myself to the task of reading anything of quality. As much reading as I had done over the years, I'd done none of the required reading of a high school or college student. And so I knew that I'd have to start my writing education by reading more widely.

Not knowing any better, I took to the classics, American authors in particular: Melville, Twain, Hemingway, Fitzgerald, Salinger. Reading these authors was important, but they were not particularly instructive about writing. The reading often felt tedious, at least on the first read; I would never have picked these books out of a pile—and so it was hard for me to see what made them great. I had neither my own developed aesthetic nor anyone else's measure for greatness. I had only one measure: Am I enjoying this? And the answer for much of it was: not really.

I broadened my selections, tried tackling some of the other greats—the Russians, the French—but my reading was haphazard, disorganized, with no natural progression that might've helped me learn anything. I slogged through Dostoyevsky with little appreciation for either the prose style or its themes, then took up Joyce and Faulkner and understood next to nothing at all.

As I was to learn, not all reading leads directly to better writing. Reading intelligently takes skill, and before such skill is cultivated, reading indiscriminately and without guidance can be frustrating and counter-productive and it can leave you trying to imitate writers you have no business imitating. It took a while for me to learn the difference between good books and books to learn writing from. The classics, I realized, as important as they are, are particularly clunky as elementary writing instruction—especially when you're your own instructor.

I did eventually find my footing, both as a reader and a writer. I realized that a book has to resonate in a certain way before it can be instructive. You don't necessarily have to like the book, but you have to get a feel for what it is attempting to do, both as a whole and in its parts.

It's hard to say at what point and with which books I began to feel that necessary resonance, but at some point I began to notice things—a page that held me captive, a turn of phrase particularly elegant, a metaphor that did exactly what it was supposed to—and I would go back and see how it was done. I began to see more clearly when a work had something for me to learn from and when it was something only to marvel at, be inspired by, but to know that it was a different sort of writing from my own, and that some voices stand only to be admired—a do-not-try-this-at-home kind of writing, best left to seasoned literary stuntmen. (Henry Miller is for me the best example of this.)

In the end, it wasn't the classics that taught me most, but contemporaries. Frank Conroy and Tobias Wolff taught me about setting up scenes, and making good use of dialogue. Mary Carr and Rick Bragg were inspiring for their exhilarating language, even if I could never hope to mimic such fluidly exquisite prose. James Baldwin's beautifully winding narrative essays, with their vivid descriptions of grit and racial despair rendered in language so effortlessly mesmerizing, put me on the lookout for artifice in my own writing, forced me to more strenuously weed out clunk, and to let my paragraphs flow with a more natural rhythm.

I also read books on writing, and some of them would prove indispensable. John Gardner's *The Art of Fiction* remains an invaluable manual on essential narrative techniques. Stephen King's *On Writing*, with its unique blend of guide and memoir, is both instructive and inspiring. Sometimes, all I needed to get me going was the image of a writer at work, or a master's thoughts on writing, and for those, the many long-form interviews in the *Paris Review* were both a treat and an impetus for getting to work.

Most importantly, after reading many dozens of works—novels, memoirs, short story collections, and essays—I learned that to write compelling prose I'd have to empty my mind and find my own voice, which would be markedly different from any author I've read—and that this is what makes writing good, not the other way around.

I had many crises of confidence while writing. There were times when I thought the whole undertaking to have been folly. I'd berate myself for thinking that an ex-Hasid with little formal education could teach himself, while nearing middle age, what others pay exorbitant sums of money to learn. If only I'd gotten that MFA, I would think, I'd know how to set this scene, perfect that awkward transition, replace a clunky metaphor with a stream of effortlessly breathtaking prose.

A crisis of confidence does nothing to make a deadline go away, though, and I had no choice but to go on. My book took four years to write, and the dual task of teaching myself as I went made much of the process tormenting. By the time I submitted that final draft to my publisher in February 2014 I had very nearly exhausted myself. But it also remains the most exhilarating work I've done in my forty years of life. I would gladly do it all over again.

This essay first appeared as part of the Jewish Book Council's Visiting Scribe *series. For more essays, reviews of Jewish interest books, book club resources, and reading lists, visit www.jewishbookcouncil.org.*

An Interview with Shulem Deen

Julie Wiener, for the Jewish Telegraphic Agency

JTA: Most memoirs of leaving Orthodoxy include an anecdote about the first time the author ate non-kosher food or violated some other fundamental rule, but yours doesn't. Do you remember those experiences?

Deen: I remember my first treif, but it was unimportant—a chicken quesadilla at a Mexican restaurant. But who cares? I was totally a non-believer by then, but there was nowhere to buy treif in New Square, and I still looked like a Hasid. As for Shabbat, I was ready to violate it way before I did. It just didn't feel like anything to me.

So you didn't half worry you'd be struck down?

That's the term people use: "Oh, I turned on the light on Shabbat and wasn't struck by lightning." I get a little annoyed when people focus so much on that. I get that first steps are important to some people who felt really constrained by the rules; to some people it's meaningful. It just wasn't for me.

Your memoir tells how, despite an initially amicable divorce, your ex-wife successfully fought to curtail your custodial and visitation rights. Could you have done anything differently to prevent that?

When I left I knew very few people who were divorced, so it never occurred to me I needed to go to a lawyer. If I had gotten a properly executed agreement on custody, visitation and all that, it would've been difficult for anyone to go to court and want to change what's been agreed upon just because my beard is no longer as long. My naivete was astonishing! Looking back, I don't know where my mind was. But I'd been with this woman fifteen years and thought I knew her. I'd gone on a journey that she watched. She didn't come along, but she was there with me, and I thought she was somewhat empathetic to what I was going through.

You also write how your children distanced themselves from you and resisted seeing you even on the few visits the courts allowed. Have things gotten any better since you finished the memoir?

It's only gotten worse. I was seeing my two boys for a while, but my youngest stopped coming a year ago. The two would come together, but when the oldest turned thirteen he stopped, and then the youngest didn't want to come anymore. He was eleven, and he would get into the car and just burst into tears. I would spend twenty, thirty minutes just trying to calm him down. After a year of doing this, I thought, do I want to do this to him? I tried to bribe him: I took him on all kinds of trips, to the aquarium and amusement parks. I bought him a digital camera, which he said he really wanted. But it wasn't getting better. So I said I'm not going to force you. I thought all these bribes would help, but he called me up a week before the next visitation was supposed to happen and left a message saying he didn't want to come anymore.

Are you hoping that at least one of your children chooses the same path as you?

If someone leaves, I want to be able to help provide what they need to make the transition. But do I want to encourage people to leave? No. I left knowing how to read and write English, knowing what it means to have a job in the outside world and interact with secular people, and even so, the transition was really, really tough. Do I hope my children will make this step? I hope they choose what feels good for them, and that one of their choices is to let me be part of their lives. I don't care whether they choose to be religious or not religious.

Is there anything besides your children that you miss about the Hasidic community?

I miss the holidays—the first two years after I left, on holidays I'd be completely torn up. Holidays in the Hasidish world, families in the Hasidish world, celebrating happy things—those are beautiful times. I have no animosity towards the Hasidic community as a collective. I have tremendous affection and sympathy for what they're trying to do.

They're trying to preserve a cherished worldview within a world that is very hostile to it. I disagree with the degree to which choice is taken away from individuals in the service of that, but I understand it.

I know you're on the board of Footsteps, a nonprofit that helps people leaving the haredi Orthodox community to make the transition to the secular world. Is there an increase in the number of people choosing to leave?

Footsteps represents anywhere from ten to twenty-five percent of the people who leave, and the number of new people who come each year is rising steadily. The fact that many of us are writing and publishing, this gives those who leave somewhat more prominence, and people within the Hasidic community are not oblivious to this, especially people who are thinking of leaving. We have people in medical school, getting master's degrees, a nice number of lawyers. It's becoming a community that has people doing things in the world, and that serve as something of an example that defies the old stereotype of the OTD [an acronym for a term that means "off the path"] person who's lost, dysfunctional, has no home, no friends, gets involved in drugs and takes up with a bad crowd.

This interview has been condensed and edited.

Shulem Deen, a former Skverer Hasid, is the founding editor of the website Unpious. His work has appeared in the *Jewish Daily Forward*, *Tablet*, and *Salon*. He lives in Brooklyn, New York.

Book design by Ann Sudmeier. Composition by Bookmobile Design & Digital Publisher Services, Minneapolis, Minnesota. Manufactured by Versa Press on acid-free, 30 percent postconsumer wastepaper.